HEALING THE CULTURE

HEALING THE CULTURE

A Commonsense Philosophy of
Happiness, Freedom, and the Life Issues

by
Robert J. Spitzer, S.J., Ph.D.

with
Robin A. Bernhoft, M.D. and Camille E. De Blasi, M.A.

IGNATIUS PRESS   SAN FRANCISCO

Cover design by Riz Boncan Marsella

ISBN 0-89870-786-2
Library of Congress control number 99-68612
Printed in the United States of America ∞

To my mother,

whose inspiration and prayers underlie

every principle in this volume

Contents

PART ONE
DEFINING "PERSON" AND "HAPPINESS"

Chapter One: Defining the Human Person

Chapter Two: Defining "Happiness"

Chapter Three: Moving Through the Levels of Happiness

Acknowledgments

My most profound gratitude for the inspiration and help of Camille E. De Blasi, M.A., who spent countless hours advising, researching, editing, diagramming, and typing two full drafts of this volume. I am most particularly thankful for her inspired leadership in starting and maintaining the Life Principles project. Without her creativity, enthusiasm, energy, and self-sacrifice in producing everything from the videotapes to the publicity pamphlets, this project would simply not have been possible.

My sincerest and profound gratitude to Robin A. Bernhoft, M.D., for his authorship of much of Chapter Ten. I am particularly grateful for the hours he spent coauthoring, encouraging, and editing the first draft of this volume. His medical knowledge, humanistic and theological insight, and incisive writing style were essential to the initiation and maintenance of this project.

I would also like to express my sincere gratitude to Human Life of Washington, which supported this project financially from its inception to the present. In particular I would like to thank Kenneth VanDerhoef for his continuous spiritual, moral, and financial support; Eileen and Jef Geller for their encouragement, prayers, and advice; my sister, Lynne Malone, who did the technical production for the Life Principles video series; and Pete and Janet Flatley, Sarah Spangler, and all others who offered their encouragement and support.

Foreword

In addition to its original purpose of providing an assessment and solution for many of our cultural problems, this book is also meant to be a resource for the Life Principles project. This project is devoted to explaining the underlying philosophy of the pro-life movement to a diverse audience.

Several years ago, when working on both cultural philosophy and the Life Principles projects independently of one another, I discovered many areas of intersection. Later I decided to combine the two projects into what has now emerged as the current draft of this book.

With respect to its use as a cultural philosophy, I have found the Life Principles to be useful in businesses, nonprofit organizations, law firms, university and high school environments, and even nursing homes and hospitals. With respect to its use as a pro-life philosophy, I have found that its uniquely rational and commonly accessible approach has had a powerful and overwhelmingly positive effect on pro-life education for the national public.

This program, with its two objectives, is more than just a written curriculum. I have developed, in conjunction with the Center for Life Principles, a video series that may be used in community organizations, church groups, university environments, and even high schools. The Center for Life Principles will assist interested people in bringing this video series to any interested group. In addition, the Center for Life Principles has developed a high school curriculum, a retreat program, a speakers' bureau, and is beginning work on a curriculum for nursing homes and hospitals.

Readers who are interested in facilitating this program in any of the above-mentioned environments or becoming members of the Life Principles team should use the information on page 347 below.

Introduction

I. An Invisible Agent of Cultural Decline

There are many positive signs in the world today, such as economic prosperity in many regions; international cooperation as markets become more open; heightened awareness of cultural diversity; increased access to education, information, transportation, communication, and technology; and improvements in health and medicine. Nevertheless, many people within our society are dismayed by what may appear to be a cultural decline. Individuals encounter numerous ethical and personal difficulties within the workplace, public officials lack the respect they once cherished, ethical relativism seems to dominate much of our thinking, depression is on the rise, divorce and family breakups are increasing, and cynicism about life and its prospects is a national epidemic. Even adolescents seem to be overcome by a malaise about life. The nation has been greatly troubled by the growing episodes of schoolchildren who shoot their teachers and classmates. One gets the impression that our culture is in desperate need of revitalization and even healing.

Although the combined efforts of government and social organizations have developed a myriad of programs to combat the abovementioned problems, these programs tend to act more like bandages than remedies. It seems there is a deeper cause of these problems. Perhaps there is something deep within our cultural consciousness that, like a rapidly mutating virus, continues to adapt itself to all superficial cures and exert itself anew.

If we are to move beyond the more insidious effects of this agent, we must begin to understand it. We must learn how to see it for what it really is. Rather than content ourselves with cataloguing its every effect, we must get to the nature of the beast. I would submit that the beast's identity is reflected in the minimalistic way we see ourselves. More precisely, it is a radically incomplete cultural attitude about what it means to be a human person.

It is hard to imagine that one "little" incomplete attitude like the one suggested above can produce so much malaise, depression, violence, confusion, and even chaos. Though it is not the sole reason for these problems, I do believe that it lies at the root of most of them. We might consider the analogy of a person from the Middle Ages coming into the twentieth century to discover that the plague that wiped out a third of Europe's population was caused by a completely invisible agent. I would like this book to be as helpful for our culture as a powerful microscope would have been for the medieval scientist. I hope that this book will serve as a sort of philosophical microscope that uses very fundamental ideas to probe the meanings, motives, values, and ideals of individuals and the cultures in which they live.

II. Materialism and the Loss of Intangibles

Materialism is sometimes associated with people who invest their life's meaning in the products of a department store or real-estate agency. Though this reflects the meaning of "ethical" materialism, it only partially indicates the meaning of "metaphysical" materialism. Metaphysics seeks to understand the ground, indeed, the ultimate ground of reality. Hence, metaphysical materialism tends to reduce reality to matter. Frequently, the term *matter* is interpreted not in light of late twentieth-century physics (for example, quantum theory, relativity theory, big bang cosmology) but rather in terms of what is tangible, clearly perceived, and clearly understood (for example, colors, solids, locomotion). This kind of materialism tends to view reality as building blocks that are clearly perceived by individuals and even clearly within their control. Unfortunately, as contemporary physicists would hasten to note, it does not describe physical reality accurately, and it certainly does not describe nonphysical or spiritual reality adequately. Nevertheless, it is a mind-set that is readily accepted by our culture because it is clear and simple and gives the illusion of control.

Most metaphysical materialists are not physicists, and hence their inadequate view of physical reality has little effect on the scientific world. However, most are moral agents with families and colleagues and are community members. Some of them are lawyers, judges, politicians, liberal educators, secondary school teachers, and members of the media. As such they influence how we think about ourselves, our life's potential, our self-worth, the quality of life, human rights, the common good, and even love, freedom, and ethics. When we ground our culture and public policy in metaphysical materialism, we advocate for not only a radically incomplete view of reality but also a radically incomplete view of human dignity, destiny, and community. As will be shown throughout this book, this undervaluation of humanity will produce the kinds of cultural problems mentioned above (for example, inferiority, jealousy, self-pity, contempt, fear, suspicion, anger, and even violent responses to minimal negative stimuli).

Metaphysical materialism is leading to a loss of the intangibles in the culture. We seem to think anything that is not visible, tangible, or perceivable through a microscope or telescope is less than real; sometimes we even think it's unreal. Consider the issue of *Time* magazine several years ago that proclaimed on its front cover that love is a "biological affair".[1] This is a rather curious conclusion in view of the fact that love, for many, is a commitment leading to a unity with another, whereby doing the good for that other is easier than doing the good for oneself. But commitment isn't very tangible. It can't be seen, touched, viewed under a microscope, or even detected by an electromagnetic test. Despite the fact that commitments are the most important realities in the lives of many people, much of the culture might think commitment, because of its lack of tangibility, has no reality at all.

The same holds true for a unity with another that makes doing the good for another easier than doing the good for oneself. Even though such unities are viewed by many to be some of the most important realities characterizing interpersonal personhood and the meaning of life, they certainly are not visible, tangible, or perceivable under a microscope. For much of the culture they may seem to be somewhat or altogether unreal. Hence, we were all relieved to learn that love is a chemical, because chemicals, after all, are visible, tangible, and even analyzable by various scientific instruments. Whew. We rescued the reality of love. Unfortunately, we had to undervalue seriously what love is and its worth in order to restore it to "reality". This undervaluation of love may direct our youth to view it as an emotion instead of a

---

[1] *Time*, Feb. 15, 1993. The cover story subtitle asserted, "Evolutionary roots, brain imprints, biological secretions. That's the story of love."

commitment and a community. In so doing, it may cause them to seek fulfillment solely through emotional highs instead of perduring commitments leading to common good through common cause. As can be seen, this opens the way for an increase in hedonism rather than generativity, which will, in turn, seriously undermine our ability to protect rights and promote the common good.

Love is not the only intangible whose value and reality are slipping away. Justice as a real quality of human persons, inalienable rights as a reality belonging to human persons, and indeed, even personhood itself seem quite doubtable. If we took a poll today among both youth and adults, I wonder how many of them would attest to the reality of these nonempirical qualities. Will this lead to a serious undervaluation of such qualities, as was seen earlier with respect to love? It seems almost inevitable.

The two life issues that this book addresses, abortion and euthanasia, are an integral part of the culture's increasing advocacy of metaphysical materialism. Diagram 1 shows not only how abortion and euthanasia have accelerated the unreality and undervaluation of intangibles (such as love, justice, and rights) but also how they have opened a moral Pandora's box that will negatively affect our view of issues such as poverty, oppression, war, and even care of the environment. As will be shown throughout this book, our view of the reality and value of the intangibles underlies every moral and cultural issue upon which the quality of our individual and communal life depends. To the extent that abortion and euthanasia accelerate the demise of the intangibles, they also accelerate the decline of every other ethical foundation and agency within the culture.

Ironically, our culture has slipped into abortion and euthanasia unwittingly, in a kind of metaphysical innocence. The so-called prochoice movement arose not out of a group of malicious individuals but rather out of a conviction that abortion and euthanasia were new options that really didn't harm anyone, because they didn't affect human realities or even reality in general. The cycle in diagram 1 shows how this metaphysical innocence gave rise to the *Roe vs. Wade* decision and the Oregon euthanasia initiative and how these, in turn, are contributing to the continued undermining of intangibles within our culture. I believe the result will eventually be moral chaos. Prevention of this moral chaos will require not only a new look at the life issues but also

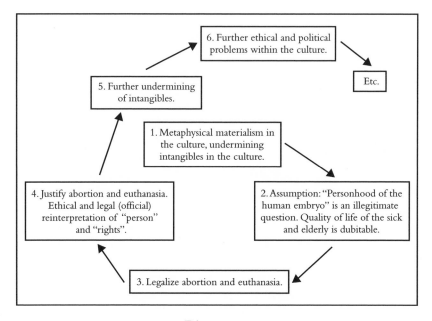

Diagram 1.

a look at the whole domain of intangibles. In short, we will not only have to reexamine what we have done in the courts and in the public domain; we will also have to provide an education that illuminates the depth and breadth of commitment, unity, freedom, love, personal dignity, rights, and the common good. This book is meant to provide a first step in this cultural project.

Let us examine the particulars of the cycle illustrated in diagram 1. As noted, U.S. and Western European cultures have experienced a host of technological, legal, and societal benefits since the end of the second world war. However, as these benefits emerged, metaphysical materialism became increasingly widespread. It seems that our increasing material well-being and reliance on technology caused us to overvalue the material and undervalue the intangible. A history of this phenomenon would be the basis for another book. Suffice it to say that this loss of the perceived reality of intangibles (box 1) led to the prevalence of two assumptions that, in their turn, gave rise to the legalization of abortion and euthanasia within our culture (boxes 2 and 3).

With respect to abortion, the legal and cultural atmosphere predating the *Roe vs. Wade* decision was filled with the popular opinion that the personhood of the human embryo is an irrelevant question. Ultrasound technology was still in its infancy, and so the human embryo seemed quite invisible and intangible. Furthermore, there seemed to be differences in appearance between the human embryo and a newborn baby. Although there were marked similarities between them, the differences in the appearances combined with the invisible and intangible nature of the embryo made the embryo seem somewhat unreal.

The same thing occurred with respect to personhood. "Personhood" refers to the intrinsic dignity of a human being, which calls forth protection by all other human beings within a society. This grounds the inalienable rights of that human being. But in a culture that has lost its awareness of the reality of intangibles, intrinsic dignity doesn't seem like a reality, something that really exists in real human beings. Rather it seems like something that I declare to be there because of my subjective decision. If intrinsic dignity is only a manifestation of my subjective decision, then human personhood is likewise only a subjective declaration. Therefore, inalienable rights would not be *real* qualities belonging to human beings by nature but would be only a manifestation of our collective *subjective* will to be generous and give people privileges that they would not otherwise have had. The seeming unreality of intrinsic dignity, personhood, and inalienable rights (now completely dependent upon our generous collective will) led to the declaration that the personhood of the embryo is an irrelevant question. Embryos and persons did not seem real outside of our collective declaration. Therefore, we needed to consult some experts to find out whether or not we *should declare* human embryos to be persons. When the experts declared that personhood was a very confusing term (not having any real correlate) and subsequently decided that we should not declare human embryos to be persons (because it seemed to reflect our political will), we eradicated the reality of both personhood and embryo in one fell swoop. It was all done in metaphysical innocence, but, as will be explained, it would have devastating consequences.

It should come as no surprise that our youth should subsequently declare that they are confused about "the intrinsic dignity of a person", that they don't quite know what we mean by that phrase. It seems so abstract and so unreal. Perhaps it would be *clearer* if we defined the value of human beings without using words like "intrinsic dignity" and "person". Perhaps these virtually meaningless abstractions should be replaced by very clear words with visible and tangible correlates such as "physical appearance", "athletic prowess", "academic performance", "verbal capacity", and so on. Does this individual look good or bad? Sound smart or dumb? Run fast or slow? Intrinsic dignity seems so unreal compared to these far more tangible qualities. Compassion for the spirit underlying the gaze of human eyes seems so vague by comparison to pride in almost heroic athletic accomplishments. We shouldn't be surprised if our youth begin to lose a sense of compassion, delight, and deep respect for the intrinsically dignified human mystery.

Above all, it should come as no surprise if young people and adults should declare that abortion isn't a real moral issue. If the personhood of the human embryo is a nonissue because personhood is an arbitrary concept, and human embryos appear very unhuman and unreal, then, in all innocence, abortion just doesn't seem wrong. Where's the harm? Obviously, if one moves beyond metaphysical materialism and begins to perceive the reality of intrinsic dignity in every being of human origin, one might become shockingly aware of a harm that betokens a moral crisis undermining every other moral foundation within the culture. More on that later.

The same innocent conjecture underlies the euthanasia movement (again, box 2). Here, the loss of intangibility in the culture does not so much affect personhood as the view of quality of life. Much of this book will be concerned with four levels of meaning and purpose in life. This will not be considered in detail here. Suffice it to say that the first level of meaning (physical pleasure and possession) and the second level (ego-gratification) are quite tangible, immediately gratifying, and emotionally intense. The third and fourth levels of meaning (concerned with contribution and love—Level 3—and transcendence and faith—Level 4) require delayed gratification, education, and subtlety, but they have pervasive effects beyond a single person, last much longer, and involve our most creative powers (for example, love, ideals, intellectual creativity, and the pursuit of the common good).

A culture that doubts the reality of intangibles will seriously underestimate the values of meaning and purpose in life for Levels 3 and 4, because those levels are, by nature, more intangible (even though they are more pervasive, enduring, and deep). Hence, this kind of culture is likely to overlook love and the common good as possible meanings of life. This culture is more likely to see career accomplishment and an excellent golf game as indicative of "the good life". As people get older, their capacity for Levels 3 and 4 increases quite markedly, but, unfortunately, their capacity for Levels 1 and 2 decreases. For example, as a grandmother's capacity to love her grandchildren and to forgive her friends for past offenses increases, her ambulatory ability and capacity for career advancement decrease. This is viewed as disastrous in a culture that has lost the reality of intangibles, because it seems like the elderly person is losing her *real* value while getting *nothing* in return. It should come as no surprise if our elderly citizens should feel useless, worthless, and, as a result, depressed. It should not amaze us if our youth undervalue the lives and qualities of our elderly citizens. Above all, it should come as no surprise if qualities like compassion, patience, forgiveness, altruism, commitment, community, and common cause should be severely undervalued. If we have erased from our minds the value of the practitioners of these qualities, we will do the same to the qualities themselves. In an atmosphere like this, it follows that we will implicitly believe that the quality of our elderly people's lives is virtually worthless.

We should also not be surprised, then, if our citizens should say that controversy over euthanasia is irrelevant. The quality of life of those who are sick or elderly seems to be worthless. Why not give them the option to kill themselves? Where's the harm? It's just a new option. As was seen above, the advocates of this position are generally not malicious. They believe that they are really giving a new and good option to the elderly, disabled, and terminally ill. However, if we move beyond the perspective of metaphysical materialism, we might become shockingly aware that we have imposed a duty to die on a very large group of our citizens who may now become convinced that they *should* avail themselves of assisted suicide because the quality of their lives is truly worthless. They may never have seriously entertained this opinion or believed that they had this duty to die prior to the legalization of assisted suicide. But now they have become convinced, through the availability of this new option, that they have a duty to dispose of a worthless life that they hitherto thought had value in the eyes of their family and friends. It is quite logical that the duty to die should arise out of our tangible bias about the meaning of life.

Let us now repeat the assumptions of Box 2:

1. The personhood of the human embryo is an irrelevant question, and, therefore, abortion is a bogus moral issue.

2. The elderly, disabled, and terminally ill have a diminished or virtually insignificant quality of life (because their more tangible qualities and powers are decreasing); therefore, euthanasia is a bogus moral issue.

In light of these assumptions, it should come as no surprise that good people, indeed, some of our best legal and medical minds, should legitimize and even legalize abortion and euthanasia (box 3). I will give a brief assessment of the history of *Roe vs. Wade* and the Oregon euthanasia initiative in the last two chapters of this book. For the moment, it need only be understood that the legalization of abortion and euthanasia had to lead, and indeed *did* lead, to a massive effort culturally to justify this legal legitimization (box 4). I do not intend to imply that this effort was malicious, but it was quite intentional. In order to get rid of our nagging doubts about some possible intrinsic dignity in the human embryo and some rights attaching to that intrinsic dignity, it became necessary to detach "person" from human being. It is obvious that a human embryo is a human being. He possesses a *uniquely* human genetic code at his single-celled stage, and he is obviously a living, metabolizing, growing being. If our society were to acknowledge that this human being possesses intrinsic dignity precisely as a human being (that is, recognized him as a human person), it would follow that this person possesses inalienable rights appropriate to his intrinsic dignity. This would have immediately raised the question of the legitimacy of abortion. Indeed, abortion would then have to be considered murder. It therefore seemed easier to let go of the question of the inalienable rights of the fetus. If the courts let go of the inalienable rights question, then the question of the intrinsic dignity of the human being would never be raised. Our cultural assumption that the personhood of the human embryo is a nonissue would, therefore, never come under reflective scrutiny, and therefore, neither would its moral legitimacy.

I am not proposing that this thinking process explicitly occurred in the minds of those who attempted to justify abortion in the aftermath of the *Roe vs. Wade* decision. However, a subconscious awareness of the inalienable rights of the human fetus attaching itself to the designation of personhood was present, and those who attempted to justify abortion shunned the designation of personhood whenever it arose. This gave rise to a peculiar turn in our popular legal and political philosophy. We began to view personhood as a matter of *subjective declaration* rather than a recognition of the *objective reality* of the intrinsic dignity of a human being. At this point, not only "person" was subjectivized, but also the intrinsic dignity of human beings, and, along with it, the objective reality of inalienable rights. As will be shown in Chapter Seven, this subjectivization of inalienable rights is not only contradictory but also perhaps the most dangerous legal/political move in which our county has ever engaged.

The legalization of subjectivized personhood, intrinsic dignity, and inalienable rights had the effect of officially sanctioning the assumptions on which this was based, namely, that the personhood of the human embryo is a nonissue, and that Level 1 and 2 quality of life should supersede Level 3 and 4 quality of life. This, in its turn, had the effect of further undermining the reality of intangibles (such as love, justice, altruism, commitment, community, and common cause). Indeed, the extremely materialistic (physicalist) assumptions in the *Roe vs. Wade* decision became almost commonplace in popular legal and political philosophy. If it is true that what becomes legal becomes normative, and what becomes normative becomes moral, then we should not be surprised that the culture would want to justify morally not only materialism but physicalism as well (box 5).

It should be expected that this further undermining of intangible realities will begin to affect all other moral issues (box 6). The vaguer and less valued commitment becomes, the vaguer and less valued justice, love, and the common good become. And the vaguer these central realities become, the vaguer and less valued the ground of ethics becomes. It would not be surprising if this dulled our youth's capacity for reasoning in virtually every ethical area. This result is particularly paradoxical because today's youth are quite idealistic, sensitized to the issues of care and kindness, and exemplify far more sophistication in their personal relationships than has been the case in generations past. Nevertheless, in spite of all this, they do seem to be less concerned and less conscientious about matters of principle. Ethics and its principles and methods seem less real and important. Commitment and long-suffering compassion seem vaguer to them. They seem to be more disposed toward self-pity. Today's youth seem to be a paradox of heightened kindness with decreased sensitivity to the intangibles that underlie the deepest aspects of ever-deepening love and commitment to the common good. If the latter should one day overcome the former through a mind-set of disappointment or dashed idealism, our culture will be in real trouble, for our youth will not have the internal capacity to bring our culture out of its decline.

It was noted earlier that abortion and euthanasia are integral to a cultural decline arising out of metaphysical materialism. Our youth are more sensitive, yet less capable of grasping or even seeing the importance of principle. They have more opportunities, yet live for meanings that are less pervasive, enduring, and deep. They seem to be far more emotionally sophisticated but are on the verge of replacing commitment and long-standing compassion with this emotive disposition. They have a heightened awareness of multicultural diversity, but are less aware of the *intrinsic* dignity of the human person. More than any other generation, they have been made aware of their rights, yet they have no sense of the inalienability of rights (that is, that certain rights belong to persons by their very nature and not by a government's declaration of them). Today's youth are performing a balancing act that cannot be sustained in the long term. If we are to give them a fighting chance for cultural survival and a legacy that will point the way to what is pervasive, enduring, and deep, we will have to recover the reality of the intangibles. We will not only have consciously to reflect upon and correct our implicit materialism, we will also have to correct all of the ethical and legal oversights that have arisen out of it. We can no longer afford to remain metaphysically innocent, and we cannot allow the negative ethical and political residuals from that "innocence" to be a part of our cultural legacy.

III. A Potential Source of Cultural Healing

The Life Principles project offers a philosophical context to facilitate the correction of cultural materialism. Though it includes specific chapters redressing the issues of abortion and euthanasia, its purpose is much larger. It is meant to provide an enriched vision of reality, persons, culture, love, and meaning of life that will not only protect the culture from the narrow and destructive effects of materialism but also give rise to a hope and vision for a more life-enhancing culture.

As will become clear, the idea of "person" is central to every aspect of culture (for example, ethics, freedom, rights, and the common good). It controls not only the way we think about these realities but also how we protect and promote them. Therefore, it was chosen as the starting point for the Life Principles project.

As noted earlier, "person" has been severely delimited by the perpetuation and justification of abortion and euthanasia and has been rendered increasingly intangible. If we are to prevent it from fading into mere myth and meaninglessness, we will have to acknowledge its objective reality through objective definition. Hence, Part One of this book will investigate how to make objective definitions (Chapter One).

Given the centrality of "person" to meaning in our lives and in the culture, we cannot afford to define it inadequately or falsely. One may say that the definition of "person" is merely a matter of subjective opinion. A "person" is what we make "it" to be. But is personhood really a matter of subjective opinion? Is there no objective ground? I intend to show that there is, indeed, a very solid and objective ground, which was discovered by the ancient Greek philosopher Aristotle (384–322 B.C.) and reiterated by many philosophers since that time right into the contemporary age. The solution lies in an investigation of human powers and ends that will, in turn, lead us into an investigation of fulfillment and happiness. Chapters Two and Three will examine the four levels of happiness, meaning, and purpose in life, giving emphasis to the third and fourth levels, which, though more intangible, are more pervasive, enduring, and deep.

Part Two will describe the third and fourth levels of meaning and purpose as they relate to the ten categories of cultural discourse. These ten categories include happiness, success, quality of life, and love (Chapter Four); suffering (Chapter Five); ethics and freedom (Chapter Six); and person, rights, and the common good (Chapter Seven). Unfortunately, because the ten categories are intangible, they too are underestimated and undervalued. This gives rise not only to superficiality but also to highly problematic conduct within the culture. An improvement in the notions of happiness and personhood should bring about a more precise and complete view of the other eight categories. These ten categories are summarized in a useful chart (Chapter Eight), which contrasts Level 1 and 2 views with improved Level 3 and 4 views. If these improved attitudes are incorporated into the minds and hearts of both individuals and the culture itself, it should produce a decrease in confusion, depression, aimlessness, violence, and other social problems. With this as our foundation, the social programs used to alleviate cultural problems will be far more effective. It would be a critical means to healing the culture.

After attempting to recover the reality of these core intangibles (which redresses the problems in box 1), the book then proceeds to Part Three, which addresses the two life issue assumptions arising out of our metaphysical materialism. Recall from section II above, that these two assumptions are:

1. The personhood of the fetus is a bogus issue.

2. The quality of life of the elderly, disabled, and terminally ill is highly dubitable.

Chapters Nine and Ten attempt to redress these assumptions by pointing to their problematic foundations (abortion and euthanasia, boxes 2–4). Whether the Court likes it or not, it has tremendous moral influence within the culture. It gives moral sanction and, in this capacity, could also sanction the wholesale violation of the rights of individuals. In brief, by its legitimization of abortion, the Court has unwittingly perpetuated

1. the subjectivization of "person", "intrinsic dignity", and inalienable rights

2. the idea that Level 1 and 2 meaning in life is more realistic because these levels are more tangible

3. a belief that unclarity about personhood and rights justifies their denial

The Court not only has moral authority; it has teaching authority as well. Its understanding (or misunderstanding) of "person" in the *Roe vs. Wade* decision will eventually trickle down through the media and the educational system into the minds of adults, adolescents, and children. If the Court's view of personhood is narrow, then the culture's definition of "person" is likely to become narrower. Similarly, if the Court's definition of "person" were elitist, then the culture's view of person-hood would likely become more elitist (see, for example, the *Dred Scott* decision, where a whole group of people was excluded from person-hood based on skin color).

The euthanasia issue is also directly connected to our view of "per-son". If the Court gives approval to assisted suicide and lethal injection, it will also inadvertently pass a negative judgment on the lives of those with terminal illnesses and, along with them, the elderly and those with dis-abilities in general. As will be shown, virtually every suicide request from a terminally ill person is reversed when pain and depression are treated.[2] Furthermore, the World Health Organization believes that pain, in the vast majority of terminal illnesses, can be completely alleviated.[3] In light of these two studies, an approval of euthanasia by the courts would con-stitute a judgment on the quality of life of the terminally ill, elderly, and disabled. Euthanasia is not for the sake of alleviating pain and depression; it is for the alleviation of an "inadequate quality of life".

Again, we must confront the myth that one "little" idea can't have all that much effect. As will be shown throughout this book, one "little" idea can have the gravest of consequences if it is central enough. Elitist views of personhood have besieged the African American population, caused genocide in Nazi Germany and the former Soviet Union, and lie at the root of virtually every form of bias and prejudice. An elitist or narrow view of personhood excludes many from the domain of rights holders, causing confusion and even violence when those who have been thrown outside of its domain clamor to get their inherent rights reinstated. But why did they have to have their rights reinstated if rights belong to individuals by their very nature? No one, no government, gives inalienable rights to individuals; therefore, no one may take them away. One can easily see the seeds of confusion, malaise, and even vi-olence in such an enterprise. One "little" idea can have immense de-structive power.

But lest I focus on the negative, I hasten to add that one "little" idea can have immense constructive power. When we define personhood

---

[2] Kathleen M. Foley, M.D., "The Relationship of Pain and Symptom Management to Patient Requests for Physician-Assisted Suicide", *Journal of Pain and Symptom Management* 6 (1991): 290.

[3] *Cancer and Palliative Care*. Bulletin of the World Health Organization, Geneva, 1990.

with great depth and breadth, when we purge ourselves of every form of elitism (especially elitism directed against the weak, the powerless, and the marginalized), we find our view of happiness, freedom, the common good, rights, and even suffering to be ennobled. Our sense of compassion, joie de vivre, creativity, and, above all, dignity, respect, and appreciation will be extraordinarily heightened. One "little" idea can do much good for individual lives and for the culture.

The Life Principles project is meant to be not an ending point but rather a starting point. It is not enough to discover the breadth and depth of personhood; it must be reinstated within the culture's consciousness. So what can we do from here?

The objective of this book may be summed up as follows. If it can be shown that the intangibles are not only real but also the most pervasive, enduring, and deep of all realities (box 1), then we ought seriously to reexamine the two moral assumptions that have given rise to abortion and euthanasia (box 2). If we find those assumptions to be incomplete, untrue, and dangerous to the advancement of our culture, we ought to correct them. If we do correct them, then we ought to consider abortion and euthanasia legitimate moral issues, and if we consider them to be such, we ought to stop justifying them as legitimate activities (box 4). If we do this, we ought to reverse the fruits of our unwitting and unfortunate mistake (box 3). And if we do this, we ought, with all our might, to reenkindle the spirit of the third and fourth levels of meaning and purpose in life, in both our youth and adult populations (box 5). This, I believe, is the key to cultural survival and advancement. It is also the key to the actualization of our full, intrinsic, human dignity. This is what we are worthy of—nothing less.

PART ONE

DEFINING "PERSON" AND "HAPPINESS"

Introduction to Part One

In order to accomplish the immense cultural project mentioned in the Introduction to this book, it will be necessary to define some central concepts well. Just as good definitions give rise to good ideas and good ideas give rise to good cultural ideals, so also do incomplete definitions (arising out of narrow agendas and political expediency) give rise to poor ideas that in turn give rise to understated and even unhealthy cultural ideals. If, therefore, this book is to make any contribution to the culture at all, it will have to be concerned with the ten major categories of cultural discourse. Two of these categories (person and happiness) will be taken up in this first part. The other eight will be taken up in Part Two. These definitions will then be systematically applied to the issues of abortion and euthanasia (Part Three) in the hopes of revealing the severe harms they cause not only to persons but to the culture. This will be concluded with a call to action.

This part will first concern itself with definition theory (Chapter One). It will show not only how to define objectively (instead of by mere arbitrary assertion), but also completely (avoiding obvious omissions which can skew whole social and cultural agendas). This will lay the groundwork for a complete and objective definition of "person" and "happiness" (Chapters One through Three). When I use the word "complete" here, I do not mean to assert that every base has been covered. Far from it. Only omniscience could produce such a definition. "Complete" here means only "not overlooking one or more of the four causal explanations elucidated by Aristotle and his contemporary followers." I select Aristotle, not because of his venerable stature within the history of philosophy, but because of his uncanny ability to set out the *broadest* possible objective explanatory apparatus I have ever seen. Many contemporary philosophers have described one or more of these kinds of explanation in much greater detail, but none seems to have grasped the breadth and objectivity of all four better than the original master himself.

Chapter One

Defining the Human Person

Introduction

I would not purport to tell anyone *who* a person is. The *who* of the person is unique, holistic, intangible, and difficult to get hold of. It might be viewed as what is uniquely Spitzer about Spitzer, that is, the way I connect with other human beings, the feelings I exude and elicit, the virtues I believe, the decisions I have made, all wrapped up into one ineffable presence communicated in a face, a glance, or even a glimpse. I intend here to get at the nature (the *what*) of "person" in its breadth and depth so that personhood may, in all ways, be protected from every form of personal and cultural prejudice. I do not mean to reduce persons to "whats", for I am aware of both my unique "who" and the "who" of others. But intriguing and life giving as this awareness is, it is quite beyond the scope of this analysis, which has as its aim the elucidation of a central concept that can be used to heighten happiness, freedom, the common good, and rights.

I. Four Kinds of Definition

There are many ways of getting at the "what" of something. These ways are systematized under what is commonly called "definition theory". Definitions may be grouped into two kinds: (1) nominal definitions and (2) real definitions. A nominal definition does not try to get at the nature of a thing. It merely assigns a particular utterance to a particular phenomenon, such as when a child learns that a cool liquid in which he has immersed his hand is *called* "water". There is nothing special about the word "water". It does not reveal anything about the substance that is called by that name. It is just an arbitrary assignment of a symbolic utterance to a particular phenomenon.

All real definitions begin with nominal definitions, but go much further. A real definition attempts to get at the *nature* of a thing. It tries to describe ways in which the phenomenon is similar to other things and ways in which it is different or even unique. Medieval philosophers were fond of using the example "man is a rational animal". What they intended to show by this was that human beings had something in common with other conscious, sentient, and self-moving beings (animality, its genus), but that human beings possessed something specific that differentiated them from the rest of animals (rationality, its specific difference). Rationality referred to a very extensive, complex power. It included not only self-reflectivity (awareness of our awareness) but also our capacity to reflect on and desire the unrestricted, the unconditional, and the perfect in love, truth, goodness, beauty, and being. It was at once the ground of freedom and morality, creativity, genius, and even the aesthetic and the mystical. How did the medievals ever come to this rich notion of rationality? Why did they believe that it represents a unique characteristic differentiating humans from other animals? Why, indeed, did they believe that it would be an invaluable clue in discovering the essence, the "what", of a human person?

In order to answer these questions, one must probe into the ancient Greek background of the medieval philosophers, most particularly Aristotle. Aristotle himself was not content with merely nominal definitions, but wanted to get at the essence or nature of things. In order to do this, he devised a method for moving beyond mere appearances to the reality, that is, to the powers and even the perfection of the powers of things. A nominal definition is content with knowing to what phenomenon (appearance) an utterance corresponds. It is really quite subjective. What do we, as a community, call a thing that is quite large; has a brown trunk, little green objects growing out of it, and roots buried deeply into the ground; and occasionally bears fruit? *We* agree to call it a "tree". No one can deny the importance of this *subjective* enterprise. Without it we would not have language and therefore would not be able to communicate. And we would certainly not be able to *explain* things in terms of real definitions.

A well-known contemporary philosopher, Bernard Lonergan, drew an important distinction between description and explanation. "Description", he noted, was the relationship between ourselves as observers and what we know through our senses (a datum). For example, "the sun is rising". Here the sun's motion relative to the observer is that of rising. Though this is a perfectly good *description*, it does not tell us about the *nature* of the sun's motion. If we are to understand its nature, we must turn to *explanation*, that is, relating one datum to other data. In this case, this would be "the earth is rotating on its own axis and revolving around the sun". Here the definer is attempting to minimize the role of the observer and to emphasize how one datum relates to other data. We are now beginning to understand *how* the sun gives the *appearance* of rising. We are no longer content with the fact that the sun appears to be rising (a true description); we are probing the nature of the real, physical motions that cause this appearance. Notice that as we move from description to explanation, we are also moving from a subjective viewpoint to a more objective, causal viewpoint. I think this reflects Aristotle's intention when he tries to differentiate definitions based on appearances (what he terms "accidents") and real definitions, which get to the heart of what causes a thing to be what it is.

There are many ways of approaching real (or explanatory) definitions. We could relate a datum to various activities, or even the magnitude of those activities. We could also relate a datum to the external causes of those activities, or even to the perfection of those activities. Before explaining each of these in detail, it will do well to understand that we have moved from the realm of appearances to activities. Explanation is not simply a process of relating data to other data. Ultimately, it's about relating activities (such as the movement of the sun) to other activities (say, the movement of the earth). Why activities? Because they reveal not only what a thing "looks like" but also what a thing can do, that is, its powers.

Power is an internal source of activity. Without it, there is no change, motion, creativity, or constructive or destructive force of any kind. It is that without which there is no activity. Now, powers can *appear* in many different ways. They could have different sizes, shapes, or colors, but when one reflects on it, it's not really the size, shape, or color that's of import, but what this reality can do. If it can't do anything, it might be interesting to look at, but for all intents and purposes, it has no causative force beyond itself. It cannot contribute or be positive in any way. For Aristotle, then, if one wanted to know what a thing was, one looked to what it could do. That's what makes it useful. That's what gives it efficacy, causative force, productivity, and positivity. The appearance of this doing, causing, productive, positive thing was quite secondary. What do you think is more important—the fact that this appearance can think rationally and act justly, or that it is six foot three and weighs 190 pounds? For Aristotle, the first indicated the reality, the substance of a thing. The second was mere accident.

Now, the power of a thing is revealed by its activities. To see what a thing can do is to know what it has the power to do. If I see a phenomenon attracting electrons to itself at a particular magnitude, I think it has the power to do this. (Let us call this the power of protons.) If I see an animal move itself to capture another animal, I assume it has a motor power. If I see a phenomenon performing sentient activities, I assume that it has sensorial powers. If I see a phenomenon writing relevant equations on a piece of paper, I conclude that it may well have rational powers. If I see a datum reflecting on the infinite, I may assume that it has the power to appreciate such an unrestricted concept.

When we observe a thing, we can get stuck just looking at its appearance, or we can shift our focus to what the appearance is *doing*. The second perspective is far more important than the first for getting at the nature of things. But we cannot stop there. We cannot merely stop at the *fact* that this object has particular powers; we would also like to know what external elements allow these powers to work and what the perfection of the powers would be. In short, if we want to know the nature of a thing, we need to understand:

1. how a particular power is similar to or different from other powers (the "what" of the power)

2. the conditions upon which a power depends for its being or activity (the "how" of the power)

3. the fulfillment or the perfection of the power (what it was meant to be)

There are technical names for each of these perspectives of a thing's power (formal cause, efficient cause, and final cause, respectively), but they are not relevant to our purpose. Suffice it to say that each perspective represents one of the forms of real definition, a definition that gets to the nature of a thing.

Let me illustrate each kind of definition in turn through the simple example of an acorn. Assume that the acorn is alive and that it is immersed in soil adequate for its germination. Most everyone could give this acorn its nominal definition. We know the kind of *appearance* that the word "acorn" is meant to signify within our particular linguistic community. But as was mentioned above, relevant as this is, it does not get to the nature of the thing. If I want to know the nature of the acorn, I must proceed to its activities. In observing those activities I notice that it is beginning to absorb water, that it must be metabolizing to some extent because it is growing, that this growth is taking on a very ordered process and eventually leads to the acorn's manifesting itself above the soil. Further examination shows me that it is performing photosynthesizing activities, that is, it is converting light energy into both metabolic activity and chemical energy. The list of activities can, of course, be expanded much further. I can look at these activities and note their similarities to and differences from other activities performed by other objects, say, rocks and birds. I can try to classify these activities according to similarities and differences. In so doing, I find myself also classifying the powers of the acorn, for its powers (its internal dynamism) are precisely reflected in the activities performed. Now I am beginning to get to the nature of the acorn, but I have not yet fully explained it. I have gotten to its "what" definition (its relationship to— its similarities to and differences from—other powers and activities), but I have not yet gotten to its "how" definition (its relationship to the conditions upon which it depends for its existence and activity) or its "fulfillment" or "perfection" definition (its relationship to the end that represents its full purpose, meaning, and destiny).

Recall that in order to know the nature of a thing, we want to *relate* it to as many *data* as possible. These relationships are not exhausted by the "what" (similarities and differences to other activities and powers). We also notice that powers have *conditions* for their existence and activity. These conditions are not simply in my mind; they really exist. They are really necessary for the existence and operation of the power. I will consider these conditions in two parts: (1) conditions for a power's existence and (2) conditions for a power's activities.

First, I will consider the conditions of existence. In the case of the acorn, the main condition of the acorn's existence is an oak tree upon which it can grow. In other words, without the oak tree, an acorn would not exist. Hence, the oak tree is a condition necessary for the acorn's existence; that is, the acorn is dependent on the oak tree for its existence.

But we do not have to restrict ourselves simply to conditions of the acorn that existed *before* the acorn (like the oak tree). We can also see conditions that are coexistent with the acorn. For example, certain kinds of cells and structures of cells are necessary for the acorn's existence. These cells, in turn, also have conditions for their existence. They depend on certain molecules and structures of molecules. These molecules depend on certain atoms and structures of atoms. These atoms, of course, are also dependent on conditions like quarks and quantum fields for their existence. And so on.

To relate a power to the conditions for its existence is to understand even more about the nature of the power. Now I not only know the powers of the acorn through its activities; I also know the conditions necessary for that power's existence. I have deeper understanding. Notice that my understanding is not subjective. I am not, here, interested in what the linguistic community *calls* these conditions, I am interested in the *real* conditions that are *really* necessary for the *real* powers to *exist*. I am seeking its objective nature, not subjective preferences.

Not only are there conditions for a power's existence; there are also conditions for its activity. Notice that just because something has power does not mean that the power will become active and do something. Thus, for example, even though a live acorn has the power to grow, that power may never become active, and so the acorn may finally wither up and die, producing a nice ornament, but never achieving its purpose or perfection (that is, an oak tree). The conditions that allow a power to become active are called conditions of *activity*. In the case of the acorn, this would be soil with a proper pH, proper nitrogen, proper nutrients, and so on. It would also include water and, when the acorn has emerged above the soil, sunlight. Obviously, this list could be expanded much further. The more I know about the conditions necessary for the power to become active, and even why these conditions are necessary for the power to become active, the more I know about the power of the acorn and, therefore, about the acorn's nature. Again, notice that I am talking not about something inside my mind but rather about something that really exists in the acorn and in its external environment, that is, real connections between its powers and its external environment, real connections between its power and the activation of its power. These real connections are not about a name but are about realities that *explain* the nature of the thing.

Knowing the "what" and the "how" of a thing is still not complete, for it embraces only a thing's past and present. Aristotle recognized that there is one more vital component that must be considered: its *"to ti en einai"* ("what it was to be" or "what it was meant to be"). At first this seems like a complex expression. But what Aristotle meant by this was a thing's full purpose, its perfection when it finally arrives at the fullest stage of its development, its fullest capacity for acting, the fullest form of its power. In the case of the acorn, this would be a fully developed oak tree.

Again, it must be emphasized that I am not speaking here about something that is only in my mind, such as my knowledge that this acorn will one day be an oak tree. I am speaking about something that is in the acorn itself, which has the power to direct the development of the acorn toward its full purpose and perfection (when, of course, all of the conditions for this development are met). There is not only a power to act within the acorn; there is also a power to direct development in a systematic, intelligible way toward a perfection that has not yet been fully actualized. This power, and even the information necessary to direct it, must be real now in order for development to occur now. Today we might talk about this information in terms of genetics and may speak of the power that uses this information to produce development as "a systematic, holistic series of cellular divisions".[1]

It is not necessary for the reader to get overly involved in the nuances of these examples. What's important is the awareness of a real, objective, informationally based guiding power that causes systematic, holistic development toward a perfection that does not yet exist. Inasmuch as this guiding *power* really exists, a perfection definition is not merely a subjective awareness of future potential; it is really existing future potential with intelligible, causative force. It is a really existing power.

It might be helpful to use a crude analogy here to make this point clear. Some readers may be familiar with the operation of a computer. The central processing unit (CPU), the random-access memory (RAM)

---

[1] See Jerome Lejeune, M.D., in *Junior L. Davis and Mary Sue Davis vs. Ray King, M.D., d/b/a Fertility Center of East Tennessee, Third Party Defendant*, "Custody Dispute over Seven Human Embryos", Aug. 1989.

and the various disk drives constitute the powers of the computer (known through the "what" definition). The other silicon chips and the electromagnetic circuitry constitute the conditions of its *existence* (known through the "how" definition). The electricity and the computer operator constitute the conditions for its *activity* (known again through the "how" definition). Finally, the *software* or the hard disk or an external drive constitutes the fulfillment or perfection of the computer in a particular mode of operation.

Notice that the software may not yet be loaded into the random-access memory. When it is not, the computer still has everything it needs to be fully operational, but that full operation cannot take place until the software is loaded. When software on a floppy disk is loaded onto the RAM it takes a bit of time for the computer to become fully operational. We would not want to say that the computer is missing any of the hard or soft elements required for its operation. All that is needed is an interaction between the two existing elements, which requires time.

If, during the loading process, I were to destroy your software and say to you, "Oh, it wasn't worth much because it wasn't in a fully operational state yet", you would probably get mad and take me to small claims court, or worse. Again, if I were to destroy the computer and say to you that it couldn't do anything yet—I had pushed some buttons and it didn't respond—you would again probably get mad. Why? Because you would realize the intrinsic value of the software and the computer. You would say that even though it takes a little while for it to become operational, it still had value.

For readers who might be interested in another, more complex but fascinating example of powers and the perfection of powers demonstrated through quantum systems, please see Appendix 1. For readers who find the example unnecessary or too cumbersome, we can now proceed directly to the definition of the human person.

II. Definition of "Person"

As was noted in the introduction to this book, an incomplete definition of "person" can adversely affect individual persons and the culture. Such an incomplete notion of "person" can lead to bias or prejudice or, even worse, to the negation of personhood in particular individuals or even whole groups of individuals. The cultural consequences of this range from confusion and depression to inequality and even violence. It is therefore imperative that we move beyond merely nominal definitions to grasp all three facets of the real definition of personhood.

As was noted earlier, definitions begin with a subjective component, a labeling, so that we might know the datum (the given) signified by a particular word. In this case, we look to the data signified by the word "person", and we see that it refers, evidently, to a being of human origin. Of course, this is an abstract generalization from a wide range of experiences. This generalization begins at childhood with associations made between the word "person" and the child's experience of particular phenomena. If we are speaking to children and we want to teach them what the word "person" means, we try to impart this range of appearances to them in the hopes that they can abstract a general category into which these different appearances can fit. "Look, Suzie, there's a 'person', a man. There's another 'person', a baby. And another 'person', an adolescent girl." After a while, Suzie gets the point and begins to see that "person" signifies a wide range of appearances that have a human origin. The gender, the race, the stage of development are not of particular consequence to "person", but having a human mother and father is. At this point, the child has formed a *nominal* definition. She knows what the human community generally means by "person". It is, at this point, still a subjective definition. This is suitable for the child, but rather insubstantial for courts, legislatures, and those having the power to create prejudice or even proscribe rights.

Before I begin the threefold process of achieving an objective definition, the reader would be well reminded that what we are accomplishing here is a process of discovery, not decision. We are trying to get to the nature of something, a nature that exists in its own right without help of any other human being's intellect or defining power. A real definition is oriented toward *discovering* what it is, how it is, and what it was meant to be. It is not *deciding* these things.

So, we begin with a "what" definition. As was noted earlier, we want to move from the appearances to the activities of the appearance. It must be remembered that appearances don't get at the nature of things; activities and powers do. We would not want to say that Joe is not a person because, as an adult, he has achieved a height of only four feet.

Unusual as this might be, Joe may well display human activities or the information necessary to produce these activities. He may, therefore, have the powers or the *to ti en einai* of these powers within him. Again, one would not want to ground Joe's personhood in how much he weighed or the color of his skin, his eyes, or his hair.

What are the distinctive powers of a human person? I will be discussing this further in Chapter Two. For the time being, it will suffice to elucidate some of the powers that belong to beings of human origin. We can, of course, see powers that human beings have in common with other animals. We have various biological desires. We engage in metabolic activity; we grow, procreate, and avoid painful stimuli. We are conscious of things outside of us. We are capable of feeling pain. We experience pleasure when certain desires are fulfilled, and we have a capacity for self-movement that is grounded in desire. For example, our desire for sustenance (indicated by hunger) can cause self-motion when we spot a delectable fruit on the tree.

Human beings also have powers going beyond those of even the most highly developed, sentient, conscious beings. I do not want to engage here in a debate about whether higher vertebrates truly experience love or experience merely a high form of affection. I also wish to avoid the question of whether higher vertebrates are self-conscious or merely conscious. This would go far beyond the scope of this book and accomplish little with respect to the definitional problem at hand. Hence, I will try to restrict myself to what most philosophers would consider to be a reasonable belief: that humans alone seem to be preoccupied with the infinite, the unconditional, and the perfect.

Of course, we cannot say for certain that an eagle is not thinking about the infinite or about unconditional truth, love, or beauty. If the eagle is, it certainly does not display frustrations about not having achieved the perfect, despair about not comprehending unconditional love, anger about not creating a perfect utopia, or frustration with the mathematical paradoxes of infinity. Eagles do not seem to cut off their ears when their aesthetic senses cannot be perfectly produced on canvases. Their awareness of the sublime beauty of music seems rather to be an oblivion. They simply do not display behaviors indicating a concern for God or the Infinite itself, for ultimate explanation, or indeed for the complete set of correct answers to the complete set of questions.

One is reminded of Bernard Lonergan's cryptic remark[2] that when nonhuman animals run out of biological opportunities and dangers (food, shelter, reproduction, avoidance of pain and predators, and even affection), they fall asleep. When humans run out of biological opportunities and dangers, they ask questions—questions about their identity, their destiny, their ideals, optimal love, unconditional truth, perfect social orders, optimal goodness, perfect beauty, and even the Infinite itself, the Sublime itself, the Mystical, the Creator, that is, God. It is not simply the ability to ask questions. It's the ability to ask questions about what is ultimate, unconditional, perfect, infinite, absolute, and eternal with respect to love, goodness, truth, beauty, and being. This is what humans seem to do uniquely by comparison with the other members of the animal kingdom. It is reasonable to believe that these powers are unique to beings of human origin. They therefore constitute part of the objective definition of "person".

It should also be noted that the above activities are linked to the goals, ideals, and perfection of the human species. They represent the full perfection of human power. Recall that Aristotle called this the "*to ti en einai*" (the "what it was meant to be") definition. I have given it the simpler label, "perfection definition", or a "perfecting, guiding power". In the case of a human person, we could therefore say that its "perfection" definition is to have access to, to contemplate, to desire, and to act upon the perfect, unconditional, unrestricted, and absolute in the areas of Truth itself, Love itself, Goodness/Justice itself, Beauty itself, and Being itself. This contemplation on these five transcendental notions could extend into mathematics, metaphysics, aesthetics, philosophy, and, of course, the spiritual, the mystical, and the religious. It can influence every goal, ideal, aspiration, relationship, thought, and action of any given human being who has achieved full actualization. Now, this signifies the perfection of a human being's powers. But the "perfection" definition is not merely concerned with the perfection of these powers; it really refers to the guiding power that moves the human being to these perfections.

This perfecting, guiding power is thought to have many causes. Some thinkers who are more materially inclined believe it to be solely genetic.

---

[2] *Insight: A Study of Human Understanding*, ed. Frederick E. Crowe and Robert M. Doran (Toronto: University of Toronto Press, 1992), p. 34.

They hold that the guiding power to all human perfections (presumably including even those that are oriented toward access to what is unrestricted, unconditional, and absolute) can be explained through a biophysical (genetic) apparatus. Other thinkers hold that even though the guiding power for most human perfections (the cerebral cortex, and a fully developed muscular structure) can be explained through genetics, the guiding power toward the desire for, and access to, the infinite, absolute, unconditional, and perfect cannot be so explained. They believe that if a power is going to guide a being toward a perfection, it must have the perfection toward which it is guiding this being, present to itself. How can something guide a being toward perfection X without this perfection being, in some sense, present ("known") to it? How can something guide a being to an "unknown" objective? It would cease to be guidance. In any case, these people believe that the guiding force toward these perfections must, in some sense, participate in the perfections themselves, that is, must participate in some unconditional or absolutely perfected quality. Since genes are *conditioned* by their biophysical parameters, these people believe that genes cannot guide a human being toward an *unconditional* objective. Hence, they hold that the guiding force to unconditional human actualization is transmaterial, that is, a transmaterial power that most refer to as a "soul".

For the purposes of this book, it does not matter whether one holds to a merely biophysical (genetic) guiding power or to a transcendental guiding power (a "soul") or to some combination of the two. The fact is that human beings *have* such a guiding power toward a transcendental perfection within them. There is abundant evidence for this guiding power. One can see it in a five-year-old who can reflect upon infinity. Again, one can see it in the five-year-old's desire for perfect love and perfect fairness (without even being trained to do this by parents or teachers). Again, one can see the perfection manifesting itself in the five-year-old's unrestricted desire to know. After answering one question about why the world is the way it is, the parent is constrained to give answers to a myriad of new questions of why *that* answer should be the way it is. One can see it in the five-year-old's fascination with the mystical (particularly in his art), and if a child grows up within a religious family, his fascination with God. If a five-year-old abundantly displays the effects of a guiding power toward a transcendental objective, why would one question that such a guiding power is operative from the very moment of his conception? We know the genetic guiding power to be operative from the moment of conception. Why, then, wouldn't the guiding powers toward this transcendental objective (whether it be genetic or a soul) be similarly present and operative? It is reasonable to believe that it is.

By combining the above steps of definition, we have the essentials of an objective definition of "person", namely, "*a being possessing an intrinsic guiding force* (whether this be merely genetic, a soul, or both) *toward fulfillment through unconditional, perfect, and even infinite Truth, Love, Goodness/Justice, Beauty, and Being*".

I believe that the above definition is *objective* because it relies only on publicly accessible data (not private, subjective data). Even though this data does rely on inner awareness or inner experience (and is therefore not sensorially accessible), I have considered it publicly accessible because it is sufficiently common to produce communication and substantial agreement. I consider the definition to be *complete* because I have allowed into the definition as much publicly accessible data as possible; that is, I have admitted the maximum amount of data about which communication and substantial agreement can be attained.

III. Some Ambiguities

It may be thought that if a particular human being does not *appear* to have reached full actualization, then that human being does not possess the above-mentioned guiding power toward transcendental perfection. As Aristotle indicated long ago, this reasoning is not valid. Empirical evidence seems to suggest that the guiding power *is* present, but that one of the conditions necessary to allow the guiding power to move the being to full actualization is not.

Recall the second kind of definition of which I spoke earlier (the "how" definition). The "how" definition refers to all the conditions necessary for a thing's existence and activity. The conditions for a thing's activity include its conditions for actualization or perfection. In the acorn example, such conditions for actualization included soil with a proper pH, proper nitrogen, proper nutrients, water, and, when the acorn has emerged above the soil, sunlight. If these conditions are not met, the acorn will not achieve its perfection (that is, the oak tree). This does not mean that the acorn does not contain a genetic code. Nor does it mean that the genetic code cannot act as a guiding power for the acorn to reach its perfection. It simply means that this guiding power is rendered ineffectual by the absence of *other* necessary factors for actualization.

In the case of a baby with cerebral palsy, one cannot conclude that the baby did not contain a guiding power toward a transcendental perfection (either a genetic one or a soul). One can only conclude that the baby was deprived of the oxygen necessary for her to *manifest* (to speak about or otherwise physically demonstrate) this transcendental perfection.

The debate about personhood intensifies as we move into the area of genetic disorders, because these seem to concern not *external* conditions for actualization but defects in the genetic apparatus (the guiding power) toward a being's full actualization. One kind of genetic disorder, like hydrocephalus, does not necessarily affect the full actualization of the human person per se. Rather, it introduces an element that could *impede* the full actualization. As the child develops, water begins to collect in the cranial area, causing retardation in the brain's development. If allowed to continue, the baby's head will be completely filled with water (thereby preventing all brain development) at birth. This disorder can be rectified by introducing a shunt in the base of the baby's skull while he is still developing in his mother's womb. This shunt allows the water to drain out of the baby's skull, thereby allowing normal brain development. Even though the problem of water in the skull has a genetic origin, the genetic apparatus is not flawed with respect to reaching its end (ordinary brain development). The guiding power is still capable of reaching its objective once the problem has been averted.

Perhaps the most difficult case is that of genetic disorders where the genetic apparatus is indeed flawed. For example, trisomy 13 (a genetic disorder) causes the child to develop in such a way that, among other possible anomalies, he never develops a cerebral cortex (a condition called anencephaly). Without a cerebral cortex, the child would not have the ability to manifest in his material body the kinds of activity that would normally indicate a capacity to desire, reflect upon, and have access to unconditional, unrestricted, absolute, and perfect Truth, Love, Goodness/Justice, Beauty, and Being (what was termed "transcendental perfection").

In this case, those who believe that the guiding power is merely material (that is, merely genetic) hold that personhood may not be present because a guiding power toward full human actualization (transcendental perfection) is really not present. Because they assume that the guiding power is completely reducible to the genetic apparatus, the absence of a genetic apparatus that can lead to a fully actualized human being means the absence of a guiding power toward full actualization. According to this assumption, human personhood would not be present.

Conversely, those who, for the reasons mentioned above, hold that the guiding power to full human actualization (transcendental perfection) is not reducible to a genetic apparatus (and is therefore connected to a soul) will hold the contrary opinion. They will assert that inasmuch as the soul is present, the guiding power is present. Therefore, a flawed genetic apparatus only necessitates that the transcendental perfection of the being cannot be *physically* manifest. Since there is no way of knowing whether or not a soul is present (because it is not physically manifest), these thinkers make recourse to either religious doctrines or spiritual/metaphysical beliefs.

The question now emerges as to whether a *belief* in the presence of a human soul (oriented toward transcendental perfection) is sufficient to know the presence of personhood. The answer to this question is that the belief is sufficient for those who have it and is quite insufficient for those who do not. We will, therefore, have to make the decision on the basis of some criterion outside the context of the regular rules of evidence, for this kind of evidence is simply not available. I would suggest a principle to which I will make recourse in the chapter on rights, namely, that when one is in doubt, one ought to err on the side of assuming personhood rather than denying it. As I noted in the introduction, the reason for making this assumption is grounded in famous court decisions like the *Dred Scott* case. In such cases, doubts about personhood led the courts to deny basic human rights to Black people instead of affirming them. The ethical and historical consequences of that assumption have had deleterious effects on a whole population and on U.S. culture for generations.

Returning to the case of the anencephalic child, I believe the most prudent course of action is to assume the personhood of the child. Even though the vast majority of such children can live no more than two weeks after birth, the culture's desire to protect even this short-lived manifestation of personhood draws a line in the sand. If we will not budge on either our definition of personhood or in our assumption of personhood in the most ambiguous cases, then we will not allow ourselves to compromise or undermine our awareness of personhood in the less ambiguous ones.

I hope that this assessment of the anencephalic child does not strike those with a materialistic interpretation of the guiding force of human actualization as hopelessly idealistic. I do not want to foist a doctrine of ensoulment on those who do not believe it. And I certainly do not intend to make any argument in this book dependent upon such a doctrine. Rather, my objective here is to set out a cultural principle worthy of everyone's consideration. This cultural principle is not concerned with assumptions about materialism, ensoulment, or the guiding force of human actualization. It is concerned with the direction in which we will err when confronted by ambiguities in the manifestation of personhood. Given what has been said about the centrality of personhood in virtually every cultural norm and ideal, and how this central notion can bring on confusion and ambivalence, or clarity and principled behavior, it would do well for both materialists and transmaterialists seriously to consider the cultural and sociopolitical consequences of erring on the side of denying personhood versus erring on the side of assuming personhood when evidence is no longer capable of determining this decision.

IV. Summary and Principles

The preceding definition of "person" and its foundations and ramifications can be summarized in the following three steps:

A. Definition

A "person" is a being possessing a *to ti en einai* or guiding impetus toward fulfillment/perfection through unconditional, perfect, unrestricted, and absolute Truth, Love, Goodness/Justice, Beauty, and Being. This definition will be considered valid irrespective of whether the above-mentioned "guiding impetus" originates from merely genetic sources, a spiritual source (for example, a soul), or both.

B. The Critical Principle

Inasmuch as *any* being should be treated with a dignity commensurate with its nature, persons should be treated with an *unconditional* dignity commensurate with their guiding impetus toward fulfillment in *unconditional* Truth, Love, Goodness/Justice, Beauty, and Being. Such a dignity acknowledges not only the intrinsic worth of a human being, but also the intrinsic *transcendental* worth of the person. This unconditional dignity is, in the last resort, the ground of inalienable rights (see Chapter Seven), which acknowledges a universal duty to protect and promote this unconditional dignity. More than this merely political consequence, the acknowledgment of this unconditional dignity grounds a *desire* for the common good and *care* for the other and so frees the heart to pursue friendship and love and a culture worthy of both.

C. The Critical Assumption

In view of the intrinsic, unconditional dignity of the human person, we can*not* in any way risk taking it away, for this dignity does not belong to us. It is *intrinsic* to the person. Furthermore, the harm done would be unconditional and absolute in its proportion (commensurate with the nature of the person). Hence, we cannot risk violating the Silver Rule (do no harm), for a harm here would constitute the destruction of unconditional dignity. Perhaps the greatest harm done to persons in human history has been to assume that a being of human origin was *not* a person (not possessing an unconditional dignity). We can see this with respect to slavery in ancient and recent times, genocide, and totalitarian political persecutions of every kind.

The only way of preventing these kinds of egregious harms is to make *the* most important and primary cultural assumption: *that every being of human origin should be considered a person.* Doubt about personhood should never be considered a warrant for denying personhood. An error in this regard could lead to every form of genocide, slavery, and political disenfranchisement based not on certain evidence but on doubt. If we as a culture do not together make this critical assumption, we risk the possibility of compromising unconditional dignity, causing irreparable individual harm, and seriously undermining our culture. The

Silver Rule (the absolute ethical minimum for any culture) could be irreparably violated, and the notion of inalienable rights rendered impotent. Given the above consequences, I must restate the critical assumption in even bolder terms: *when in doubt, err on the side of assuming and according personhood to every being of human origin, whether or not the activities of that being manifest the above transcendental qualities of personhood.* Failure to do this will simply cause us to repeat the errors of history.

The rest of this book will be devoted to explicating these steps. First, I will examine the heart, for it is not sufficient to make the above critical assumption from a purely mental point of view. We must care about it enough to defend and promote it. We need not only the heart's *understanding* but also the heart's *conviction* (the disposition of our wills). Secondly, I will probe the above intrinsic, transcendental nature of the person so that the unconditional dignity of persons (including ourselves) can be more clearly appreciated and appropriated. Thirdly, I will look at how this view of the human person affects the nine other major categories of cultural discourse (happiness, success, self-worth/quality of life, love, suffering, ethics, freedom, rights, and the common good). Fourthly, I will look at how this view of dignity and personhood affects the inalienability of rights, the intrinsic ordering of rights, and our view of the common good. And finally, I will look at how the issues of abortion and euthanasia undermine all of the above in the individual harms they cause, the implicit duties they impose, and the redefining of the ten categories of cultural discourse. The net result is a deep wounding of the culture.

In view of the fact that people intend such good things for one another, and in view of the little and great acts of love that are daily manifest in our lives, in view of the many acts of kindness, delight, and friendship that characterize our lives, and in view of our desire for the common good and to enter into common cause toward that good, the above cultural harm seems so unnecessary, indeed, another one of history's tragic flaws. If we are to let our better side overcome this tragic flaw, we must together make the above critical assumption an integral part of both our minds and hearts. Once taken seriously, it will liberate our vision of the intrinsic, transcendental dignity of personhood leading to a horizon that will not allow for the individual and cultural harms we now face.

Chapter Two

Defining "Happiness"

Introduction

After coming to an objective definition of "person", one might ask, "Why should we concern ourselves with the matters of the heart?" The answer is that even though an objective definition gives solidity, stability, and certitude, it does not give freedom. Even though it gives evidence and grounding, it does not move one to care or concern. If we do not make an earnest attempt to set our hearts free, indeed, if we do not even know how to set our hearts free, we will not be able to move our most objective, most correct, and most complete ideas into reality. We'll be all dressed up with no place to go.

I. The "Heart"

In the posthumous collection of notes entitled *Pensées*, Blaise Pascal observes, "The heart has reasons that the mind knows not of." [1] Most of us have an intuition about what this might mean, but we need more than an intuition, for the culture, the common good, and the future of rights are dependent upon the reasons of the heart and the mind. Inasmuch as Pascal was a mathematician, his view of the "mind's reasons" was probably related to geometrical demonstration, algebraic proof, mathematical definition, the setting of postulates, and so on. In fact, this barely touches the surface of what can be known by human beings. As noted in the previous chapter, the Neoplatonists recognized knowledge outside the spatio-temporal, mathematical, and even imaginary domain that they termed "the five transcendentals" (being, truth, goodness/

---

[1] Blaise Pascal, *Pensées* (1670).

55

justice, beauty, and "the one"). Moreover, poets have recognized yet another "transcendental", namely love, which philosophers and theologians have frequently spoken of as an ultimate objective of humankind. Pascal saw that there was a dimension untouched by the domain of objective definition theory, logic, and mathematical demonstration. He believed his beloved mathematics had to be complemented by these transcendentals in order to achieve the full depth and breadth of understanding and judgment. Through this complementary relationship, the heart "awakens" the mind as the mind awakens the heart. Witness, for example, the great physicist and astronomer Sir Arthur Eddington, who in his famous work *The Nature of the Physical World* makes a defense of mysticism as a consequence of his own scientific inquiry:

> We all know that there are regions of the human spirit untrammeled by the world of physics. In the mystic sense of the creation around us, in the expression of art, in a yearning towards God, the soul grows upward and finds the fulfillment of something implanted in its nature. The sanction for this development is within us, a striving born with our consciousness or an Inner Light proceeding from a greater power than ours. Science can scarcely question this sanction, for the pursuit of science springs from a striving which the mind is impelled to follow, a questioning that will not be suppressed. Whether in the intellectual pursuits of science or in the mystical pursuits of the spirit, the light beckons ahead and the purpose surging within our nature responds.[2]

Just as Eddington reached the final frontier of scientific inquiry, another kind of knowing was awakened within him. He began to sense mystery beyond limit, a light beyond mathematical reasoning. Instead of feeling closure or an emptiness beyond mathematics, he sensed a *being* beyond mathematics that infused it with a reality much greater than the mathematics could define. In his pursuit of truth, Eddington *allowed* his other mental faculty to be awakened, to absorb passively and be filled by the mystery beyond Schrödinger's and Einstein's equations, and found himself in a state of appreciation and awe rather than in a state of demonstration and control. This experience of awakening extends also to the pursuit of goodness, justice, beauty, and love.

---

[2] Sir Arthur Eddington, *The Nature of the Physical World* (Cambridge, England: Cambridge University Press, 1929), pp. 327–28.

Perhaps the most important function of the heart is to seek meaning and purpose in life. If one attempts only to find meaning and purpose through what Pascal called the "mind", one will likely limit one's view of reality (and therefore of "person") to what is clearly perceivable and tangible. But if one complements the mind with the heart, one's horizon will open upon Eddington's mysticism in the equations of physics, the mystery perceived in the glimpse of a sunset over the ocean, the ecstasy felt in a Brahms symphony, the call felt in the simple song of a bird, or even time slipping to its still point in the midst of profound camaraderie. The heart really does have reasons that the mind knows not of, and when these two realities work inclusively, the full range of human ideals, desires, passions, commitments, wisdom, hopes, freedom, indeed, even the common good, seems to find a breadth and a depth that it never had before. The human spirit comes alive. It sees things anew, finds profound meaning and hope where before it may have had little. Above all, it gives a different vision of the human *person*. The recognition and valuing of the knowledge of the heart can set one free to see persons in a completely new light—in the light of mystery, in the desire for the unconditional and the unrestricted, in the boundlessness of curiosity, in the profundity of the desire for perfect love, in the quest for perfect beauty, and even in the longing for perfect goodness and truth.

II. The Effect of the "Heart" on the Culture

What does the above mean about the definition of "person" and its effects upon "rights", the "common good", and the good of the culture? Everything. For as the heart goes, so goes the definition of "person". And as the definition of "person" goes, so goes the definition of "rights" (see Chapter Seven), and as the definition of "rights" goes, so goes the definition of the "common good". And as the definition of the "common good" goes, so goes the *real* welfare of the culture. Will the culture contribute or detract from the development of human beings? Will the culture lead to greater unity or disarray? Will it promote peace or hatred? Equality and dignity, or bias and prejudice? Will it seek a solution to its problems in truth, love, goodness, beauty, and being, or rather in lies, hatred, injustice, depravity, and annihilation? It all depends on whether our hearts are in the trim, whether we use our hearts to open up our vision of the human person or to narrow it. It all depends on whether we really care about the person we have perceived, whether "person" and "rights" are merely legal abstractions, or whether they are the most objective yet mysterious realities within our worldly purview.

In the Introduction to this book we saw that if the culture is to lead toward greater possibilities and opportunities for humankind (instead of the opposite), it will have to have the most complete and objective definition of "person" possible. Now it is apparent this task will require both knowledge of the mind *and* knowledge of the heart.

The mind liberates the heart and the heart liberates the mind. If our vision of personhood and of individual persons can be caught up in this ongoing interdependent cycle, we can be sure that we will see dignity wherever it may be, that rights will not be a mere legal abstraction, and that the common good will be fired by a passion and a vision that will surprise even the greatest optimist. A culture cannot help but benefit from this. The upcoming four levels of happiness are intended not only to awaken the heart, but also to produce a complementarity of mind and heart that will open upon a truly respectful, responsible, and benevolent culture.

III. Four Levels of Happiness, Desire, and Purpose in Life

To know one's desires is to know one's purpose, since both are oriented toward fulfillment and perfection. Every desire seeks fulfillment. It is at once an emptiness and an anticipation toward something that it does not have. It is filled with purposefulness toward this objective, toward what will eliminate the emptiness, toward what will fulfill. The correlation between desire and purpose is so intimate that one can make any one or more of one's desires into one's entire identity or purpose in life. For example, I can turn my desire for comfort into my sole purpose in life. Or, I could turn my desire for admiration into my purpose. Likewise, love or truth could also be my purpose in life. Therefore, wherever there is desire, there is purpose; and wherever there is purpose, there is the potential to seek complete actualization and identity. Whether this desire be superficial or sublime, it can become the limiting conditions or the horizon for my entire purpose and even for myself.

Desire is not linked only to purpose; it is also linked to happiness. In general, when my desires are fulfilled, I am happy. When my desires go unfulfilled, I am unhappy. Perhaps the most general definition of happiness is "the fulfillment of desire" (whether that desire be superficial or sublime). Likewise, the most general definition of unhappiness might be the nonfulfillment of desire: frustration, continual heartache, and yearning. In sum, happiness is linked to desire; desire to purpose; and, therefore, happiness to purpose.

The forthcoming discussion of happiness/desire goes by many names. Many philosophers refer to these concepts as purpose in life or happiness. Others call them the four powers of a human being. Some psychologists have called them fulcrums of identity, dimensions of self-actualization, or markers of growth. Some theologians have identified them with phases in the journey of the soul or levels of spiritual life. Sociologists, anthropologists, historians, and writers have likewise classified them under still different names, which simply reflect different perspectives on the same reality.

One can see these four levels of happiness in the works of such diverse thinkers as Plato[3] and Kierkegaard,[4] Aristotle[5] and Jaspers,[6] Augustine[7] and Buber,[8] Viktor Frankl[9] and Abraham Maslow,[10] and Thomas

---

[3] See, for example, Edith Hamilton and Huntington Cairns, ed., *The Collected Dialogues of Plato* (Princeton, N.J.: Princeton University Press, 1973): *The Republic*, books VI and VII (pp. 720–72); *Phaedrus* (pp. 475–525); and *Symposium* (pp. 526–74).

[4] Søren Kierkegaard, *Works of Love: Some Christian Reflections in the Form of Discourses*, trans. Howard and Edna Hong (New York: Harper and Row, 1962); *The Sickness unto Death: A Christian Psychological Exposition for Upbuilding and Awakening*, ed. and trans. Howard and Edna Hong (Princeton, N.J.: Princeton University Press, 1980); *The Concept of Anxiety: A Simple Psychologically Orienting Deliberation on the Dogmatic Issue of Hereditary Sin*, ed. and trans. Reidar Thomte (Princeton, N.J.: Princeton University Press, 1980); and *Either/Or: A Fragment of Life*, trans. David F. Swenson and Lillian Marvin Swenson (Princeton, N.J.: Princeton University Press, 1944).

[5] See, for example, Richard McKeon, ed., *The Basic Works of Aristotle* (New York: Random House, 1941): *De Anima*, book III (pp. 589–603); *Nichomachean Ethics* (complete).

[6] Karl Jaspers, *Way to Wisdom*, trans. Ralph Manheim (New Haven: Yale University Press, 1954) and *Reason and Existenz*, trans. William Earle (New York: Noonday Press, 1955).

[7] St. Augustine, *Confessions*, trans. F. J. Sheed (Indianapolis: Hackett Publishing, 1993).

[8] Martin Buber, *I and Thou*, trans. Ronald Gregor Smith (New York: Charles Scribner's Sons, 1958); *Paths in Utopia*, trans. R. F. C. Hull (Boston: Beacon Press, 1958).

[9] Viktor Frankl, *Man's Search for Meaning: An Introduction to Logotherapy*, trans. Ilse Lasch (Boston: Beacon Press, 1992); *Man's Search for Ultimate Meaning* (New York: Insight Books, 1997); *The Doctor and the Soul: From Psychotherapy to Logotherapy*, trans. Richard and Clara Winston (New York: A. Knopf, 1965); *Psychotherapy and Existentialism: Selected Papers on Logotherapy* (New York: Simon and Schuster, 1967).

[10] Abraham Maslow, *Motivation and Personality* (New York: Harper and Row, 1970); *Toward a Psychology of Being* (New York: Van Nostrand Reinhold, 1968); *Religions, Values, and Peak-Experiences* (New York: Penguin Books, 1970).

Aquinas[11] and Lawrence Kohlberg.[12] One may also see them in the Scriptures of Christianity, Judaism, Islam, Hinduism, and Buddhism. Throughout the last 3,500 years one can see them recur again and again in the cultures of North and South, East and West. They are most deeply reflected upon, yet often times most forgotten—the most obvious parts of our common heritage and yet the most esoteric. They reflect not only what moves us in our heart of hearts but also the ideals toward which we aspire, the relationships we seek, the worth we attribute to ourselves and others, our sense of well-being, of hope, and of groundedness. They are at once the sources of our sense of autonomy, self-possession, self-communication, love, self-transcendence, faith, and even communion with a higher power or God. We return to them more often than any other concept or image. Our lives are imbued with them.

Common sense tells us that no sane person seeks unhappiness. Aside from masochism or significant depression, each of us chooses actions we hope will make us happy. Unfortunately, we are often disappointed. Finding happiness is not so easy. The world is full of options that promise happiness. Some actually deliver; many do not. Some deliver fairly well for a while, but decay ultimately into boredom, emptiness, or pain.

Is there any guide to happiness more helpful than trial and error or the all-too-fallible advice of family and friends? Is there anything objective enough to predict happiness most of the time? Something useful to most people? Could such a general guide to happiness even be possible? After all, people's tastes vary. Some find excitement or pleasure in actions that others consider boring or disgusting. As the saying goes, "one man's meat is another man's poison". Is there any way to understand happiness in general or to predict what will "work" for large numbers of people?

---

[11] Saint Thomas Aquinas, *The Summa Theologica of St. Thomas Aquinas*, trans. Fathers of the English Dominican Province (New York: Benziger Brothers, 1947); *Treatise on Man*, part I, questions 75–102 (vol. 1, pp. 363–505), and *Treatise on Habits*, the first part of part II, questions 49–89 (vol. 1, pp. 703–985); Vernon J. Bourke, *Summa contra Gentiles* (Garden City, N.Y.: Image, 1956), book III, chaps. 1–48 (vol. 3, pp. 34–162); and *Treatise on Happiness*, trans. John A. Oesterle (Notre Dame, Ind.: University of Notre Dame Press, 1964).

[12] Lawrence Kohlberg, *The Psychology of Moral Development: The Nature and Validity of Moral Stages* (San Francisco: Harper and Row, 1984); *Moral Stages: A Current Formulation and a Response to Critics* (New York: Karger, 1983); *The Meaning and Measurement of Moral Development* (Worcester, Mass.: Clark University Press, 1981).

People use different guides in their search for happiness. Some rely on a sense of inner comfort and limit themselves to those activities with which they feel "comfortable". Others find comfort boring, preferring challenge to complacency, and claim that discomfort may not only be overcome but might even be a necessary precursor of deep, lasting happiness.

The search for the principles of happiness is an old one, for the desire to avoid unhappiness goes back to the beginning of human history. It was first systematically addressed by the Greeks, thousands of years ago, and rearticulated by medieval and modern philosophers. These philosophers experienced the same types of unhappiness as we do today, the same failed dreams, the same frustrations and miseries. However, with their uncanny powers of observation, they discovered an underlying logic to the cycles of happiness and unhappiness that seems remarkably modern. They noticed that not all routes are equally likely to arrive at happiness. Some satisfy deeply, others less, some not at all. Some fulfill for a while, like candy, but ultimately produce unhappiness. These philosophers explored the underlying reasons for these differences. They found principles that allowed them to predict not only whether any particular activity would likely make most people happy but also how long it would remain effective and whether it would generate logical consequences that could destroy happiness in the long run. Their system remains surprisingly reliable.

These philosophers observed that types of happiness could be ranked. What they called "lower" forms of happiness had the advantages of being immediate, intense, and apparent, but suffered from being short lived and relatively narrow in focus. "Higher" forms of happiness had the advantages of being pervasive, enduring, and deeply satisfying, but the disadvantages of being more abstract and less rapidly attained than lower forms, and frequently took more effort. Lower forms of happiness were generally more material or physical; higher forms were generally more emotional, intellectual, or spiritual. The lower levels of happiness tended to break down into one form of crisis or another. The very highest levels managed to avoid crises altogether.

Philosophers throughout the ages sought to draw their students away from the lower levels of happiness to the higher levels of happiness, appreciation of which generally requires some developmental maturity. They sought to train hearts and minds to prefer those forms of happiness that are deeper and more lasting over those that are superficial and intense but short lived.

In my study of the history of philosophy and developmental psychology, I have noticed four major groupings or levels of happiness. The first and most basic level of happiness (in Latin, *laetus*) comes from an external stimulus. It interacts with one or more of the five senses, gives immediate gratification, but does not last very long. A sensorial pleasure like an ice cream cone or a possession like a new car can impart immediate gratification from these stimuli. In this book, I will call it *Happiness 1*.

The second level of happiness (in Latin, *felix*) comes from ego gratification. *Ego* in Latin means "I". This kind of happiness comes whenever I can shift the locus of control from the outer world to myself. Hence, whenever I win, gain power or control, or gain admiration or popularity, I feel happy. I feel as if my inner world is expanding. My control relative to the outer world is enhanced. I will call this level *Happiness 2*.

The second level of happiness does not exhaust the scope of human desire. As was noted above, we also desire love, truth, goodness/justice, beauty, and being. These desires initially manifest themselves as a desire to contribute. The second kind of happiness tried to shift the locus of control to the self. In the third level of happiness (in Latin, *beatitudo*) we try to invest in the world beyond ourselves. We want to make a difference with our lives, time, energy, and talent. I will call this level *Happiness 3*.

Strange as it may seem, the third level of happiness still does not exhaust the scope of human desire, for as was noted above, humans not only desire *some* love, goodness, truth, beauty, and being, they can also desire *unconditional, perfect, ultimate,* and even *unrestricted* Love, Goodness, Truth, Beauty, and Being. In the context of faith, one might call this the desire for God. But even if one does not have faith, one can treat it as an awareness of a seemingly unconditional horizon surrounding human curiosity, creativity, spirit, and achievement. As noted in Chapter One, this particular desire differentiates humans from all other animals. I will call this level *Happiness 4* (in Latin, *gaude*).

Part Two of this book will demonstrate how these four levels of happiness dramatically affect our viewpoints on every important personal and cultural issue we face. The level of happiness we tend to live for will determine how we view success, what we mean by quality of life, what we think love is, how we interpret suffering, the system of ethics we live by, and how we understand freedom, rights, and the common good. Part Three, in turn, will show how our views on these categories will determine the personal and cultural policies we form, specifically on abortion and euthanasia.

At present, however, we must complete our investigation on the definition of personhood and happiness. As noted above, the purpose of Life Principles is not merely to give an objective definition of personhood. Important as this task is for developing an adequate definition of rights and the common good, it does not provide the freedom to put it into practice. This freedom comes from what I termed "the heart" (the inner conviction and desire arising out of one's meaning in life, which reaches its completion in the awareness and pursuit of the five transcendentals). An objective definition of "person" will provide a clear access to the truth, but it will not provide the conviction, desire, and freedom to act on this truth. If we are to arrive at a definition of "person" that provides both conceptual objectivity *and* the desire and freedom to act, we must explain the above four levels of happiness (purpose in life), which, in turn, will provide an access way to freedom of the heart. This will be the purpose of Chapter Three.

Chapter Three

Moving Through the Levels of Happiness

Introduction

The objective of this chapter is to help individuals understand the four major interior driving forces within their lives (the four levels of happiness) and to act upon this understanding in a way that will be beneficial to them and to the culture.

Diagram 2 gives a brief summary of the four kinds of happiness mentioned in the previous chapter. Recall that the first level (for example, a bowl of linguini), though immediately gratifying, intensive, and quite apparent, is not very pervasive, enduring, or deep. In contrast to this, the fourth level (grounded in the five transcendentals) produces very enduring, pervasive, and deep happiness and good, but it is not very intensive and frequently requires a search and delayed gratification. The purpose of education from the days of the Greek Academy to the present has been to help students to move from the immediately gratifying to the enduring, from the apparent and superficial to the deep, from the narrow and intensive to the pervasive. This is why these four levels of happiness have found their way into so many philosophies, psychologies, sociologies, and anthropologies. They are not simply part of our inner makeup. They are really a culmination of many cultures' reflections on the common good and the purpose of education. Let us proceed.

I. The First Level of Happiness and Its Crisis

Happiness 1 is essentially material, or physical. It results from physical pleasure and possession, such as the simple, sensual gratification one may obtain from eating a bowl of linguini or driving a new car. Simi-

		Ultimate Good
4	Objective:	Participate in giving and receiving ultimate meaning, goodness, ideals, and love.
	Characteristics:	Good is ultimatized. Principles include ultimate Truth, Love, Justice, and Beauty.
	Gratification:	Eternal
		Good Beyond Self
3	Objective:	Do good beyond self.
	Characteristics:	Principles include justice, love, and community. Intrinsic goodness is an end in itself. Decisions are focused on the greater good.
	Gratification:	Long term
		Personal Achievement/Ego
2	Objective:	Ego centeredness, be better than, gain advantage.
	Characteristics:	Promotion of self is primary; personal power and control are key. Jealousy, fear of failure, contempt, isolation, loneliness, and cynicism.
	Gratification:	Short term
		Immediate Gratification
1	Objective:	Maximize pleasure and minimize pain.
	Characteristics:	Obligation is to self alone. No desire for common, intrinsic, or ultimate good. Lack of self-worth, fear of tangible loss/harm, boredom.
	Gratification:	Immediate

Diagram 2. Four Levels of Happiness

larly, soaking in a hot tub, lying on a beach, having a massage, or other bodily pleasures generate Happiness 1, as does relief of hunger, thirst, or pain.

Happiness 1 is concrete, direct, quick in onset, and often quite intense. Properly understood and pursued, Happiness 1 is thoroughly enjoyable. Its chief drawback is superficiality, which often generates boredom for those who limit themselves to this level. Material things are insubstantial because human beings do not seek merely material perfections or ends. They need far more than this. Indeed, as we have seen, they even seek the perfect, absolute, unrestricted, and unconditional in the five transcendentals. Materialism and pleasure are enough to satisfy the body, but they fail to reach the deepest parts of the human consciousness.

Most persons who attempt to live entirely at the level of Happiness 1, singlemindedly pursuing possessions and pleasure, eventually experience intense feelings of emptiness—a state I call *Crisis 1*. The person in Crisis 1 is plagued by boredom, loneliness, and a sense of meaningless lack of direction. The questions "What's it all about?" and "Who am I?" are asked often in Crisis 1, without apparent answer. Persons in Crisis 1 may anesthetize their pain by intensifying their pursuit of pleasure and possessions. This approach, however, seldom works for long and often makes Crisis 1 even more intensely painful.

Why should this be? While various possible explanations exist, Crisis 1 suggests that the demands of the human spirit are broader and deeper than those of the body. If human beings were only material bodies, then physical gratification ought to satisfy completely and permanently. But it obviously does not.

Human beings need more than the satisfaction of material desire. Developmentally, as children find their material needs met, they seek higher levels of emotional and psychological integration. They focus first on ego needs, then move on to more abstract levels of development. Interestingly, both Eastern and Western ancient systems of ranking levels of happiness and crises coincide closely with our modern understanding of human psychological development. Further, it seems that the crises actually serve an important developmental function: just as each of the lower levels of happiness generates a specific crisis, so each crisis opens the way to the next higher level of happiness.

In Chinese, the pictogram for crisis contains the pictogram for opportunity. Hence, the boredom and emptiness of Crisis 1 create the opportunity (and motive) to reach beyond the materialism of Happiness 1. The pain of Crisis 1 pushes the person toward the second level of happiness, ego gratification.

II. The Second Level of Happiness and Its Crisis

The second level of happiness is a vital stage of human development. It involves the creation, through personal achievement or success, of a robust sense of self-esteem. Happiness 2 starts early in life. Small initial successes combine with childhood achievements like forming an identity independent of parents, and adolescent breakthroughs like finding one's own special niche, to make possible balanced growth into maturity.

Happiness 2 in adulthood comes from self-advancement, from activities that, for example, make one seem more successful, better looking, or more powerful than others. These satisfactions are "higher" than Happiness 1, for they are not purely physical; they chiefly involve the ego.

Most adolescents learn reasonably well to balance the apparent conflict between the demands of ego and those of relationship, learning that their sense of worth can as easily be based on healthy interactions with others as on personal success. Unfortunately, however, some people set up a false antagonism between self and other. Happiness 2 becomes a problem for this latter group, usually in late adolescence or early adulthood. Typically, these individuals get stuck in the preadolescent belief that their own egos are the center of the universe. Since they fear healthy relationships as threatening the centrality of their egos, they avoid sound, mutually reinforcing, adult relationships. Instead of moving on to higher happiness through love, regrettably, these people base their entire sense of self-worth on subordinating others to themselves. They seek to extract admiration from others and to gain and exercise power over them.

A healthy adult sense of Happiness 2 assumes a level of success and ego gratification sufficient to maintain a stable sense of self. However, it combines reasonable ego strength with a willingness and ability to derive much of its sense of worth from relationships based on giving, sharing, and ultimate purpose and faith (Happiness 3 and 4, respectively). Unhealthy Happiness 2, in contrast, features relationships based on power, popularity, and even domination.

Happiness 2, healthy or unhealthy, focuses chiefly on obtaining comparative advantage for the self—on advancing the self, on pushing the self to the top, on comparing the self with others. The "comparison game" has intrinsic difficulties that usually lead to crisis. The specific form of crisis depends on the degree of success obtained within the comparison game. The intensity of crisis varies with the degree to which self-worth is perceived to be based on Happiness 2.

If Happiness 2 becomes exaggerated, most people will find it to be unbearable, for one will invest virtually all of one's self-worth in comparison, in continuously struggling to be better than others. Serious problems begin to emerge as one discovers that continuously improving success (which is required in order to gain continuous comparative advantage) is almost impossible to sustain.

As a person moves from adolescence to young adulthood, he can turn his purpose away from Level 3 and 4 identities and become almost fully invested in a Level 2 identity. He can begin to think that the *only* things that will make him happy, the *only* things that will give him purpose in life, the *only* things that will give him self-worth are winning, popularity, and power. These three objectives require substantial achievement by comparison with others. Hence, one is forced to achieve in order to find happiness, purpose, and self-worth in life.

Notice that in Happiness 2 one is not achieving to make a difference or to love; one is not achieving in order to experience the transcendentals more profoundly, but *only* to win and gain popularity and power. Hence, achievement is relegated to the pursuit of Level 2 satisfaction alone. One must use all of one's wits, education, talents, and energy to gain comparative advantage, popularity, and power. This has three distinct *dis*advantages, which may be illustrated through the example of Barbara, a bank executive. The first disadvantage concerns taking one's mind off achieving for the sake of others. Here, Barbara, who has appropriated a compulsive Level 2 identity, finds herself almost unconcerned about making a difference with her life or having a net positive effect on her family, friends, community, and workplace. She ignores her fundamental desire to make the world a better place, to use her talents and energy on creating something good and positive. In short, she finds herself expending all her energy on *self*-aggrandizement rather than positive contribution. Instead of using her creativity, love, and talents to make a real positive difference in her own little (or great) part of the human community and human history, she spends all that she is and has on calling attention to herself. She begins severely to underlive her life, underuse her talents, and underactualize her destiny. Objectively, her life contributes less, means less to others, and has less effect on the world. She implicitly recognizes this and begins to feel profoundly empty, though she frequently does not know explicitly why. An apathy and boredom begin to emerge from which she tries to escape through even greater wastes of time (new Level 1 delights enhanced by a peculiarly adolescent take on the world).

The second disadvantage concerns personal relationships. Barbara's exaggerated emphasis on being better than others, being admired, and gaining power grows wearisome. At best, people grow tired of her exaggerated self-concern; at worst, they write her off as hopelessly superficial. Though they try to be well mannered about it, she nevertheless feels their judgment and slowly begins to see them withdrawing. Even though she implicitly recognizes people's judgments and withdrawal, her exaggerated ego needs compel her to override her thoughts about self-correction. She begins to build up a myth about how people really enjoy her as a power seeker, how they really have to grovel at her feet, how they really know their subordinate place and feel great about groveling. "People naturally want to bask in my light", Barbara tells herself, when all the while they really are becoming progressively more repulsed. They are trying to find nice ways of telling her that something is amiss, that she's really not a god, but just someone with a lot of talent. They want to convey that a relationship based solely on acknowledgment of her superiority is not enough. They would like a little bit of dignity and respect and, if possible, a tinge of friendship or love. But Barbara cannot hear this because she *wants* her ego to be more important than the friendship. As people begin to withdraw, she becomes more bitter. As she becomes more bitter, they withdraw all the more. She begins to develop a rather cynical and contemptuous outlook on them and on life.

The third disadvantage concerns a panoply of negative emotions that arise when Barbara narrows her life to three outcomes: winning, losing, and drawing. As Barbara invests progressively more of her self-worth and identity in comparative advantage, popularity, and power, she focuses almost exclusively on questions like "Who is more popular? Who is less popular? Who has more control? Who has less control? Who is advancing more, and who is advancing less? Who's winning, and who's losing?" These questions exhaust her range of possible purposes in life. She has altogether forgotten about positive contribution, love, the transcendentals, and faith. All she cares about are comparisons, and the three outcomes of these comparisons (win, lose, and draw) begin to give rise to a sense of self-negation and anxiety.

With respect to the first outcome, losing the comparison game, the prospect of losing sends chills down the spine, depriving the loser of respect, identity, and meaning. Recall that the *only* thing that matters to this person is winning, admiration, and control. Hence, losing a small contest, a promotion, or some admirability feels like a loss of identity, self-worth, and purpose. Achieving less, for this person, does not mean "achieving less". It means loss of self. The resultant effect is at the very least apathy, and at worst depression. This depression is frequently accompanied by jealousy.

Consider the example of Sam, a surgeon. Sam, a very talented surgical resident, believes that his life draws its meaning from the fact that he is the best resident in his training program. When a new resident, Alice, proves even more technically proficient than himself, Sam begins to suffer fits of jealousy and depression. His sense of superiority is replaced by an inappropriate fear of inferiority; he begins to imagine that his coworkers secretly disdain him. He hates Alice; he hates himself. He turns to Happiness 1 (sex or drugs), but the pain remains.

Sam's anger grows more intense, despite psychotherapy. He has invested his entire identity in winning the comparison game. As a loser, he feels empty and without value; he has been deprived of the admi-

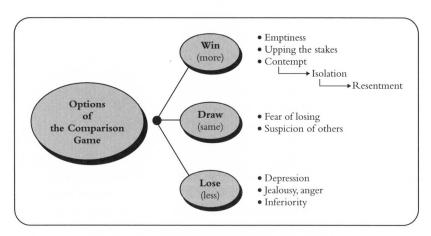

Diagram 3. Crisis 2: The Comparison Game

ration he so deeply desires. He shouts at nurses for charting errors. He hates patients who develop complications, seeing in them a reproachful comment on his ability. At night he turns his anger on himself and considers suicide.

Sam's downward spiral threatens himself and those around him. His regression to Happiness 1 becomes boring. Pressed to an extreme, it may even weaken his surgical abilities, earning him the professional contempt he fears. He finds it hard to climb out of his self-created hell.

One might think that the *second option of the comparison game, winning,* would bring on happiness. After all, one has made Level 2 goals one's *sole* source of purpose, identity, and happiness. There can be no doubt that one will experience *short-term* happiness from one's achievement and progress, but eventually this becomes overshadowed by what I term the "upping the stakes game", emptiness, and contempt.

With respect to the upping the stakes game, let us consider the case of Ben, a businessman. Ben has achieved much in his life. He has been promoted to the executive level and enjoys wide respect with his accomplishments. But as he has moved up, he finds himself with less and less potential to move higher. There are fewer places in the higher realms, and he is feeling a little less energetic and creative. All this gives rise to a period of less advancement. Because Ben has invested his entire self-worth in advancement, he needs to advance *more* with each promotion period. As the promotions begin to pass him by (even though he has a high position, is incredibly productive, and is incredibly well respected), the "more" that he so desperately needs for self-worth is simply not accessible. He begins to feel the emotions of the loser. First, he thinks of his life as worth *less* because he is not advancing *more*. He sees himself as not going anywhere. He thinks that his life has lesser quality, that people are respecting him less, and that he is just "the same old humdrum Ben" that he was a year ago. He feels less admired, less in control, and as a consequence begins to feel a malaise, and then even a depression. It's harder to get up in the morning. He feels less excitement about life, and he doesn't get the same ego highs he used to get as people looked admiringly at him when he would walk down the corridor. Anxiety begins to overtake him, and even a sense of inferiority. Most of his friends would be absolutely shocked to find out that he feels inferior because they do not judge him to be so. Nevertheless, that is what he believes, and therefore that is what he feels.

Ben begins to grow jealous of others who are progressing within the company, even those who are making very small incremental increases by comparison with his already high stature. They are making progress, and he is not. That makes all the difference. This jealousy eventually translates into impatience, judgmentalness, and anger. He puts people down to make himself feel good. He does not acknowledge people for their successes. He can't stand to do this, because it reminds him of what is not happening to him. People begin to lose respect for him as a person, even though they still admire him for his accomplishments. Ironically, he believes that they have lost respect for his accomplishments, because he has forgotten all about his personal qualities. He does not value these personal qualities. They are mere nothings by comparison with another promotion or advancement. Slowly but surely, Ben the Success convinces himself of his decline, his worthlessness, and his inferiority and contents himself with a few good glasses of scotch to overcome his sense of depression, malaise, and jealousy. People are bewildered. They say he's changed. And indeed, he has. Objectively, he is no less of a success. Subjectively, he is terribly unhappy and becoming less and less of a person to whom people can relate.

There is a second consequence of the upping the stakes game. Ben is likely to cultivate a great deal of ego sensitivity. Because he is so obsessed with people's admiration for him as his sole indicator of purpose, identity, and self-worth, he can never lose face in public. He cannot laugh at himself. He can't even afford to be a human being. He has to portray an image of himself as perfectly admirable, which means, of course, that he has to portray the image of being perfectly infallible and perfectly put together. He has to be the exemplar of the perfect person with a perfect life. Indeed, he would feel best if people envied his life, but knew that they really couldn't become quite as perfect as he is. They would have to stand at a distance and think what it must be like to be that perfect.

What is the one thing that Ben can't tolerate? A little hole, even a pinprick, in that massive ego façade. Ben has not only built up an incredible façade; he has also built up a complete intolerance to any challenge to it. If he should make a mistake in public, if he should manifest something less than perfect admirability, if he should show himself to belong to the ranks of ordinary humanity, he would lose his very self. He has predicated himself on his admirability, not on his likability. He wants people to believe that he has worth because of his vast superiority, not because of his contribution to others or the world. To lose admirability is to lose himself. When a terrible incident of weakness first occurs, he feels a quiet desperation, but represses it. After all, he must remain cool in public. However, when he returns home, he begins to swear at himself, curses the mistakes he made, increases his alcohol consumption, and sometimes feels like inflicting physical pain on himself (for example, by hitting a wall). In rare cases, he feels tremendous self-pity accompanied by suicidal impulses. All this because of a little mistake? All this because he was exposed to be like mere mortals? Yes. All too frequently, yes.

Before proceeding with Ben's other problems, I would like to remind the reader that I will extensively discuss the remedy to these problems in the next section. For the time being, let us proceed to the other anxieties that arise out of winning the comparison game, namely, emptiness, contempt, and cynicism. With respect to emptiness, it was mentioned earlier that all of us have a need to make a difference to somebody or something beyond ourselves. When we do not do this, we judge our lives to be less significant to the world. Our lives seem to matter less, to be underlived, not living up to their full potential and positivity. Eventually we begin to *feel* this judgment of ourselves. It takes the form of emptiness or self-alienation. Ben, for example, looks at himself in the mirror, and it seems as if he has little substance or value. He feels a deep anxiety in the pit of his stomach, but feels powerless to give himself substance. He doesn't believe he really has substance, because he doesn't believe his life really matters. He tries to escape this anxiety by *filling up* on a surrogate like food or alcohol or other creature comforts. If these don't work, he tries to induce a trancelike state by absorbing himself in television or pursuing ever-enhanced excitement and adventure. In the end it never seems to be enough, and the haunting feeling of emptiness continues to rear its ugly head.

The only solution to Ben's problems is to find a purpose in life that really does make his life matter (a contribution, a creative endeavor, an act of love, or something similar), for then he will feel his life and his person to have substance. But failing this, the emptiness will persist and deepen.

Last, but not least, Ben is also likely to be mired in contempt. If the only things that matter are being admired and gaining comparative advantage, then (in his "better moments"), as a winner, Ben is likely to feel contempt for those who have not made it as far as he has. He will secretly disvalue first the life and then the person of those with lesser stature. Even though these people may be contributing far more to their families, friends, community, and even colleagues at work, even though these others may be far more creative and contributive, Ben will believe that their lives are less worthwhile because they simply haven't advanced as much. After a while, he begins to believe that these "inferiors" have only one purpose, and that is to acknowledge his superiority over themselves. Ben does not want to associate with these people except to receive obsequious servility. If he will deign to be seen with them, if he will spend his valuable time with them, it will have to be made worthwhile by their expressing his intrinsic superiority. If they will give him several hits of admiration and appropriately grovel before his superior position and talent, they will prove themselves to be useful. But God help them if they should actually expect some of his time without at least a bow or a curtsey. Ben will just have to show them who matters and who doesn't. This can be easily accomplished by either ignoring them, putting them down, or simply undermining all of their efforts at creativity and contribution. If Ben can make their lives seem trivial or their purpose in life insignificant, he will have done his job well. These inferiors will then know their true place, and Ben can proceed to other more high-minded endeavors.

If these people, however, should become "uppity" and insist on the fact that their lives do have meaning, that their contributions are significant (perhaps even more significant than Ben's), or if they should declare that they and others have intrinsic dignity, Ben will have to take immediate action to correct this threat to his identity, meaning, and purpose in life. Furthermore, he will have to redress this absence of admiration. He may at first attempt to show off a few more of his accomplishments. Perhaps these uppity folks need a little bit more evidence of his intrinsic superiority. But if that does not work, Ben will just have to find a way of not simply putting them down, but, if possible, smashing them into the earth. After years of practice, Ben should be able to accomplish this with remarkable facility. Unfortunately, these uppity people will not like Ben's destructive propensities. If they don't actively resist it, they will simply move out of the way. One thing is certain: they will not give him the admiration after which he is pandering. Ben will feel at once isolated and outraged. This, in turn, will give rise to cynicism about both life and other people. What a joy it is to be a winner when the only thing that matters is winning.

Before proceeding to the solution to these problems, *the third outcome of the comparison game (drawing)* must be discussed. What can be expected if I invest my entire identity in winning or gaining popularity and control, but only "measure up"? I'm not really winning or really losing, but rather just keeping my head above water, keeping up with the herd. Let's take the example of Sophie, a software engineer.

Sophie has defined both her self-worth and identity in terms of being an outstanding software engineer. She works in a firm with many other bright people, and because she holds this identity in such high regard, she needs to be well thought of in order to have a successful life and high self-worth. The fact that she is among bright people causes her to think that she is merely mediocre, and so she progressively brands her life as such. After a while she begin to lose energy. She's not getting the kind of satisfaction she needs from her job. As she progressively loses her zeal for life, she also notices a bit of anxiety creeping in. She anticipates that she will not be too much further than she is today. The anxiety begins to grow when she notices some younger software engineers moving up on her quickly. She fears not only that they could overtake her but also that they might actually render her superfluous. Given her high investment in this identity, this thought causes her far more anxiety than simply being demoted or losing a job. She really believes that her *whole* self is being threatened. The progress of these younger people causes her to lose sleep and sometimes to wake up terrified that she may not have an identity, or worth, or even a self someday. People would no longer be impressed by her merely mediocre qualifications. They might be even chidingly disdainful about her slip from mediocre glory. The anxiety causes Sophie to play politics and withhold information from these colleagues. She will never admit that they are doing a good job. She is able only to find fault in their performance. She finds herself becoming progressively more manipulative, quick tempered, and defensive. At night she is utterly suspicious of her colleagues: *I know what they're trying to do. They're trying to steal my glory.* Because her entire self-identity is fixed on her profession, she plots in her bed at night, thinking about how to keep the invaders out. It suddenly occurs to her that even her husband is trying to steal her glory.

He really wishes that she would fail, because that would give him an upper hand in the relationship. She also becomes quite convinced that her friends are doing the same. Indeed, the entire world seems to be ganging up on her.

Needless to say, Sophie is not happy. She has only two ways out. She can either become more proficient at software engineering *or* invest herself in an identity other than software engineering, an identity not derived so much from comparative advantage as from the contribution she can make to family, friends, community, colleagues, employees, and ideals.

Even though I have presented the various negative emotional states of the comparison game through three hypothetical persons (Sam, Ben and Sophie), it is not uncommon for one person to experience all three sets of emotions even within a day or two. Changes in life's circumstances and mood swings can push a person from the upping the stakes game to depression, and from contempt to inferiority, with every form of emptiness, suspicion, and fear in between.

If we are to move beyond these emotional states (which are also self-negating), if we want to improve our relationships with others (from the most intimate to the least intimate), if we want to accomplish more in life, reach for what is truly worthy of us, to enkindle a spirit that makes us feel alive opening upon horizons of great adventure and opportunity, we must stop playing the comparison game. For even though we have invested our entire selves in being admired, our actions and emotions cause us to be admired less. Even though we have invested our entire selves in being competitive, we find ourselves to be less competitive and more reliant on cutting corners to get the competitive edge. Even though we have staked our identities on being strong and confident, we find ourselves undermined by emotions that induce in us precisely the opposite. We simply must stop playing the comparison game.

Before progressing to the way out of the comparison game, it will do well to remind the reader that the vast majority of people who move into the comparison game do so without malice. Most, when they were children, made an unconscious choice to pursue comparative advantage and admiration as the major ground of their identity. As they got older, it became an almost exclusive ground of identity. By the time they reached their early twenties, they found themselves quite adept at playing the comparison game, though the ramifications of it kept haunting them. Eventually, for lack of any other identity, they decided that it was worth the pain to themselves, colleagues, family, friends, and culture to put on a good front and continue the game in "earnest". It would be so simple to attribute malice to these people, but in point of fact they are not malicious; they are merely acting out of a compulsion that has its roots in an unconscious decision of early adolescence. If this innocent compulsion is to be laid to rest, we simply must stop playing the comparison game.

III. The Third Level of Happiness: A Way Out of the Comparison Game

By now it should be obvious that one cannot really "win" the comparison game. Unfortunately, it is not that easy to stop focusing exclusively on comparison, for these values are deeply imbedded in our minds. That being true, most people find that a brief abstinence from comparison leads them to believe they are "better than" those who still play the comparison game. The insidious logic of Happiness 2 is inescapable, unless we replace comparison with something positive.

The most effective strategy is to look for *the good beyond self*. Instead of contemplating self, or personal position, we can try to make a difference to some cause or person. We all have a desire to make the world a better place. We all yearn to contribute to something greater than ourselves. Idealism is not a charming affectation; it is a basic human drive. We have a basic need to use our talents to enhance humanity. If we get to the end of life and find that we have given nothing to humanity, we will plumb the depths of despair.

If, for example, I achieve the ripe old age of eighty and one day ask myself the question, "Now what was the difference between the value of my life and that of a rock?" and I answer, "Let me think about that for a while", or even, "Not much", I will probably be in incipient despair. I could not stand to think that my life did not or does not matter. If this should even occur to me, I would lose purpose, self-worth, and perhaps even the drive to live. Conversely, when I believe that my life does matter, that there is external evidence or validation of my worth, that people or even the community have benefited from my time, effort, creativity, and talent, I feel like I have really lived my life to the full, that my life was not wasted, but indeed was optimally spent.

This gives me a sense of spirit and well-being that translates into even greater creativity, love, and effectiveness.

A. Five Fundamental Attitudes

The secret to stopping the comparison game lies in achieving a higher viewpoint on five fundamental attitudes. These attitudes are so fundamental that they represent at once what we are looking for and living for. What we are looking for turns out to be what we are living for, and what we are living for conditions what we are looking for.

Though we must stop the comparison *game* (focusing *exclusively* on comparisons for our identities), we cannot stop making comparisons, for that would require either ignoring or cutting off one of our fundamental desires. Level 2 desires, like Level 1, 3, and 4 desires, are *built into us*. These desires seek specific fulfillments or perfections. These fulfillments/ perfections orient human powers toward themselves. When these powers arrive at their given fulfillment/perfection they stop operating.

Recall what was said in Chapter One about Level 4 desire. This desire has a specific fulfillment or perfection *built into* it (that is, for unconditional, perfect Truth, Love, Goodness/Justice, Beauty, and Being). Our awareness of this perfection guides our human powers toward this perfection. Inasmuch as this desire is incompletely satisfied, we continue to use our powers to seek its fulfillment.

Ego desires (Level 2) work in a similar way. There are certain fulfillments/ perfections built into our "ego power" (self-consciousness). Because these fulfillments/perfections are built into us, we are aware of them. Hence, we pursue achievement, competitive advantage, admiration, and power to attain the fulfillment of this power. *We can't simply turn it off.* Thus, despite our best efforts, we always will make comparisons. We will seek to achieve more, to gain respectability, comparative advantage, and so on.

Are we then stuck in the comparison game? No. As many philosophers have discovered, we can make our Level 2 desires healthy by removing the "*only*" from them. As noted earlier, there is nothing wrong with Level 2 per se. It leads to achievement, excellence, self-esteem, and the like. However, when I begin to think that this is the *only* fulfillment that is worthwhile, when I believe that this is the *only* thing that will make me happy or give me a meaningful, well-lived life, then

I will become compulsive, find myself immersed in the anxieties of the comparison game, become angry at myself, and sometimes even become self-destructive. This obviously will have very negative consequences on my relationship to others and even on the actualization of my goals and ideals. The point here is I *cannot* stop Level 2 desires from operating powerfully in my life, but I *can* stop the comparison game by stopping my *exclusive* focus on Level 2.

The way to accomplish this is to add Level 3 and 4 objectives to Level 2 desires. Hence, what gives me meaning in life is not simply achieving, but rather achieving *for* a Level 3 or 4 objective (for example, a good for my family, friends, community, or church). Again, I would not reduce my meaning in life simply to being better than others, but rather to being as good as I could be in order to do a good for my family, society, ideals, and so on. The same can be said for achieving respectability (admiration) and the use of power. If I want to be respectable (credible) in order to do a good for others, it will have very different consequences than if I simply want to be respected. The latter makes respectability the *end* of my life. It makes me compulsive about getting more respectability. In contrast to this, if I want respectability in order to do a good for others, that good is the *end* of my life, and respectability is merely the *means* (the vehicle) to achieving this end. Notice that when respectability is merely a means (when it's in its proper place) it produces neither compulsion nor the anxieties of the comparison game. There is a peace about it. Notice too that my friends and family treat me differently. They seem implicitly to understand that my respectability is attached to the good I'm doing. Thus, they do not view it as arrogant, and therefore they do not resent or resist it.

Diagram 4 shows how to integrate Level 3 and 4 objectives into our Level 2 desires. This will stop the anxieties of the comparison game by turning our desire for achievement, comparative advantage, and respectability into a powerful tool for the good, even the transcendent good, beyond ourselves. The moment we focus on this good as our true end, our lives, relationships, and emotional states begin to improve immediately. Diagram 4 is broken down into five fundamental attitudes. The left column identifies the kind of attitude. The second (middle) column explains the Level 2 objective of this attitude. The third column explains the Level 3 and 4 objective of this attitude, which transforms the Level 2 desire from being self-destructive to being instrumentally constructive. Thus, the third column shows the precise focus that will

Kind of Attitude	Level 2 Objective	Level 3 and 4 Objective
1. View of meaning	Better than others Comparison only	Good for others Contribution (making comparison healthy)
2. View of others	Looking for the bad news in others	Looking for the good news in others
3. View of relationships	Being over and against others Threat→ manipulation/blame→ suspicion	Being with and through others Common cause→ enjoyment→ team
4. View of self	Object self only: treating people as objects, not as whole human beings	Subject self (making object self healthy) Appreciating people as human beings (e.g., for their intelligence, sincerity, honesty, compassion, creativity, value)
5. Overall viewpoint	Viewing people and life as problems	Viewing people and life as opportunity, mystery, and adventure

Diagram 4. What Am I Looking (Living) For?

remove compulsion and anxiety from our Level 2 desires, putting an end to the comparison game.

One of the regrettable features about human desire is that we focus on the lower levels of desire more. Why? Because we don't have to think about them as much. It is easier to think about a Level 2 desire *only* than to think about a Level 2 desire being a means to a Level 3 end. Human beings simplify, and hence they tend to focus exclusively on Level 2. This has the peculiar effect of turning Level 2 only into a kind of periodic default drive. When our psychic energy is low, when we are thinking about other things, we turn to Level 2 only by default. We focus on what is easier to see.

Does this mean that we are likely to be stuck in Level 2? No. But we do have a predisposition to Level 2, which means that we do have to take certain measures to make sure that we are not enslaved to this predisposition. Our very freedom and livelihood depend on this. What measures can we take? We can do everything to make the Level 3 and 4 objectives as *concrete* and *specific* as possible. This will be discussed later.

Let us begin with the *first and most fundamental attitude*, namely, the one concerned with meaning and purpose in life (the first row). Left to itself, our Level 2 desire will cause us to seek the "better than" (comparative advantage as an end in itself). Hence, we begin to become obsessed with such questions as "Who's achieving more? Who's achieving less?" "Who's better? Who's worse?" "Who's more popular? Who's less popular?" "Who's got more control? Who's got less control?" "Who's winning? Who's losing?" Notice that the moment we make achievement an end in itself (instead of making it a means to a good beyond ourselves) it becomes comparative. Once it is an end in itself, the only thing that matters is "more". I have to get even more with each passing day. I have to have more than other people. I have to be *seen* to be having more than others. Now the compulsion begins.

As noted above, we cannot simply stop our Level 2 desires. Therefore, we must turn the Level 2 desire into a means to a Level 3 and/or Level 4 end. In this case, we need to make the "better than" the means to the "good for others". If we can simply list the various contributions we can make to family, friends, work, or community, and make these the ends of our achievement, competitiveness, respectability, and the like, we will notice our anxiety level drop and our relationships improve. Above all, we will notice a marked improvement in our capacity to achieve goals, for these goals will now be viewed as opportunities instead of problems.

Try this out for yourself by taking the following "at home" test. This test is important for making the above truth your own. If you find that the above advice really does work in your life and the lives of your family, friends, and colleagues, then act on it as if your very life depended on it. If it does not apply, simply ignore it until the day on which anxiety overtakes you. Then take a second look. Here's the test:

First, start at the center column in diagram 3c. Pretend that the sole purpose of your life is achievement, winning, admiration, and control. Allow yourself to feel the "ultimate" impact of these questions: "Who's achieving more? Who's achieving less? ..." Now, ask yourself three questions:

1. What's your anxiety level like?

2. How are your relationships with others? Do these others know that they are being treated as mere objects of comparison instead of as subjects of contribution?

3. Is life a problem or an opportunity and an adventure?

With respect to the last question, you might gauge your response by assessing how you look at your calendar in the morning. Is it something like this? "That person will be a hassle. That meeting will be a waste of time. That course of action is sure to go nowhere ..."

If so, it may indicate that your fundamental view of life is somewhat problematic. Alternatively, if you are saying, "That person, though he has some problems, also has potential. That meeting, though it will probably have its nonproductive moments, could lead to some creative endeavors. And that course of action, though it may have fatal pitfalls, could in fact produce interesting connections and results", then you might consider yourself an opportunity seeker.

Now, if you find that your answers to the above three questions are overwhelmingly negative and that asking the questions is provoking anxiety, switch your perspective and start making your Level 2 desires reach out to Level 3 and 4 ends. The way to start this is to take out a sheet of paper and begin writing down the area where you feel you have the most contribution to make. Remember, Level 3 and 4 objectives are more intangible than Level 2 objectives, and in view of the many goals and projects involved in your life, you will probably be inclined to simplify matters by letting go of Level 3 and 4 objectives. Therefore, it is necessary to make these objectives as concrete and specific as possible. This is accomplished by writing them down and recalling them at least twice per day. Begin by writing down the ways in which you can contribute to different family members. What are the ways you could make life better for them? Proceed to your friends, moving from the most intimate relationships to the least intimate. Then think about the ways you could contribute to your colleagues at work and your employees. Look at the ways your creativity, ideas, and energy could contribute to your workplace, your community, or even to the larger society. Once you have finished this list, put an asterisk behind the four contributions on which you want to concentrate first. Now, say to yourself, "This is why I'm here on this earth. This is why I was born, and this is what gives me purpose." Ask yourself the same three questions again: (1) Anxiety level? (2) Relationships with others? and (3) Life as opportunity or problem? Has your perspective changed? Do others know that your perspective has changed? Has it begun to influence your capacity to achieve your goals?

Now proceed to the second attitude in the second row, namely, one's view of others. Again, you might notice that the Level 2 desire tends to act as a default drive. The bad news seems to be easier to notice than the good news. In fact, it's so much easier to notice that we often give it our undivided attention, which translates into our focusing almost *exclusively* on it. It is so easy to find ourselves focusing on what is irritating, weak, stupid, insensitive, and unkind. After all, the bad news is somewhat painful and calls attention to itself. Painful experiences seem to have more immediacy than edifying ones, though edifying experiences have much more far-reaching effects. As we focus on the more urgent, painful experience, it becomes more and more important. Hence, the perspective of "person as problem" overtakes the perspective of "person as mystery". We finally resolve not to waste any more time seeking opportunities because the problems are too overwhelming. If we do not stop treating the bad news as an end in itself, we will appropriate a very cynical attitude not simply toward people in general but also to our deepest intimates.

The way out of this is to make Level 2 serve Level 3 and 4 objectives. How? By looking for the good news in the other and making this good news the main goal of seeing even the bad. Again, the easiest way of making this Level 3 or 4 attitude concrete and specific is to write it down and review it at least twice per day.

This point may be illustrated by taking an at home test similar to the one mentioned above. When you return home, look at your spouse or your children or your best friend, and start by allowing your default drive to have a field day. Let yourself be maximally irritated by every weakness and every boring or stupid utterance. Allow this perspective to drift into your memory of the person so that you are vividly recalling every irritating, weak, stupid, and unkind feature manifest throughout your many years of relationship. Ask yourself the following five questions (the first three are similar to the ones mentioned earlier):

1. What's your anxiety level like?

2. How is your relationship with this other person? Does the person implicitly know that you are looking for the bad news (even though you haven't announced it)? Is this person defensive? Hurt? Incensed? Starting to play games or to "get even"?

3. Is this person a problem? Do you see this person as fundamentally bothersome, annoying, or even malicious? Or rather, is

this person intriguing, worthy of being a partner in common cause toward a common good? Is this person a mystery? Do you find that it requires a tremendous amount of energy to look for something good in this person, or do you find it relatively easy to see, acknowledge, and be drawn to the good?

4. What's your impatience level like? Prescinding from the times when you are tired or pressured, are you snapping at people, outraged by their "incompetence"? Or rather, do you find it relatively easy to be patient with them in their all-too-human weakness?

5. What's your judgmentalness level like? Do you believe that most people can make mistakes, or do you take offense at the smallest errors, saying that the other person should be more vigilant about being perfect? Prescinding from very grievous offenses, is it very hard to forgive people, or easy? How many judgments per day do you think go through your mind? Compare this number to the number of judgments of yourself.

If this perspective is getting you down, you might want to switch it so that your Level 2 perspective is oriented toward a Level 3 or 4 objective. The easiest way to do this is to look for the good news in the other. Again, it is essential to make this concrete and specific. So, take out a sheet of paper and begin writing down the good news: (1) the little good things that this person *tries* to do, (2) the great good things that he tries to do, (3) the goodness of his presence, his friendship, his kindness, even his delightful idiosyncrasies (delight is not a characteristic of children alone). Also, write down his strengths, aspirations, ideals, even the mystery of his being. Now focus on this and say to yourself, "This is who my *friend* really is." Now funnel the bad news through this concrete perspective of the good news. Ask yourself the above five questions all over again. Has anything changed for the better? Are your relationships improving? Are patience, tolerance, and generosity much easier? Are people problems, or are they mysteries?

At this point one might be thinking, "I can't be looking for the good news all the time. Sometimes I have to evaluate people, and I shouldn't be looking solely for the good news. I also have to hold certain friends and family members accountable. I can't turn into Pollyanna and ignore what I'm not supposed to see." Don't worry. You will still *see* the bad news. After all, it's the default drive; it's what you will turn to first; it's what irritates; it's what calls attention to itself. But the question is not "What do you *see*?" It's "What are you *looking* for?" If you see the bad news when you are looking for the bad news, the impatience level, judgmentalness level, and problematic perspective, will intensify tremendously. However, if you see the bad news when you are looking for the good news, your patience level, tolerance, and generosity will win the day.

Prior to my present position, I was a professor for over fifteen years. I had to correct papers and grade students all the time. It was never a difficulty for me to see the bad news. If a student was setting up an equation improperly or misplacing commas, I always seemed to notice it immediately. When I was looking for the bad news (allowing my default drive to have a field day), I would be quite angry by the time I reached the tenth misplaced comma. I wanted to draw a red line across the paper and write, "I give up. Go to the writing center and get a life!" However, when I saw the same bad news while *looking for* the good news, I would be just as easily inclined to write, "You know, you have perfectly good ideas. Indeed, at points, you are quite profound and creative. When you misplace commas, you are distracting your reader and undermining your credibility. Why not go to the writing center and get a little help with this simple problem? It will be the best hour's investment you could possibly make." Which comment do you think would have been more effective in reaching and doing good for the student in question?

Notice that the first attitude (the first row in diagram 4) affects the second attitude. If I have to be better than you in order to achieve meaning, self-worth, and happiness in life, I will probably not want to see the good news in you, for every bit of good news in the *other* removes happiness, purpose, and self-worth from me. Hence, looking for the good news with a Level 2 perspective alone requires enormous energy and is very likely to fail. Alternatively, if I derive purpose and happiness from contributing to others and from entering into common cause with others, I will find it much easier to see the good news in them. I want to see the good news because I want to pursue something worthy of me with that other. I want to pursue the common good. Hence, looking for the good news in another becomes easier and more apparent. Even if the bad news is also apparent, I am still looking at it in connection with the bad news, and *that makes all the difference.*

The third attitude (the third row) is determined by the selection made with respect to the first two attitudes. If I allow my default drive to dominate, giving rise to an almost exclusively Level 2 focus, I will view relationships fundamentally as a threat. I will look at you as if you are against me, threatening to take away my identity, my purpose, my happiness, and even my reputation. Notice that though this feeling could be based on objective evidence, most of the time it is not. I do not sit down and list all of the ways in which Betty has truly threatened my livelihood and reputation throughout the last ten years and *objectively* conclude that she is therefore a threat. I assume that Betty is a threat based on an undifferentiated feeling arising out of my perspective of having to be better than her and looking for the bad news in her. Notice also that I am probably not being malicious. It is unlikely that I would want to cause harm to Betty (simply to see her suffer) or that I am plotting her demise in order to elevate myself. Rather, I am more likely to be compulsively *defending* myself from the undifferentiated threat that she (and all other competitive people) pose to me when my identity is invested almost exclusively in Level 2 fulfillments. What are the consequences of this almost predetermined attitude toward Betty? There are five of them.

1. I treat Betty with suspicion. (How else can I treat her? She's a threat to my identity, purpose, happiness, and self-worth.)

2. This suspicion causes me to control either her or the situation in which she can affect me. I turn, therefore, to manipulation, blame, game playing, negative remarks, cynicism, and undermining.

3. Betty begins to react to me in an equally defensive way. Seeing my aggressive, defensive behavior, she feels compelled to protect herself and so begins to defend herself aggressively, causing me to be even more suspicious and even more manipulative and controlling.

4. This causes the breakdown of open communication. Betty begins to hoard information, hide her true opinions, and, if necessary to defend herself, to give slightly misleading information.

This, of course, confirms what I have suspected (compulsively) all along.

5. The relationship now devolves into an exercise in game playing where each person becomes progressively more passive aggressive until aggressive aggression begins. Attempts are made to insult the other subtly and sometimes even to hurt the other overtly. The negativity eventually results in complete withdrawal or an overt fight.

Needless to say, spouses, intimate friends, acquaintances, and even corporate teams will be significantly hurt by this compulsive dynamic. Conversely, if one gives the first two attitudes Level 3 and 4 objectives (that is, looking for contribution/common cause with the other and looking for the good news in the other), the opposite dynamic will most likely occur. It is not guaranteed, however, because both parties in the relationship must have similar Level 3 or 4 propensities. If there is a mutual pursuit of Level 3 and 4 objectives, the fivefold result of the relationship will be precisely the opposite of the one mentioned earlier:

1. Instead of treating Betty with suspicion, I treat her with trust. Inasmuch as Betty is not a threat to me, and I want to enter into common cause with her, I will be predisposed to trust and tolerate her when she makes mistakes. The common cause we serve, plus my ability to see the good news within her (in the service of that cause), opens me to her trustworthiness. I find that I do not have to suspect her unless her behavior or intentions should change somewhat dramatically. Since trust is the precondition of all open communication, teamwork, and public commitment, the other four consequences follow like the night the day.

2. Instead of trying to control Betty and the situation in which we work, I begin to focus on the common good in our mission or common cause. I want Betty to make that same common good her focus as well. In order to keep this common focus alive, we work around each other's weaknesses and insensitivities, try to support one another when we are tired, and keep an open mind to suggestions that are different (and would be threatening if my ego sensitivities were high).

3. Instead of reacting to me defensively, Betty now reacts to me with overt concern for both me and our common cause. Though this concern could begin in a very superficial way, it tends to grow as one begins to adjust oneself to another's habits and propensities over the course of time.

4. Instead of communication coming to a halt, communication is substantially enhanced, causing not only good teamwork but also enhanced creativity and energy in our mutual association.

5. Instead of game playing, Betty and I are able to manifest a higher degree of commitment to one another and to our common cause, causing our friendship (in the personal domain) to increase, or causing our collegiality, teamwork, and synergy (in the workplace) to increase.

With respect to the fourth attitude (the fourth row), there are two ways of looking at myself: the "object self" and the "subject self". By the "object self", I mean things about myself. Hence, I focus on what I have, on the clothes I'm wearing, the car I'm driving, the degrees or grades I received, the books I wrote, the awards I gathered, and so on. Notice how most things in the object self can be *compared* to similar traits in others' object selves. When the object self becomes the sole focus of one's identity, one tends to emphasize the esteemable self to the *exclusion* of the likable and lovable self arising out of one's subjective perspective.

The "subject self" represents the core identity of the human subject. I can't point to its characteristics, and it is very difficult to compare it to similar traits in others. It is the particular quality of my presence and friendship. It is manifest by a benevolent glance, by my concerned look and my unconcerned look; it informs my ideals, values, commitments, beliefs, loves, passions, and everything else that involves my intangible core identity. It is my "Spitzerness". One does not want to associate the distinctive, identifying personal essence of "Spitzer" with things, abilities, and accomplishments. The personal essence is manifest in my presence, in the way I connect with others, in the way I make others come alive through my friendship, presence, and concern. It's the ethos I exude both in private and in public. It is what makes me to be likable as distinct from what is merely admirable or esteemable. It's what gives me a depth of character rather than a mere surface appearance. It's what other people can connect with on the deepest possible level. It's what gives rise essentially to empathy.

As usual, the Level 2 disposition constitutes the default drive. If I allow it to dominate my perspective, it will become my exclusive focus. When this occurs, I will tend to value my résumé more than my likable or empathetic self, my accomplishments more than my presence and depth, my skills and functions more than my intrinsic dignity and worth. This has an immediate effect outside of me. If I do not value the subject self in myself, I will surely not value it in others. If I am blind to another person's presence, friendship, dignity, or character, I will be blind to his likable self. And if I am blind to that likable self, I will find it extraordinarily difficult to be concerned about his person, let alone to be a friend. This will alter the way I pursue friendships. Instead of emphasizing the dignity that gives rise to concern, that gives rise to care, and that in turn gives rise to commitment, I will emphasize the admirable, the respectable, the useful, and the humorous. There is nothing wrong with these last four. Indeed, they are a part of every friendship. But if they are the *only* characteristics that constitute a friendship, the friendship will never grow on a personal, dignifying, concerned, committed level. This eventually will come back to me, for others will recognize my choice of the object self (to the exclusion of the subject self) and will, in turn, be forced to admire me rather than like me or (in the case of deeper friendships) love me. The way I treat others will proclaim, "I really don't want you to like me or love me; just admire me. Just esteem me. That will be sufficient." Don't worry. Others will comply. But the absence of concern, care, and commitment will produce a bit (or perhaps a lot) of loneliness.

What's the way out? As noted earlier, one does not have to give up the Level 2 perspective (the object self). One cannot do so, because the drive is built into us. Indeed, it's the default drive. The way out is constituted by making a concrete and specific appraisal of one's subject self. You might want to sit down and, for a moment, acknowledge your presence, friendship, and interpersonal personhood (the way you connect with others). This should not be a narcissistic reflection, but rather an acknowledgment of your own likability equivalent to the recognition of others' likability. Can you be a friend to yourself in the way that others are friends to you? Can you be at peace with your *self* in the way that you can be at peace with others? The acknowledgment of one's own intrinsic worth and dignity, which opens upon the acknowledgment of one's inner substance, helps to overcome self-alienation and bring about a peace that flows quite naturally to others. If I am at peace with myself, it helps me to be at peace with others. If I believe in my own intrinsic worth and dignity, I will believe in the dignity and worth of others. These others in turn will reflect my concern back to me if they also have a sense of their subject self, which will, in turn, give rise to deep and enduring friendships.

Conversely, if I have no appreciation of my intrinsic dignity (dignity apart from the *things* about me), I will begin to view myself as a mere object of comparison and eventually reduce myself to a mere problem. I will become a problem to myself and will undoubtedly present problems to others, who will, in turn, reflect that back to me. The loss of committed love in this culture is probably attributable more to the loss of the likable self (to the contentment with mere admiration) than any other source.

The fifth attitude (row 5) is only a summation of what has come before. It is like our world view. If we focus on the middle column (the default drive, which, if uncorrected, will become our *exclusive* focus), we will become problem centered. With respect to the first attitude, if I have to be better than others in order to have purpose, happiness, and identity in life, I will find myself viewing life as a "problem". Similarly, if I am focusing on the bad news in the other, I will find the other to be a problem. Thirdly, if I am focusing on the threat posed by relationships, I will find relationships to be a problem. And finally, if I focus on my object self alone, I will eventually "thingify" myself and find myself to be a problem. Slowly but surely a sense of gloom begins to arise. This is complemented by self-pity and boredom (in my relationship to myself) and pessimism, scepticism, and cynicism in my relationship to others and to the community. This will make me somewhat difficult to live with. People will withdraw, and so I will have to find *things* about me to get people to reconstitute relationships on the basis of admiration alone. But the dominant perspective will reemerge again and again. Life, others, relationships, and even self are dominantly, no, predominately problems. What a joy. Regrettably, this is the end product of my default drive, *if I do not add Level 3 and/or 4 objectives to it.*

If I do endeavor to use my Level 2 drives for Level 3 or 4 ends I will find myself moving in the opposite direction. Instead of being a problem, life becomes more of an opportunity and an adventure. Obviously, one will not stop having problems. Real problems will emerge from real people in real life circumstances, but I will not be predisposed to *viewing* my life as a problem. This opens my vision to the opportunities and adventures around me. This will thereby help me to solve problems, to see human potential, and above all to see human dignity and mystery. This perspective does not foreclose, but enhances the recognition of the *real* opportunities, potential, and mystery in the world around me. This cannot help but make me more creative, spirited, contributive, patient, peaceful, self-secure, and, in the case of friendship, loving. I will accomplish far more, create far more, and, in the end, be far more happy.

B. The Essence of the Third Level: Love

Choosing the Happiness 3 side of the dichotomies is the beginning of Happiness 3. Happiness 3 finds its fruition in love. In order to explain this, it is necessary to give an initial definition of love. Love is looking for the good news in the other, leading to the acceptance of the other as a lovable self, giving rise to the desire to be with the other and to do good for the other, giving rise to a unity with the other, whereby it is just as easy (if not easier) to do good for the other as to do it for self, which yields mutual acceptance, shared being and doing, and interpersonal unity.

Love is not a stoic act of will in which one heroically overlooks the nastiness of the other. I do not look at the bad news in the other, noting all of his weak and irritating features, and then say, "It is my Christian duty to love that irritating, boorish, weak, and inferior thing. Therefore, I will, I will, I really will!" Clearly enough, there is no love in that. This is simply the comparison game on skates.

Evidently, love must begin with looking for the good news in the other. From this, love grows quite effortlessly. True love revels in the good news, while "stoic love" focuses on the bad news and congratulates itself for looking beyond it. Sometimes the good news may seem remote or inaccessible, particularly when the other is acting mean spirited or difficult. Even then, true love enables one to recall the good news and remember that the other is the good news and not the transiently apparent bad news.

The lovability of the other draws me out of myself and makes me want to give myself to the other. The greatest gift I can give is my acceptance. Acceptance means letting the other into my inner world, letting the other matter to me. Love approaches unity when it becomes just as easy, if not easier, to do something for the other as to do it for myself. Parents, for example, often find it easier to do things for their children than for themselves.

True love is about giving and reciprocity. The spirit has an inherent need to create something of value outside itself. We do this in relationships. A deep relationship may become a unity, which might be termed *interpersonal personhood*, in which the connection between two persons takes on a life of its own. Each discovers that part of his personhood is derived from that connection. The person is not merely an autonomous island, but interpersonal, connected to others with varying degrees of affinity.

The care of the other, the other's response and being, switch something on inside me—they ignite my spirit. Further, I ignite the other, and I know it. *My* care and response make the other come alive, and I enjoy providing this good. It seems to justify my existence. I feel I contribute something important to the other, that I have left an effect that could last an eternity. Alone, I am a mere shadow of myself—a shadow of what I could give, of what the other could make come alive in me. But in relationship, I come alive. From the ego perspective of the second level of happiness, personhood may appear autonomous, but from the love perspective of Happiness 3, personhood is interpersonal. Pure autonomy would seem to be the emotional equivalent of amputation.

Deep interpersonal unity becomes a living entity; our *me's* meld into an *us*. The relationship becomes an interpersonal person. When this degree of unity occurs in marriage or deep friendship, it becomes necessary for the friends or couple to find a common vision or shared cause larger than themselves, for a relationship, like an individual, must reach beyond itself or wither. There are many goods beyond "ourselves": common projects or ideals, children, or the community, to name a few. Relationships not oriented to larger purposes often stagnate. Lovers can look into each other's eyes with such infatuation that they become for each other the pool of Narcissus—they gaze so deeply that they fall in and drown.

While infatuation is to be expected in newlyweds, the healthy marriage grows beyond that stage. Couples whose relationship has grown beyond infatuation will tend to include others within their unity (although each is capable of relating separately). They will extend some of their mutual acceptance to others, including them within the family circle. Conversely, infatuated couples not only will exclude outsiders; they also will avoid goals beyond each other. Without connections to others, with no thought of good beyond themselves, their relationship becomes an island no more self-sufficient than that of an autonomous individual, just twice as big.

To be fulfilled, love must move beyond itself to a greater good. The greater good need not be a person: Happiness 3 can also be experienced through serving a cause or an ideal. A relationship that does not reach out to a shared goal loses its connection with the world. When we are not a part of the whole, we feel great alienation. Without external connection, a relationship lacks objective validation of its worth. Like an individual, an "interpersonal person" without a larger purpose feels empty and useless. Relationship is not, therefore, an end in itself. It is a means toward love and good.

Relationships that do not grow remain superficial. Growth requires commitment. Intense growth requires commitment of the whole self and reciprocity from the other. Without commitment and reciprocity, friendships cannot grow. Friendships do not have to grow; they can remain superficial. Indeed, superficial friendships are safer; they risk little emotion. Commitment to depth risks rejection, but offers the rewards of love and deep joy.

Deep relationships involve sharing and mutual dependency. Sharing, however, is not necessarily caring. In codependency, for example, the partners share neuroses or dysfunctional traits. But sharing and dependency can also be positive, if positive values are shared. Mutual dependency based on shared love, generativity, and goodness is healthy. Indeed, such sharing and mutual interdependency are the essence of interpersonal personhood. As we commit more deeply to one another, more of our respective selves comes alive; we actualize our interpersonal being, increase our sense of purpose, and find great joy. Since we mean so much to each other, an element of mutual dependency is unavoidable.

The third level of happiness lies in experiencing the good beyond self. Most people find this level through deep, committed love or through service to a cause. Both breadth and intimacy are necessary as one grows in Happiness 3 love. However, breadth and intimacy need not grow proportionately. Some people's love may grow more in breadth, becoming more inclusive: Mother Teresa's love welcomed, accepted, and encompassed a new multitude of people each morning. Other people's love may tend toward intimacy, in which they achieve a depth of commitment, knowledge, care, and unity with one person. This depth of intimacy creates a new reality that reaches out toward children, the community, or some other common goal. Breadth and intimacy are both valid; neither is better than the other.

Reaching for Happiness 3 does not in any way imply spurning all the joys of Happiness 1 and 2. It is true, of course, that the emotional direction of Levels 1 and 2 (toward self) is opposite that of Level 3 (toward the other), but the states are not mutually exclusive. One can live in Happiness 3 and still experience the pleasures of Levels 1 and 2. Indeed, Happiness 3 often enhances the pleasures of Happiness 1 and 2. Ice cream tastes better when one is in love. We grow into Happiness 3 when our primary goal is not to grab gusto for ourselves, but to allow the pleasures of Happiness 1 or 2 to accomplish good outside ourselves, for someone else. In so doing, we find the deepest pleasure.

IV. The Third Crisis and the Fourth Level of Happiness

In light of the above, it might seem that human actualization can be complete through the achievement of Level 3. Alas, this is not the case, because human beings are greater than this. We will now see that the transcendental nature of the human desire for truth, love, goodness/justice, and beauty gives rise to a third crisis (the category error), which, despite the pain it produces, leads to the fullness of human actualization.

It was noted in Chapter One that human beings are self-transcendent by nature. Their desire for truth, love, justice, beauty, and being can be satiated only by what is perfect and unconditional. We could therefore say that full human actualization must include access to, desire for, contemplation of, and interaction with the perfect, unconditional, unrestricted, and absolute in the areas of Truth itself, Love itself, Goodness/Justice itself, Beauty itself, and Being itself. This contemplation could extend into mathematics, metaphysics, aesthetics, philosophy, and, of course, the spiritual, mystical, and religious. It can influence every goal, ideal, aspiration, relationship, thought, and action of any human being who has achieved full actualization.

Before probing the nature of the third crisis, I will probe more deeply into the power of human self-transcendence in six particular areas.

A. *The Power of Human Self-Transcendence*

The power of self-transcendence is manifest in six areas: (1) the human, unrestricted desire to know; (2) the human desire for unconditional love and to love unconditionally; (3) the human desire for perfect justice/goodness and to be perfectly just/good; (4) the desire for perfect beauty; (5) the desire to be at home in all that is; and (6) faith (a desire for relationship with God).

Though faith requires a choice, the other five manifestations of self-transcendence seem to be intrinsic to human beings. The first five manifestations lead one to the brink of the faith choice, but do not push one into it. Though all six manifestations of self-transcendence give rise to every form of human striving in knowledge, love, art, justice, and faith, they can lead to problems in living out the Happiness 3 (H3) ideal, for they sometimes incite human beings to seek ultimacy, perfection, the absolute, the unconditioned, and even the infinite and eternal in those things that are by nature imperfect, conditioned, finite, and transitory. Let us call this a "category error" (the third crisis). This leads to a host of problems ranging from dashed idealism to dashed romanticism. The result is generally an undermining of H3 and a cynical return to H2 or H1. Before considering these problems, I will briefly discuss each of the six manifestations of self-transcendence giving rise to the fourth level of happiness and purpose in life.

1. *The unrestricted desire to know* is manifest in children who persistently query, "Why is that?" One gives an answer, and they ask the further question, "Well, why is that?" One gives another answer, and still they ask, "Well, why is that?" They are likely to go on forever until one says, "Be quiet now, you're overeducated." This seemingly endless process of querying shows that human beings recognize the inadequacy of answers. They see that a particular answer is not fully explanatory, and since they want complete explanations, they proceed to ask yet another question. This process will likely continue in a freely inquiring

subject until one has the complete set of correct answers to the complete set of questions.

Human beings are not seeking merely pragmatic knowledge (for example, "How can I get more food with which to live?"). They seem to want to know just for the sake of knowing, and they seem to be endowed with a desire for complete explanation. They recognize when they have not arrived at this point, indicating that they are always beyond any answer at which they have arrived. Human beings have the remarkable capacity of knowing that they do not know; yet one must ask, how is this possible unless they have some awareness of what is beyond what they already know?

Many contemporary philosophers (such as Emerich Coreth,[1] Bernard Lonergan,[2] and Karl Rahner[3]) have concluded that human beings have a prethematic awareness of complete intelligibility. They believe further that complete intelligibility really exists and that every particular answer to every particular question is ultimately grounded in it. A completely intelligible being contains within itself every answer to every question that could ever be raised about it. This *reality* frequently goes by the names of "unconditioned Truth" or an "unrestricted act of understanding" and is frequently associated with "God" (see below, section IVB). These philosophers further believe that human beings have a "sense" of this perfect, complete Truth. This "sense" is not knowledge or a clear idea; it is only a prethematic awareness of the perfect Truth, which ultimately grounds the intelligibility of any imperfect or finite truth. This awareness incites human beings unceasingly to ask questions until they have arrived at the perfect and unconditioned Truth.

Those with faith interpret this to be the human's sense of God (given by God to human beings). Hence, they believe that the human self-transcendent quest for knowledge comes from God and can find fruition only through union with God.

2. Similarly, philosophers have long thought that human beings have a "sense" of *perfect and unconditional love*. Not only do we have the power

---

[1] Emerich Coreth, *Metaphysics*, trans. Joseph Donceel (New York: Herder and Herder, 1968), pp. 103–97.

[2] Bernard Lonergan, *Collected Works of Bernard Lonergan: Insight*, ed. Frederick E. Crowe and Robert M. Doran (Toronto, Canada: University of Toronto Press, 1992), pp. 657–708.

[3] Karl Rahner, *Spirit in the World*, trans. William Dych, S.J. (New York: Herder and Herder, 1968), pp. 163–230, and 387–406.

to love (that is, the power to be connected naturally to another human being in profound emotion, care, self-gift, concern, and acceptance); we also have a "sense" of what this profound interpersonal connection would be like if it were perfect. This sense of perfect love has the positive effect of inciting human beings to pursue ever more perfect forms of love. However, it has the drawback of inciting human beings to *expect* ever more perfect love from other human beings. This generally leads to dashed romanticism and to the slow decline of relationships, which can never grow fast enough to match the perfect and unconditional expectations of the participants. As will be noted below, this expectation leads to one of the main problems arising out of H3.

What is the origin of this "sense" of perfect, unconditional love? As with the desire for perfect Truth, many contemporary philosophers believe that there exists a transcendent, unconditionally loving reality that is present to human beings, giving them a sense of what love could be. It allows human beings to be beyond any imperfect manifestation of love, causing at once a striving for more and a dissatisfaction with what is. This unconditionally loving reality goes by the names of "Love itself"; the "idea of Love itself"; "perfect, interpersonal subjectivity"; "the ground of perfect, interpersonal subjectivity"; "the ground of interpersonal connectedness"; and, for those with faith, "God" or "the loving God".

3. As with the "sense" of perfect and unconditional Truth and Love, philosophers have long recognized the human desire for *perfect justice or goodness*. Not only do human beings have a sense of good and evil, a capacity for moral reflection, a profoundly negative felt awareness of cooperation with evil (guilt), and a profoundly positive felt awareness of cooperation with goodness (nobility); they also have a "sense" of what perfect, unconditioned goodness/justice would be like. Human beings are not content simply to act in accordance with their conscience now; they are constantly striving for ways to achieve the more noble, the greater good, the higher ideal; they even go so far as to pursue the perfectly good or just order.

This desire for perfect goodness/justice can be seen in children. An imperfect manifestation of justice from parents will get the immediate retort "That's not fair!" Adults do the same thing. We have a sense of what justice ought to be, and we believe others ought to know this. When this sense of justice has been violated, we will just as easily respond in our minds with "That's not fair!" A violation of this sort always seems particularly acute. We seem to be in a state of shock. We really expect that perfect justice ought to happen, and when it doesn't, it so profoundly disappoints us it consumes us. As a result, we can feel outrage toward God, toward other human beings, toward social structures, and so on.

As with our "sense" of perfect and unconditional love, our sense of perfect and unconditional goodness/justice has both a good side and a bad side. The good side is it fuels all our strivings for an ever more perfect social order, a more just legal system, and greater equity and equality; it even fuels our promethean idealism to bring the justice of God to earth. The bad side of this "sense" of perfect or unconditional justice is that it incites our *expectations* for perfect justice in a finite and conditioned world, which normally means that our promethean ideals are dashed. This causes disappointments with the culture, the legal system, our organizations, and even our families. We seem always to expect more justice and goodness than the finite world can deliver, and it causes outrage, impatience, judgment of others, and even cynicism when it does not come to pass. This, again, is one of the major problems arising out of living at H3 (see below, IVB).

What is the source of this "sense" of perfect justice/goodness? This desire for perfect justice in the world, and even the promethean desire to save the world? This desire to be the "ultimate hero"? As with perfect and unconditional Truth and Love, many philosophers believe that that there is a transcendent, unconditionally good, just reality. It goes frequently by the names of "Goodness itself", "the ground of human social connectedness", "the idea of perfect Justice", and, for those with faith, "God". In the famous allegory of the cave in *The Republic*,[4] Plato likens this reality to the sun, which is the source of all light and even the source of all shadows. From the time of Plato, many philosophers have called this reality "the really Real". It is more real than the world of changing things and far more real than the world of the shadows. In any case, these philosophers believe that human beings have a "sense" of this perfectly just/good reality that allows them to be beyond any imperfect manifestation of it. Inasmuch as they are always aware of what is

---

[4] See Edith Hamilton. *The Collected Dialogues of Plato* (Princeton, N.J.: Princeton University Press, 1963): *The Republic*, book 7, chapter two.

beyond any imperfect manifestation of justice, they continually strive for, and expect, the more perfect.

4. One need not read the nineteenth century Romantic poets, listen to the great Romantic composers, or view the works of Romantic artists to see the human capacity to idolize *beauty*. One need only look at the examples of simple dissatisfaction with beauty in our everyday life. We don't look good enough, and neither do other people. The house is not perfect enough, the painting can never achieve perfection, and the musical composition, though beautiful beyond belief, could always be better. Once in a great while, we think we have arrived at complete ecstasy. This might occur upon looking at a scene of natural beauty: a sunset over the water, or majestic green and brown mountains against a horizon of blue sky, but even there, despite our desire to elevate it to the quasi-divine, we get bored and strive for a different or an even more perfect manifestation of natural beauty—a *little* better sunset, or another vantage point of the Alps that's a *little* more perfect.

As with the other three transcendentals (perfect Truth, perfect Love, and perfect Goodness/Justice), human beings seem always to have a prethematic awareness of what is more perfect. It incites them to the desire of this more perfect ideal. This desire has both a good and a bad effect. The good effect is that it incites the continuous human striving for artistic, musical, and literary perfection. We do not passively desire to create; we passionately desire to create, to express in ever more beautiful forms, the perfection of beauty that we seem to carry within our consciousness. We do not simply want to *say* an idea; we want to express it beautifully, indeed—more beautifully, indeed—perfectly beautifully. We do not simply want to express a mood in music; we want to express it perfectly beautifully. This striving has left a legacy of architecture and art, music and drama, and every form of high culture.

The bad effect is that we will always grow bored with any imperfect manifestation of beauty, which causes us to try to make perfectly beautiful what is imperfect by its nature. It is true that a garden can achieve a certain perfection of beauty, but our continuous desire to improve it can make us grow terribly dissatisfied when we cannot perfect it indefinitely. One is reminded of the tourist going through the gardens of Versailles exclaiming, "Enough garden, already. What's next?" or a very beautiful woman, who despite tremendous vanity harbors a secret knowledge and resentment of every "defect" in herself, or the music lover who proclaims, "I've heard Brahms too many times."

Where does this sense of perfect beauty come from? As with the other three transcendentals, many philosophers suspect that there exists a transcendent reality that is perfectly beautiful. This transcendent reality frequently goes by the names of "Beauty itself", "the ground of the artistic muse", "the idea of perfect Beauty", "unconditioned Beauty", "Glory itself (*Herrlichkeit*)", "the ground of perfect ecstasy", and, for those with faith, "God". These philosophers also believe that human beings have a "sense" of this transcendent reality that allows them to be aware of beauty beyond any of its imperfect manifestations. This causes at once the striving to create the beautiful and even the more beautiful. It also causes us to expect perfect beauty where it cannot be found, leading to yet another problem associated with living at H3.

5. Perfect harmony with totality: being at home. Human beings also seek a perfect sense of harmony with all that is. They not only want to be at home in a particular environment; they also want to be at home with the totality, at home in the cosmos. Have you ever felt, as either a child or an adult, a sense of alienation or discord—a deep sense of not belonging? You ask yourself, "What could be the source?" and you look around and see that at this particular time you have a good relationship with your friends and your family. Your work relationships seem to be going fairly well; community involvements have produced some interesting friends and contexts in which to work. Yet something's missing. While you do feel at home with family, friends, office and organization, you don't quite feel at home in a *general* sense. You feel like you are out of kilter with, and don't belong to, the *totality*. And yet, all the *specific* contexts you look at seem just fine. You feel an emptiness, a lack of peace, yet there is absolutely nothing you can put your finger on.

Many philosophers would identify this feeling with a human being's "sense" not only of the totality but also of some initial sense of harmony or peace with the totality—a "sense" of perfect home, a sense of home amidst the whole of reality without any taint of alienation. This sense of alienation from the totality also has both a good side and a bad side. The good side is that it presents a call to seek ever greater and deeper forms of harmony (peace within the world). The bad side is the confusion and discontent that it brings. I do not understand why I feel this lack of peace, this emptiness, this sense of not belonging, and so I tend to feel animosity toward those groups who can do nothing for me when I'm feeling it. One may look at his own wife and think, "Although I feel at home with her, she can do nothing for this peculiar sense of emptiness." Her inability to help induces frustration in him, and she is baffled by this seemingly inexplicable frustration. Again, one could realize that his best friend, who seems to bring comfort in so many human situations, cannot help him to belong, to fit in, to feel at home in this universal sense. And so he displays his frustration and restlessness at her powerlessness. Relationships have a way of taking a downward turn in these circumstances because we are trying to extract from them what they cannot give. The only way out, seemingly, is to find perfect home and harmony with all that is.

What gives rise to this "sense" of perfect home in the totality? Again, many philosophers would assert that there exists a transcendent reality that is itself perfect peace (perfect home). This reality goes by the name of "perfect Harmony", "Harmony itself", "the idea of perfect home", "the Eternal Order" and in some cases overlaps in name with "unconditional love", "Love itself", and "the ground of interpersonal connectedness". Again, many of these philosophers associate this transcendent reality with "God". These philosophers further believe that human beings have a "sense" of this transcendent reality that enables them to go beyond any particular or imperfect feeling of home or peace that may arise in any specific context. This gives rise to a striving for more perfect peace. In some religions, this "sense" of perfect peace is identified with the unitive or mystical experience.

6. The above five manifestations of self-transcendence provide the *basis of human faith* (a relationship with a personal God). If the above philosophers are correct, and the human "sense" of the perfect and unconditioned comes from a transcendent reality that is perfect and unconditional Truth, Love, Goodness/Justice, Beauty, and Home/Peace, then the human proclivity toward faith seems quite natural, for despite the different tenors of Truth, Love, Goodness/Justice, Beauty, and Home/Peace, they are all held together by one fundamental similarity: they seem to be perfect and unconditioned by nature. Long before philosophers attempted to prove that all these transcendentals were one and the same reality, human beings had a tendency to blend them all together because of the perfection and unconditionedness they "sensed" in them. They felt that all reality participated in this perfect,

transcendent reality that is Truth, Love, Goodness/Justice, Beauty, and Home/Peace by its nature. This came to be known eventually as "God" (monotheism).

As philosophy developed, the perfect and unconditioned was associated with the unrestricted and the infinite. It was also associated with creation as human beings began to sense, and later to prove, that an actual infinity of past time (and achieved infinity) was contradictory and therefore impossible. Therefore, a Creator of finite past time,[5] which Creator would have to be outside of time, was associated with this unrestricted, unconditioned, perfect, transcendent reality. These various attributes were then seen intrinsically to be interrelated, which gave rise to a host of proofs for God's existence beginning with Plato,[6] Aristotle,[7] Augustine,[8] and Aquinas,[9] until the current day (Etienne Gilson,[10] Jacques Maritain,[11] Bernard Lonergan,[12] Mortimer Adler,[13] James Ross,[14] Alvin Plantinga,[15] and even mathematicians such as G.J. Whitrow,[16] to name only a few). It therefore took on a variety of interrelated names given by theologians, philosophers, physicists,

[5] See Appendix 2 for a full explanation.

[6] *The Republic*, books 6 and 7.

[7] Richard McKeon, *The Basic Works of Aristotle* (New York: Random House, 1941): *Physics*, book θ (pp. 354–94), and *Metaphysics*, book λ (pp. 872–88).

[8] Augustine, *The Trinity*, trans. Stephen McKenna (Washington, D.C.: Catholic University of America Press, 1963), XIV 15, 21; XV 21, 40; XIV 7, 9; and *Confessions*, trans. R. S. Pine-Coffin, book X, 6–27 (Penguin Books: London, 1961). See also, Etienne Gilson, *The Christian Philosophy of Saint Augustine*, trans. L. E. M. Lynch (New York: Random House, 1960).

[9] Thomas Aquinas, *Summa Theologica*, trans. Fathers of the English Dominican Province (New York: Benziger Brothers, 1947–1948, I, Q.2, art. 3, pp. 13–14; and *On Being and Essence*, trans. Armand Maurer, C. S. B. (Toronto: The Pontifical Institute of Mediaeval Studies, 1968), pp. 53–57.

[10] Etienne Gilson, *The Elements of Christian Philosophy* (New York: The New American Library, 1960), pp. 46–94.

[11] Jacques Maritain, *An Introduction to Philosophy*, trans. E. I. Watkin (Kansas City, Mo.: Sheed and Ward, 1944), pp. 190–93.

[12] Ibid.

[13] Mortimer J. Adler, *How to Think about God* (New York: Macmillan, 1980), pp. 69–111.

[14] James F. Ross, *Philosophical Theology* (New York: Bobbs-Merrill, 1969), pp. 182–95.

[15] Alvin Plantinga, *Faith and Philosophy* (Grand Rapids, Mich.: Eerdmans, 1964), pp. ix, x, and 100–102.

[16] G.J. Whitrow. "The Age of the Universe", *British Journal for the Philosophy of Science*, 5 (1954–1955): 215–25, and *The Natural Philosophy of Time* (London: Thomas Nelson and Sons, 1961). Also, "On the Impossibility of Infinite Past Time", *British Journal for the Philosophy of Science*, 29 (1978), pp. 39–45.

mathematicians, and simple people of faith: "the Creator", "Pure Being", "Unconditioned Existence", "Being itself", "Power itself", "Unconditioned Power", "Timeless Power", "the First Cause", "Ultimate Ground of Being", "Creator of Being".

As noted above, Plato and his followers referred to the objective of this desire as Being itself, Goodness itself, Truth itself, and Beauty itself, which he implies are one and the same being. Augustine (a Neoplatonist) and his followers view Plato's transcendentals as *attributes* of an infinite, absolutely unique, ultimate ground of being (God).

Physicists since the time of Aristotle have frequently associated it with an Uncaused Cause, a First Cause, an Unmoved Mover, a First Mover, and a Creator. The creation event has been configured in a multiplicity of ways throughout the ages and now is particularly rich in light of the possibilities suggested by quantum and big bang cosmology.

Obviously, this ultimate reality has been reflected on by others besides philosophers and physicists. Its most wide ranging reflection takes place in faith and religion. Though not all religions personalize the Ultimate, most do, because love, goodness, justice, and home have an interpersonal quality and seem to reveal, therefore, an interpersonal dimension of the perfect, unconditioned, unrestricted Creator. Hence, faith not only sees this Being as a perfect, unconditioned Cause of all else that is; it also attributes consciousness, self-consciousness, intelligence, personal identity, and even interpersonal identity to it.

Most faith traditions go beyond this. They associate love with the interpersonal consciousness of the Ultimate. This generally results from an intuitive awareness that love is one of the highest powers, if not the highest power, in human beings, making it likely that the Creator could not be completely devoid of it. If the Creator created human beings ultimately to be fulfilled through love (through interpersonal personhood), it seems likely that the Creator would not only have to be cognizant of this ultimate form of fulfillment, but even in some way possess it. This loving, interpersonal, unconditional Creator is normally given a name such as "God" or "the Lord".

In many faith perspectives, God is recognized to be more than a loving Creator. God is interested in the lives of human beings, for human beings are thought in some way to be made in the image of God or to share in some finite way in a divine power (for example, creative intelligence, the cognizance of good and evil, love, freedom, even the very desire and recognition of infinity and eternity). God's love is manifest not only in sharing God's power and life with human beings, but also in leading human beings to the fullness of life, including eternal life in the divine domain. Human beings respond to God's loving initiative through prayer, worship, knowledge (in sacred texts), and trying to live a life commensurate with God's will. This constitutes a relationship that philosophers characterize in a variety of ways: the infinite passion of faith (Søren Kierkegaard),[17] creative fidelity (Gabriel Marcel),[18] I-Thou (Martin Buber),[19] and so on.

Whether or not one calls the Ultimate a "Higher Power", "Unconditioned Power", "Uncaused Cause", "Timeless Being", "Infinite Being", "the Creator", "Conscious Deity", "Limitlessness", "Unrestricted Being", "Loving God", or "Triune God", or even if one does not believe in an Ultimate, all human beings seem to have one thing in common: a *desire* for the unconditional, perfect, absolute, and ultimate, which makes all finite and transitory beings incapable of fulfilling it.

B. The Third Crisis (the Category Error) and Its Resolution

In section IVA, I showed that the human desire for unconditional Truth, Love, Goodness, Beauty, and Being at once inspired human creativity and striving (positive effect) while inciting us to expect perfect satisfaction from imperfect realities (negative effect). Sometimes we can carry this negative effect to an extreme by expecting a human being to be the perfect satisfaction of all five desires for the unconditional, for example, "Would you please be perfect and unconditional Truth, Love, Goodness, Justice, Beauty, and Home for me? And I will do my best to be the same for you, because my love is true?" Obviously, true love has been confused with perfect and unconditional Love, which will sow the seeds of its own destruction. One, of course, does not stop there. If you can supply all these things to me, and I can do likewise, why not just sum it

---

[17] Søren Kierkegaard, *Concluding Unscientific Postscript*, trans. David F. Swenson and Walter Lowrie (Princeton, N.J.: Princeton University Press, 1941), pp. 224 and 262–66; and *Fear and Trembling*, trans. Walter Lowrie (Princeton, N.J.: Princeton University Press, 1954), pp. 90–93.

[18] Gabriel Marcel, *Creative Fidelity* (New York: Crossroads, 1982).

[19] Martin Buber, *I and Thou*, 2nd ed. (New York: Charles Scribner's Sons, 1958).

all up and ask, "Would you please be perfect and unconditional happiness, meaning in life, and being for me? And I will do my best to be perfect and unconditional happiness, meaning in life, and being for you." The annals of human love, thereby, are transformed into the annals of human tragedy.

By the time one begins to sort out this misidentification between true love and perfect and unconditional Love (if, indeed, one really does do this), the relationship once filled with care, natural connection, kindness, delight, self-gift, and joy has turned into dashed expectations, frustration, disappointment, and sorrow. This, of course, only gradually manifests itself. As the first signs of imperfection, conditionedness, and finitude begin to emerge in the beloved, I show slight irritation but have hopes that the ideal will soon be recaptured (as if it were ever captured to begin with). But as the fallibility of the beloved begins more acutely to be manifest (they are not perfectly humble, gentle, kind, forgiving, self-giving, and concerned with me in all my interests), the irritation becomes frustration, which, in turn, becomes dashed expectation: "I can't believe I thought she was really the 'One'." Of course, she wasn't the One, because she is not perfect and unconditioned. Nevertheless, the dashed expectation becomes either quiet hurt or overt demands, both aimed at extracting a higher level of performance from the beloved. When she does not comply, alas, perhaps the relationship should be terminated.

I, for my part, also have a rather large responsibility to live up to, for I have implicitly promised that I would do my best to be perfect and unconditional Truth, Love, Goodness/Justice, Home, Peace, happiness, meaning in life, and Being for my beloved. Despite the fact that my love is true and I am quite certain that I can fulfill my beloved's every desire, I have found myself experiencing certain shortcomings in this regard, requiring that some rather elaborate façades be constructed. These could turn into outright lies if need be, or, if I'm good at it, I could just continue to hide the real me from my beloved. Regrettably, I slip up. She inexorably finds out little details leading to other little details, which open the way to self-exposure. "I hate her nosiness . . . her prying into my subjectivity. Her incessant desire to want to get in and see my weakness. It will not happen. Yet, I think she might see it."

Clearly enough, this relationship is not going to grow, if it is able to last beyond five tumultuous years. The root problem was not with the authenticity of this couple's love for one another. It did not arise out of a lack of concern, care, responsiveness, or desire to be self-giving, responsible, self-disciplined, and true. Rather, it arose out of a false expectation: "Would you be the perfect and unconditioned for me? And I'll be the perfect and unconditioned for you." In the words of faith, "Would you be god for me? And I'll be god for you."

Why do we fall prey to what seems to be such an obvious error? Because our *desire* for love and to love is unconditional, but our *actuality* is conditioned. Our desire is for the perfect, but our actuality is imperfect. We as human beings, therefore, cannot satisfy one another's desire for the unconditional and the perfect. If we do not have a *real* unconditional and perfect Being to satisfy this desire, we start looking around us to find a surrogate. Other human beings at first seem like very good surrogates, because they display qualities of self-transcendence. Hence, we confuse one another for the perfect and unconditioned and undermine the very relationships that hold out opportunities for growth, depth, joy, common cause, and mutual bondedness.

We do not stop at trying to extract all six aspects of transcendentality from other human beings, we also attempt to extract them from imperfect and conditioned manifestations of truth, goodness/justice, beauty, and home/peace. With respect to truth, history is replete with examples of brilliant men and women trying to find the perfect and unconditioned in philosophy, science, mathematics, and literature, but there always seems to be some unanswered question that gets in the way of perfect intelligibility being fully manifest. There always seems to be some flaw in what could otherwise have been a perfect system. These disenchantments have, on many occasions, brought the brilliant from the heights of complete self-confidence to the depths of dashed rationalism, causing them to protect invalid ideas and systems beyond their time. Something has gone awry in these authentic and dedicated seekers of truth. Again, the problem is not with the thirst for truth and knowledge and the love of the process of inquiry, but rather with trying to extract perfect and unconditioned truth from an imperfect and conditioned world.

With respect to goodness/justice, one need only look at last year's newspapers to find a host of well-meaning, dedicated, and generous men and women who have tried to extract the perfect and unconditioned from the legal system, the ideals of social justice, and social institutions dedicated to the common good. The despairing rhetoric of dashed idealism and cynicism does not belong solely to early Marxism; it can be found in public defenders who decry the legal system for prosecuting the innocent, and victims who vilify the very same system for letting the guilty go free. It can also be found in educators who criticize the educational system for not setting strong enough standards and in community advocates who tear down the very same system for making the standards too high and too exclusive. Who is right? Aren't both parties well intentioned, committed, looking out for the good of society, trying to help? Again, the problem seems not to be so much one of searching for justice and goodness but rather for seeking perfect and unconditioned justice and goodness in an imperfect, conditioned world.

One can see the same problem manifest in the artistic community. When one reads the biographies of great artists, musicians, and poets, one senses the tragedy with which art is frequently imbued. What causes these extraordinarily gifted men and women to abuse themselves, to judge themselves so harshly, to pour themselves so totally into their art? Perhaps it's when art becomes a god, when one tries to extract perfect and unconditional Beauty from imperfect and conditioned minds and forms.

In sum, all of the above cases manifest the problems arising out of H3 people trying to extract the perfect and unconditioned from an imperfect and conditioned world. If we are to stop torturing ourselves, to cease becoming cynical about what is most precious in our lives—our beloveds, ideals, knowledge, and creativity—if we are to stop undermining ourselves in every pursuit that holds out the potential for self-transcendence, we must make sure that the objective for which we are searching can be found in the domain in which we are looking. We cannot be looking for the unconditioned in the domain of the conditioned.

For those with faith in a personal God, this would mean, quite simply, "Let God be God, and let creatures be creatures." The way to overcome the problems associated with self-transcendence (if one has faith) is to pray to the loving God, to establish a deeper relationship with God, and to include God in every aspect of one's journey. Not only will God be the Ultimate that one really seeks; God will be the source of grace and love drawing the person of faith to the divine life, which is the *only* life that will satisfy.

If one does not believe in God, one still cannot escape the above-mentioned problems. But one cannot call upon God or faith to solve them. Therefore, these problems can only be mitigated by an act of negation: "I will *not* make anything that is imperfect, conditioned, or finite into an unconditioned, perfect Ultimate."

C. Faith

Readers not having faith may want to skip these sections and proceed directly to Chapter Four. For those with an interest in faith or in seeking faith, the following may prove helpful as a means to overcoming the third crisis.

As noted above, our powers of self-transcendence do not constitute faith. Our awareness of and desire for fulfillment in unconditional and perfect Truth, Love, Goodness/Justice, Beauty, Harmony/Peace, and even God do not, in themselves, constitute a relationship with a personal God. They form only the interior *basis* for such a relationship. Augustine was enamored of Plato's transcendentals long before his conversion to Christianity. Indeed, history is replete with examples of great thinkers (for example, Blaise Pascal,[20] Edith Stein,[21] C. S. Lewis,[22] Jacques Maritain,[23] Simone Weil[24]) who have discovered within themselves an insatiable desire for perfect and unconditional Truth, Love, Goodness/Justice, Beauty, Harmony/Peace, and God. Yet this desire, and even love of the transcendentals, was not enough. What drove these great thinkers to move from an awareness of a transcendent reality to faith? *A recognition of the fact that they could not bring themselves to this transcendent*

[20] Blaise Pascal, *Pensées* (1670).

[21] Edith Stein, *Edith Stein, a Biographical Essay and the Way to Know God*, by Teresa Benedicta of the Cross, ed. Edith Stein Center (New York, Edith Stein Guild, [1981]); *Collected Works of Edith Stein: Sister Teresa Benedicta of the Cross, Discalced Carmelite* (Washington, D.C.: ICS Publications, 1986-); *Knowledge and Faith*, ed. L. Gelter and M. Linssen, trans. Walter Redmond (Washington, D.C.: ICS Publications, 2000).

[22] C. S. Lewis, *The Abolition of Man* (New York: Macmillan, 1947).

[23] Jacques Maritain, *Existence and the Existent* (Garden City, N.Y.: Doubleday, 1956); *On the Use of Philosophy: Three Essays* (Princeton, N.J.: Princeton University Press, 1961).

[24] Simone Weil, *Lectures on Philosophy*, trans. Hugh Price (New York: Cambridge University Press, 1978); *Oppression and Liberty* (London: Routledge and Paul, 1958); *On Science, Necessity, and the Love of God*, trans. Richard Rees (New York: Oxford University Press, 1968).

Reality, which was their heart's true desire, by themselves. Try as they did, they could not think themselves into it, nor could they love themselves into it or win their way into it. Through great works of justice, the harder they tried the more they spun their wheels, until they came to an awareness of their *need* for the transcendent Reality to come to them. They needed Emmanuel (God with us). These thinkers confronted an untraversable abyss that could only be crossed by an unconditional, transcendent Reality.

Once they discovered this *need*, they could not run from it. They had to cease playing the "self-sufficiency game". They even had to acknowledge that they could not be the center of their own universe and that they could not, by themselves, satisfy the ultimate yearnings of their hearts. They could not make themselves happy without a transcendent Reality because their hearts' longing was precisely for this. Augustine phrased it well when he noted, "For Thou hast made us for Thyself, and our hearts are restless until they rest in Thee."

Acknowledgment of need is difficult for most of us, for it is an act of both humility and vulnerability, yet it seems unavoidable if we are to allow the transcendent Reality to come into our lives and hearts. It is ironic that the very moment we come to appreciate our transcendental dignity through our awareness of the perfect, unconditional, transcendent Reality we need an act of humility to bring this awareness and dignity to fruition. Awareness of our transcendental identity and dignity could be a source of great pride, but it cannot last for long, for we cannot give ourselves what we yearn for. A humble search followed by humble acceptance and humble love is the only way to enter into the perfect and unconditional satisfaction for which our natures yearn.

This humble acknowledgment of need requires a decision. We can't just slip into it. We must deliberately choose to ask God to come into our lives, to guide us to what we cannot give ourselves. This can be done through a variety of different prayers such as, "Lord, I need you", "Lord, I invite you into my life", or "Lord, I love you". Perhaps the most poignant is, "Thy will be done", where one entrusts oneself to the infinitely loving, good, and truthful will of God while working to actualize this will in one's life and in the world.

This faith decision (expressed through these or similar prayers) is not made in a vacuum. It begins with the acute awareness of the transcendent Reality, which causes our desire for unconditional Truth, Love, Goodness, and Beauty to function. Without this transcendent Reality being present to us, we would have no desire for it, for every desire requires an awareness of its objective. The very fact that we desire unconditional Truth, Love, Goodness, and Beauty points to our prethematic awareness of a transcendent Reality, which had to come to us because we, in our finitude, could not give it to ourselves.

As Augustine recognized long ago, God's presence in us causes us at once to feel empty and continuously to be creative and positive (by enabling us to see beyond every boundary of truth, love, goodness, and beauty). Our most creative moments are, therefore, linked to our emptiest moments. The very source of our creativity is the source of the third crisis. Our intrinsic inclination to move toward the sublime is fraught with discontent, but it is a discontent imbued with truth, namely, the truth that neither I nor anyone else except God can ultimately satisfy my yearnings. This discontent is, therefore, the truth about humility, creaturehood, and imperfection set into the horizon of perfect satisfaction, which can be ours through God alone.

In sum, faith seems to be built on a four-layered foundation. These layers represent a dialogue between God and a person:

1. *God's invitation.* God's presence to us, which gives rise to our yearning for unconditional and perfect Truth, Love, Goodness/Justice, and Beauty. This is the source of our creativity in intellection, love, ethics, politics, art, philosophy, and the spiritual. Yet it is also the source of emptiness that beckons us from Level 1 to Level 2, from Level 2 to Level 3, from Level 3 to Level 4, and ultimately to the recognition of the need for the God who comes (Emmanuel—God with us).

2. *Our response—part one: the key decision of human freedom.* Once we recognize that we cannot get to the perfect and unconditional objective of our heart's desire, we have only two options: we can proclaim that life is absurd (because we can never achieve the objective of our fulfillment), or we can *believe* that this objective of our fulfillment exists as a reality outside of ourselves (because we, in our conditioned nature, are aware of this unconditional objective). If we recognize the paradoxical structure of our existence (namely, that we are aware of something that we should not be able to be aware of by our conditioned nature alone), we will be inclined to believe in the Reality that stands as the source of our desire for unconditional and perfect fulfillment.

3. *Our response—part two: our choice to ask God in*. The above inclination toward belief is not sufficient for faith. Faith also requires an act of accepting God into our lives. This is done through a humble acknowledgment of need, which helps us to overcome the myth of self-sufficiency. Spontaneous prayers such as "I need you", "I accept you into my life", and above all, "Thy will be done", reflect our choice to put ourselves into the unconditionally true, good, beautiful, and loving will of God. These prayers can be said twenty times a day for the rest of our lives, which allow us to move ever more deeply into the Reality that grounds all truth, goodness, love, and beauty and so grounds our ultimate satisfaction through one another and the Reality itself.

In conjunction with the decision to accept God into our lives is an almost insatiable curiosity about God. It provokes a need for revelation. We begin to ask questions such as: Does God really make good come out of all suffering? Does God's providence orchestrate the whole panoply of free agents to their best possible end? How does prayer work? One cannot help but think that if God is unconditionally loving, then God not only would know of our need for answers to these questions, but also would willingly provide them through some form of self-revelation. This could come in the form of prophetic utterances in a sacred text, in God's presence among us through his spirit, or even through his presence among us through the flesh. The point is, an unconditionally loving God would not leave us orphaned. We seem instinctually to know this and respond by searching for the word of God, reading it, appropriating it, filling our hearts with it, submitting to it, following it, and ultimately surrendering to it.

The need for community and public worship also seems to be awakened by our decision to believe and accept God into our lives. This community not only provides support in times of need and for growth and faith; it also provides the vehicle through which we can serve the needs of others in faith. Ultimately, this community, when it reflects the love of God, provides a little glimpse of the home, harmony, and peace for which we yearn. It is a vehicle through which God works to respond to this transcendental desire. Hence, we frequently join such communities, attach our family lives to them, and involve ourselves in the various projects that serve the needs of the world beyond us.

4. *God's response to our response*. God responds to our response first with a sense of being at home. God overcomes our emptiness, our feel-

ing of being alone in the totality, and our sense of self-alienation. When we reflect on it, we see that in the past we could not get beyond these feeling by ourselves. Try as we might, the feeling of not being at home was not in our power to overcome. But suddenly, in our humble act of belief and acceptance of God, in our prayer "Thy will be done", the feeling of being profoundly alone is so radically overcome we actually feel charged up, filled with fervor, alive in a way that we never felt before. Naturally, we can get used to this higher degree of life and spirit. But then the moment when self-alienation is overcome, there is no mistaking how different life is through the grace of God. "Did I acquire peace on my own?" the sceptic may ask, followed by the further question, "Well, if I did, why couldn't I ever do that before?"

Although peace itself may have been felt before, the depth of peace that comes with "Thy will be done" will be experienced as quite unique. It will manifest itself not only in explicit feelings of joy (what C. S. Lewis called "stabs of joy")[25] but also in new and unfelt proclivities. One will notice deeper and broader vision, better judgment, and better productivity, and above all, one will notice that the five attitudes in section III above, leading to Level 3 fulfillment, are finally attainable. It is a curious thing that attitudes such as "living for contribution", or "looking for the good news in the other", or "living for and entering into common cause toward a common good beyond myself" are so difficult to incorporate into our everyday lives. I think the reason for this is that these attitudes (which bring so much peace) require peace. The peace that comes from God provides that necessary impetus to keep starting anew and to move more deeply into those attitudes that ultimately enable us to live life as an opportunity, adventure, and mystery instead of as a problem. We can see the peace of faith through its effects. If we orient ourselves toward those Level 3 attitudes and allow the God of love to help us in this endeavor, the peace that is beyond all understanding will bring to completion what we have been otherwise powerless to do.

Once at home abiding in a deepening peace, opening upon contribution and love, human understanding becomes shaped by the knowledge of the God of love. It is not simply in knowing God's attributes,

---

[25] C. S. Lewis describes this initial experience of God as "stabs of joy" in the autobiographical work *Surprised by Joy: The Shape of My Earlier Life* (New York: Harcourt, Brace and World, 1955).

but more importantly in knowing God's heart speaking to our hearts in tones of patience, kindness, mercy, peace, and comprehensive vision, which draw us ever closer to the virtuous life we desire in communion with every being of human origin.

These three gifts of God's response finally bring with them profound happiness. Though it is not complete, it is profound enough to betoken what that completeness might look like. It is a happiness imbued with a vision and unity with God that overcomes every form of self-alienation. It is a still point erupting upon the dynamism of love. It is the joy of care come fully alive, given to us by God, and reflected by us back to God. It is the entrance into the unconditional Truth, Love, Goodness/Justice, Beauty, Being, and Home that we have always desired. But not only this, we will be able to give it to one another through the uniqueness of our own personhood for all eternity through the generous favor of the God of love. At last, a happiness betokening the completion of our transcendental desire through the unconditional actuality of God. At last, a happiness from the dynamic, unique, and completed gift of ourselves to one another. And what is love, after all, but gift of self? If this is true, then sublime joy must be contained in this completed, unique gift of self.

V. Some Supplemental Prayers to Enhance the Life of Faith

Spontaneous prayers (short prayers of petition) can be very helpful in bringing God's grace into particular situations. These prayers will be further explicated in Chapter Five, but a few that can be helpful in times of fear or uncertainty are the following:

"Lord, make good come out of any potential harm in this situation."

"Lord, make good come out of whatever harm I might have done."

"Lord, snatch victory from the jaws of defeat."

"Lord, you are the just Judge, the merciful Judge. You take that person, and that situation, and take care of them. I don't want to be dominated by this any more."

"I give up, Lord. You take care of it."

It must be stressed that with the fifth prayer, one is not giving up *on life*; one is giving up *to God*. This prayer is particularly useful when one is trying to "figure oneself out". As one proceeds to look at all the things that might have caused a particular personal propensity, one might begin to trace it to causes A, B, and C, which, in turn, may have been caused by X, Y, and Z, which, in turn, may have been caused by D, E, and F. Most people, after a while, begin to feel overwhelmed because they know they really do not have perfect control over who they are, what's going to happen, or even what's happened to them. For those with faith, it is not necessary to have this kind of control. Let God take care of it. God wants to take care of it.

Letting God take care of the situation will produce a peace far more powerful than the peace we can produce on our own. God's peace is grounded in his grace, which extends far into a future over which we have little control. When he gives us this peace, it is imperative to take it, to abide in it, and to live our lives in trust of that grace. Rough times could still be ahead, but by trusting in this grace, we can be sure that God's will is already bringing good out of this fearsome situation.

Furthermore, grace can help to control the flare-ups that come with impatience or ego sensitivity, for I now no longer have to rely solely on the attitude of contribution to help overcome these sensitivities. I can rely on God's grace working through my desire to accomplish the divine will in the world.

It was noted above that one could become inordinately attached to an inherently conditioned objective. When this conditioned objective fails to satisfy, it could produce frustration and even obsession, leading to a general dissatisfaction and malaise about life. Prayer can help one to move beyond such attachments by revealing that the only reality capable of satisfying one's desire for the unconditioned is an unconditioned reality, namely, God.

Prayer not only opens the way to an awareness of God's loving presence in life; it also allows this loving presence to show forth the truth about who one really is, what one is really destined for, and what can help to satisfy one's longings. God's presence is an automatic dose of reality.

If my attachments are particularly intransigent (through romantic or even mythical idealization), I will generally run from prayer. Frequently when one is poised for flight before prayer, when one wants to run away from solitude with God, one is usually confronting an attachment—a kind of falsity within oneself. My suggestion is to stay with prayer and stay with God even if the discomfort is substantial. How? (1) Ask God to enable you to see the attachment that is disturbing you. (2) Ask to see the truth about this attachment's capacity to satisfy you. (3) When God's healing calm comes, take it and journey with God beyond the attachment to what is really worthy of you. Even though this process may seem like an eternity, it may take only ten minutes. Walking with God through these three stages can enable one to do what one cannot do by and for oneself.

As was noted above, pride is perhaps the most insidious and problematic impediment to positive change. It seems that we need new H3 habits in order to get beyond the pride that undermines these new habits. Pride seems to catch us up in a vicious circle, which bespeaks the need for grace to move beyond this inhibitor that so frequently leads to a fall. Though there are many suggestions that can be made, ranging from listening to God's word in the Scriptures to worshipping within a faith community, I will here make only one.

This concerns the prayer of which I have spoken most frequently: "Thy will be done." As I have noted above, this prayer brings God's peace and calm and enables us to move beyond attachments and fear by letting go into God's providential hands. His peace and calm are essential to the freedom to see myself as I really am. I don't have to be the Messiah, I don't have to be the greatest, I don't have to be an ultimate, and I don't have to make other people think that I am, because God is at the center of my universe, and God is taking care of what I cannot do for myself. When people confront me and ask, "Spitzer, how worthy are you?" I can simply respond, "As worthy as God wants me to be, and I suppose that's enough." I don't have to worry about being *more* worthy. I certainly don't have to worry about being *most* worthy.

"Thy will be done" does not vitiate my desire to make contributions (H3) when it brings this peace and calm. It frees it to see clearly what is true and what is false, what is worthy of pursuit and what is not, what will lead to life and what will lead to death. Peace does not kill zeal; it purifies it. Calm does not enervate; it energizes. The peace of which I speak does not come from an absence of pressure or fear. It is a peace filled with Truth that is so grounding, I no longer need to trumpet my success, to build a myth, or to garner others' approval of it. "Thy will be done", said at the beginning of the day and frequently throughout the day, is God's peace filled with grounding Truth, energizing me to contribute, befriend, achieve, compete, and create.

In the vast majority of religious traditions, God is looked upon as loving and good. God's will is likewise viewed as loving and good. Indeed, God's infinite providence orchestrates the panoply of human activities toward the good of all. Since God's will respects human freedom, human beings can act against what is loving and good, yet God will work through even this to bring out the most loving and good result. This activity of God's is so complex no human being or group of human beings could even begin to understand how and why it moves to its unconditionally loving end; yet, people of faith know that in the *long term*, this is precisely where it will lead. All suffering, in the long term, will lead to growth toward the good; all darkness will, in the long term, be turned into light. God will not give us trials that his grace will not help us to overcome. Indeed, that grace will always bring about a growth, peace, goodness, love, unity, and joy. After many years of living a life of faith, I can say without question that God's will is not only trustworthy but also beautiful. Even though my trials are not immediately resolved in the ways that I would like them to be, they are eventually resolved in ways much better than I could have ever made them.

I frequently have the inclination to tell God, "Here's how to resolve this fearful situation. I took the liberty of outlining a fourteen-step plan so you could clearly see how best to make good come out of this situation. I also thought you wouldn't mind my including a timetable for the plan along with it." Needless to say, God's plan leads to places that I cannot lead myself and respects other people's freedom and needs. Not being God myself, I am generally unable to accommodate all of this, and so God sometimes allows my plans to fall on hard times (thank God).

The point here is God's will is not a sword of Damocles; it is not impending doom. It is not a hardship that I cannot endure. God is not a stoic, thinking to himself, "I'm going to load some more suffering on Spitzer because he needs to get tougher." God is not a sadist who says, "What does not kill him will make him stronger." God is not waiting around to get even with people for things that they have done fifteen years before. God is gentle and humble of heart. That is what it means to be unconditionally good and loving. Therefore, we do not have to cower and grovel before God's will. We need to trust in it: trust in its awesome beauty, its unconditional power to bring goodness out of the seeming limitless diversity of so many people's lives; trust in the affection that the Hebrew prophets termed *"hesed we emet"* (a parent's love for a child). If we know what unconditional love is for our children, how much more does God manifest this for all of us who turn to God?

Living the life of faith will bring deep experiential conviction about the truth of trusting in this unconditionally loving will, and it makes the essential prayer "Thy will be done" an even more efficacious conduit of grace in our lives. I say this prayer before I give talks or write books, indeed, before I even look in my calendar. It gives me peace, for I do not want to be successful at something that is not God's will. I would, quite frankly, rather have it crash and burn. But I do want to be successful at whatever *is* God's will, for then I know that I will be a conduit for goodness, love, and truth in the world. The third and fourth levels of happiness simultaneously come into my life through the coincidence of God's grace and this little prayer made in faith.

This prayer brings peace, and with peace comes the power to do much and to do much well, to have a net positive effect on the world while at the same time being competent and efficacious. It is a prayer that brings all four levels of happiness together through the peace that is beyond all understanding.

VI. Ramifications of the Four Levels on the Notion of "Person"

It may by now be obvious that the way one views happiness/meaning in life will affect what one is able to see, or even wants to see, in a person. At the end of Chapter One, I noted three tenets for enabling the notion of "person" to heal the culture. I also noted that an inadequate notion of "person" could severely undermine the culture, rights, and the common good. In Chapter Two I suggested that the "heart" has its own reasons, which could add concern and care to our objective understanding of personhood. Without the heart's reasons (grounded in the four levels of happiness), we would be left with objective understanding alone, which seems quite inadequate to the task of leading the culture to a higher actualization of freedom, rights, and the common good. In light of what has been said above about the four levels of happiness, it may do well briefly to review the three tenets about "person" given in Chapter One:

1. *Definition.* A "person" is a being possessing a *telos* or guiding impetus toward fulfillment/perfection through unconditional, perfect, unrestricted, and absolute Truth, Love, Goodness/Justice, and Beauty. The definition will be considered valid irrespective of whether the above-mentioned "guiding impetus" originates from merely genetic sources, a spiritual source (for example, a soul), or both.

2. *The critical principle.* Inasmuch as *any* being should be treated with a dignity commensurate with its nature, persons should be treated with an *unconditional* dignity commensurate with their guiding impetus toward fulfillment in unconditional Truth, Love, Goodness/Justice, and Beauty.

3. *The critical assumption.* The only way of preventing egregious harm within the culture is to make *the* most important and primary cultural assumption: *that every being of human origin should be considered a person.* Doubt about personhood should never be considered a warrant for denying personhood. An error in this regard could lead to every form of genocide, slavery, and political disenfranchisement based not on certain evidence, but on doubt, which, in turn, would severely undermine the Silver Rule and the notion of inalienable rights. Given the above consequences, we must restate the critical assumption in even bolder terms: *when in doubt, err on the side of assuming and according personhood to every being of human origin, whether or not the activities of that being manifest the transcendental qualities of personhood.*

The perspectives of Level 3 and Level 4 allow a deep understanding and care for these three tenets. Though one would be able intellectually to understand these tenets with a Level 1 and Level 2 perspective, it probably would not make an impact sufficient to produce care and concern. Hence, the above definition would seem like an interesting philosophical idea, but not an *ideal* essential to the well-being of one's children, relatives, friends, culture, and society. One can see how a Level 3 or 4 perspective would make the above definition come alive. It could be a catalyzing moment for the recognition of one's own personal dignity and purpose in life, which in turn could lead to a deep concern for the same in others. However, without this Level 4 or even Level 3 perspective, this definition, though not considered unreasonable, would not be viewed as central to one's self-worth and goals in life. I might say, "I suppose I do have an unmitigated thirst for fairness and love, but I don't have time to think about these kinds of abstractions right now. I need to balance my checkbook." This is why the heart has reasons that can liberate the mind.

PART TWO

THE TEN CATEGORIES OF CULTURAL DISCOURSE

Introduction to Part Two

The heart's reasons (grounded in the four levels of happiness) affect not only the notion of "person" but also eight other significant categories. These categories influence the way we interact with society and view the progress of our lives: success, self-worth/quality of life, love, suffering, ethics, freedom, rights, and the common good. These categories take on radically different meanings in accordance with one's dominant view of happiness. They also seem to feed into and interact with each other in the order listed above. Diagram 5 indicates how this interaction is likely to proceed and thus shows how any given person is likely to care about and interact with the culture and the social order.

The first notion to be affected by one's choice about happiness/ purpose is "success". For example, if I choose Happiness 3 to be my

Meaning in Life Happiness (Heart)	Success	Quality of Life (Self-Worth)	Love	Suffering	Ethics	Freedom	Person	Rights	Common Good
H4	S4	QL4	L4	Sf4	E4	F4	P4	R4	CG4
→	→	→	→	→	→	→	→	→	
H3	S3	QL3	L3	Sf3	E3	F3	P3	R3	CG3
→	→	→	→	→	→	→	→	→	
H2	S2	QL2	L2	Sf2	E2	F2	P2	R2	CG2
→	→	→	→	→	→	→	→	→	
H1	S1	QL1	L1	Sf1	E1	F1	P1	R1	CG1

└─────── Individual ───────┘ └─ Cultural ─┘

Diagram 5.

fundamental purpose in life, then I will very likely shape my view of success in life around it. This view of success will, in turn, influence my view of "quality of life". I make judgments about my life every day. Are things going well? Am I progressing? Am I using my time well, or am I just wasting my time? Are my talents being utilized, or are they un-derutilized? Notice how this view is linked also to my sense of self-worth. If I believe that I am underutilizing my talents and time, I will believe that I am underliving my life, which will cause me to under-estimate my worth or value. Conversely, when I believe that I have a good quality of life, that I am using my time and talents to the full, that I am hyperliving my life, I will judge my worth and value in a way that gives spirit, creativity, and energy.

This view of my self-worth will, in turn, affect my view of "love". We all know the cliché, "The person who does not love himself will be unable to love anyone else." Love may be defined as "gift of self". There-fore, the kind of love I manifest will be determined by the kind of self I want to give away. And the kind of self I want to give away will be determined by the kind of self I have appropriated through my view of purpose and success in life.

My view of purpose, success, self-worth, and love will combine to influence my view of "suffering". Everyone needs to see purpose in suffering (that is, to see some good for self, others, or the culture in that suffering). If we did not, we would become incurably depressed. But if we see purpose in pain and negation, if we see a positive horizon for self or others, we will not only develop resilience; we can actually move beyond the suffering to new heights of freedom, commitment, love, and self-transcendence.

One's view of purpose, success, self-worth, love, and suffering, in turn, influences one's view of "ethics". If I, for example, have a Level 3 purpose in life (desiring to use my time and talents to contribute to as many facets of the world in as many ways as I can), I will likely have a corresponding Level 3 view of self-worth, love, and suffering. This, in turn, will motivate me to acquire habits that will help me to achieve this contributory objective (and to avoid pitfalls to achieving it). The ancients called these good habits "virtues". The pitfalls they called "vices" or "deadly sins".

The more one loves contribution, and the people to whom one con-tributes, the more one will love the virtues (habits) that help to promote this. That same love will, in turn, make me more wary of the vices that threaten it. As will be explained, a Level 2 perspective of happiness, self-worth, love, and suffering will give rise to a more restricted view of virtue and vice than a Level 3 perspective. Similarly, a Level 4 perspective will give rise to an even more enhanced view of virtue and vice.

The combined viewpoint of purpose, self-worth, love, suffering, and ethics now influences the notion of "freedom". Freedom could be divided into "freedom from" and "freedom for". "Freedom from" tends to resist commitment. I will see freedom as the escape from constraint and the promotion of independence. Alternatively, "freedom for" views commitment as empowering. I do not wish to escape constraint, but rather to engage in whatever discipline is required to actualize what is pervasive, enduring, and deep.

The various levels of happiness/purpose will also influence the culture. The culture (which transmits our societal values, virtues, and goals) is perhaps most influenced by the concepts of "person", "rights", and the "common good". The concept of "person" is the most important because the notions of "rights" and "common good" are directly dependent on it. The way the culture views "person" is the way it interprets "rights" and the "common good". Narrow notions of "person" lead to equally narrow notions of "rights" and the "common good".

This brief outline of the interrelationship among the ten major categories should indicate the importance of the connection between the four levels of happiness and the life issues. The next four chapters will be devoted to exploring each of the major categories in detail. If we truly want to protect inalienable rights of all citizens, if we truly want the common good to supplant mere egocentric interests, if we really want our quality of life to be enhanced by generative and transcendental concerns; indeed, if we really want our beliefs about ethics and freedom to influence the way we live, then we will have to come to the best possible understanding of "person" and then, using true freedom of the heart, live out of that understanding so that our common welfare may flourish.

Chapter Four

Happiness, Success, Quality of Life, and Love

Introduction

Our view of happiness influences our view of success (how we view a life well lived), which, in turn affects our view of self-worth and quality of life. These attitudes, which determine how we relate to ourselves, influence our view of love (how we relate to others).

I. Success

One of the ways we explicitize our view of happiness is to talk about our view of a "successful life". Defining "success" shows us what we really think we should achieve or what our goals ought to be. The absence of these goals could be viewed as a life underlived or wasted. Important as this term is for the whole meaning and direction of our lives, most people never take the time explicitly to define it. They may have some thoughts, feelings, and intuitions about it; they will sometimes exclaim, "I am a success", or "My life is a failure"; they may have unexplained feelings about failure or success; but these feelings arise out of a history of expectations from parents or friends, peer pressure, signals given by teachers or coaches, impressions picked up from television or music, or some interior need for status, affection, or acceptance. These *implicit* signals frequently form a structure of goals that guide individuals in everything from choice of career to choice of spouse. As has been noted above, it can also determine happiness or unhappiness, a sense of direction or aimlessness, strong identity or weak identity, underliving life or optimally living life. Hence, we must not only get a sense of what makes us happy and where we look for happiness; we must also translate this into our view of success.

The more we explicitize "success", the more reflective, contributory, and loving we can be.

Just as there are four levels of happiness, so there are also four levels of success. *The first level of success* transforms the first level of happiness into the criteria for a life well lived. Hence, accumulating many possessions, pleasures, creature comforts, food, wine, and the other epicurean delights would constitute a life well lived. As I'm going though my life I would *feel* as if I had accomplished my purpose if I had visited the world's great spas, or perhaps stayed in five-star hotels in most countries throughout the world, tasted the finest foods, had drunk the best wines, and had six different residences for all occasions of weather.

One's view of success converts one's view of happiness into a life pattern, or a kind of momentum. Until dissatisfaction arises (from the first crisis), one could overlook the vast majority of one's powers, potential achievements, feelings, contributions, experiences, perspectives, and loves. A society that embraces and promotes this view of success would show symptoms of unhappiness, emptiness, and lack of regard for the common good.

We cannot wait for the discontent and emptiness of the first crisis to dislodge us from superficiality. This method could take so long that one might come to grips with underliving one's life only at the age of sixty. Thirty-five or forty years could have been spent on a treadmill or in a dream world that simply did not address questions about contribution, dignity, or love. As was noted in the previous chapters, possessions are not enough. They can be comfortable, but they cannot fulfill. They can help me to escape from emptiness, but they cannot cure it.

Thus, it is incumbent upon citizens with a greater and deeper recognition of the value and potential of human life to ask friends, neighbors, and family to reflect upon and explicitize their views of success. We must make the options known. We must show them ways of achieving them all. We must all be mentors for one another. Failure to stimulate this process of reflection allows superficiality, with its accompanying feeling of emptiness, to perdure. This leaves only one choice for our friends, to escape into new pleasures and possessions, that is, to further entrench themselves in the superficiality that vitiates them. To stimulate the process of reflection, however, is to empower our friends with a new view of their potential and a new hope for life. If this new view takes hold, they will never be the same again, filled, as it were, with a new sense of purpose, depth, creativity, and passion for life.

The second level of success follows from the second level of happiness. It transforms the values of the comparison game into the criteria for a life well lived. Again, this view of success is rarely recognized in the context of other alternative definitions. Nevertheless, one can tenaciously hold onto it, feel it, and believe in it as if one had spent years reflecting upon and choosing it. What makes a life well lived? Having more accomplishments, status, popularity, and higher position than others. Having *more* and being *more* is success. As was noted in the previous chapter, the second crisis can dislodge one from this view, but it takes so long, causes so much human misery, so much breakdown in relationships, and so much time and talent wasted. Again, it is incumbent upon us to help our friends and culture put this second level of success into the context of the other three so that it can be clearly seen for what it is. We must be persistently Socratic in order to be good friends and culturally responsible. We must ask, "What do you mean by 'success'?" or "Why do you feel successful?" or "Why do you feel your life is a failure?" "Is this all there is to 'success'?" Can a failure on one level be a success on another? Can one and the same event in our lives be both success and failure? So long as we allow this all-important term and its all-important feelings to remain enshrouded in interior mystery, we eschew our duty to friends and to culture, to the weak and the strong, to those with a voice and those without, to children and adults, to our present and to our future.

The third level of success transforms the third level of happiness into the criteria of a life well lived. If people have reached the third level of happiness, they ought to make this contributory view of life as specific as possible. They need to remind themselves in writing and through friends which contributions and relationships constitute their reason for being. They might want to sit down and write the names of the children, family, friends, colleagues, employees, community members, and so on to whom they have the opportunity to contribute. How can I touch the lives of these people through an act of listening, a letter, a smile, an act of friendship, or a commitment? How can I make the world a little safer? How can I alleviate a little of the world's suffering? How can I improve a few of the world's institutions? How can I bring about greater unity, learning, hope, spirit, and concern? What are the *opportunities* for *positivity*?

If this view of success is explicitized, it will surely give rise to a more positively contributory life. While it alleviates the emotive crisis of the comparison game, it will lead to greater dynamism and focus while it deepens friendships and collegiality.

No matter how empowering and enlightening this view of success is, it has an Achilles' heel. It plays into a fatal flaw in human idealism. It makes us yearn for an ideal of Love, Truth, Goodness, and Beauty that we cannot produce and that others cannot produce for us. It leaves us open to disappointment, frustration, dashed romanticism, and dashed idealism. It tempts us to think we can do it all ourselves, to believe too much in our own perspectives and accomplishments, to exaggerate our already overly exercised belief in our own heroism. The third level of success compounds and accelerates our heroic self-image. The hero begins to eclipse the humility and gentleness of love, and soon the little moments of care, compassion, delight, and empathy are replaced by the very serious agenda of actions toward heroic purpose. The ability to laugh at myself is replaced by the seriousness of my projects. Something is lost. I'm too central, my project too important. Little people are too easily ignored. The pace of contribution replaces the opportunity for simple love and delight.

The fourth level of success counteracts these problems because it brings a universal perspective to the fore. If one has faith, one might call it "God's perspective". When one sees oneself amidst the whole panoply of human freedom and human good, one tends to take oneself and even one's problems much less seriously.

Recall that a Level 3 view of success is open to a kind of messianism where one's exaggerated heroic feelings have a twofold negative consequence: (1) they allow a Level 2 view to creep back into one's consciousness and to undermine one's Level 3 view (for example, "My life is more important than that other person's" or "I am doing much more for humanity than others"); and (2) this forces me to be more central to the purpose of others' lives than any one human being can possibly be (for example, "I have to be mentor, rescuer, parent, and friend to all 500 people on my Christmas card list"). Aside from the inevitability of failure and burnout, one is likely to drive all one's friends to the brink of despair with an ever growing heroic self-indulgence and arrogance.

The only way to transcend these negative consequences is to immerse oneself in a universal perspective where one is not the center of the universe. If one has faith, this is accomplished by letting God be the center not only of the physical universe, but also of all personal and interpersonal universes. In this perspective one does not have to be the mentor and rescuer of all. One does not have to have superior advice to other mentors. One can work side by side with other human contributors. One can even rejoice in the successes of others who have had positive effects in the world. If one has faith, one can thank God for the positive contributions one has made without having to think, "My contributions are better than hers" or "My life is better than his". This universal perspective, then, not only helps to remedy the problems of failure, burnout, and arrogance; it also helps us to rejoice in goods not produced by us and not even related to us. In short, it produces an empathy similar to that of a little child who begins to laugh because everyone else in the room is laughing, although he does not understand why. This empathy of joy brings Level 3 to its healthy fulfillment, for now my passion and energy are turned to doing *the* good for the other before *my* good for the other. When we can rejoice in the good for its own sake before we rejoice in our having done it, we not only will form a community toward the common good but also will experience a unity and empathetic solidarity that bring the joy of friendship to a new level. From the perspective of faith, this love is what God intends for the world.

It should be repeated yet again that we are the primary instruments of bringing this perspective and love into the world. If we see the immanent problems of messianism and exaggerated heroism undermining the good that we do, we must call it to one another's attention. This need not be done in a self-righteous way. It need not be done even in a specific way. It is sufficient to present the above generalities to our friends and children and allow them to apply them in specific ways to their own lives. Pointing out specifics ("Aha, you just manifested some messianic behavior, some elevated self-importance—you hypocrite") is generally very counterproductive and just as hypocritical as the hypocrisy pointed out. It is better to form a community of reflection about general principles wherein we all, recognizing our own weaknesses, progress slowly toward a detachment from ego that will bring hypocrisy to a silent end. Those with faith will say, of course, that this is possible only with God's grace, that is, with the assurance of Unconditional Love manifest in unconditional patience, kindness, forgiveness, gentleness, and peace, *leading* me to where I cannot lead myself. Whatever one's view, failure to move toward this universal perspective will generally result in heroism undercutting its own virtue amidst hypocrisy.

II. The Relationship Between Self-Worth and Quality of Life

Human beings judge themselves several times a day. This judgment may come in the form of explicit questions and answers such as "Is my life progressing well? Am I living up to my expectations?" Or it may come in the form of a hunch or a feeling, whereby either I feel good about myself, my life, and my progress, or I don't. This judgment process either empowers one to do more, be more creative, have more energy and more joy about life, or it vitiates one, takes away one's energy, creativity, and capacity to associate. Therefore, it affects the way one views love, friendship, suffering, and freedom and what one is looking for in all these areas.

One may not have an explicit or conscious view of self-worth/ quality of life, but one certainly has an implicit view, and this implicit view may be most easily seen by looking at one's view of happiness, or even what one is pursuing in order to achieve happiness. The objective of this section is to indicate how one's view of self-worth/quality of life affects (1) how one feels about oneself (self-esteem/self-love) and (2) one's view of love. This will directly impact one's interpretation of suffering, ethics, and freedom.

With respect to Level 1, if one restricts one's happiness or purpose in life to what is sensorial and external, one is also likely to restrict one's self-identity and self-image to the domain of things, chemicals, physical properties, and external agents. This has four major consequences. First, it restricts my dignity. If I view myself as only a clump of chemicals, I will tend to think I have a dignity commensurate with merely inanimate, manipulatable objects.

Secondly, it will affect the goals I seek. If I view myself predominately as an aggregate of chemicals, I will probably imagine that the most I can do with my life is acquire sensorial pleasures, avoid sensorial pains, and possess and extend myself through external things: "A good cigar is what makes life worth living." "Eating at Michelle's makes life really worthwhile." "What would life be without a Mercedes E-class with leather upholstery?"

Thirdly, I will tend to believe that others judge themselves on the same basis as I do, and therefore I will mistakenly presume that most people will be impressed and pleased by a multitude of sensorial pleasures and external possessions.

Fourthly, I will make judgments about other people's worth or value (their esteemability) on the basis of how many pleasures they indulge in or how many possessions they have.

Several problems emerge with this very restricted view of self-worth/quality of life. First, I reduce my life's *purpose* to *"getting"* or *"having"*. It forces me to "thingify myself", thereby blinding me to the real possibility of unconditional Truth, Goodness/Justice, Love, and Beauty in my life. I spend most of my psychic energy and my waking hours overlooking the whole domain of *"doing"* and *"being"*. I am virtually oblivious to creativity, love, justice, contribution, and even the arts, not to mention the transcendentals, the eternal, the absolute, and faith. I'm simply too busy for such things. This limited viewpoint is really forcing me to underlive my life.

The second problem concerns my view of *myself*. When I "thingify" myself, I think the tangible and the pleasureful are what really matter, and hence I miss the most intangible and therefore the deepest parts of myself. I don't value my esteemable self, nor do I value my likable self, nor my lovable self. Indeed, I may be completely unaware of these integral dimensions of myself. Do people admire, like, or love me? I'm too busy with the material world ("the real world") to be concerned with these things. Regrettably, I see only about one-tenth of who I am or could be.

The third problem is that I will value others in the way that I value myself. Hence, I will judge others according to their material pleasures and possessions, while being oblivious to their esteemability, likability, or lovability. Inasmuch as love begins with noticing the lovable in the other, love at this stage is severely weakened. Furthermore, if friendship is based on noticing the likable in the other, friendship would also be severely undermined.

Clearly, this viewpoint underestimates my potential, my self-worth, and my assessment of others. Since I do have the capacity and desire to live for more than these things, it does come back to haunt me. As will be shown, it reduces my view of love to the merely physical, forces me into an epicurean view of suffering and to a pleasure/utilitarian form of ethics, and limits my view of freedom to "escape from constraint".

If one identifies one's self-worth with pleasure and possession, one will have little tolerance for material deprivation, illness, weakness, and pain. This will make aging a problem, for one will accentuate these negative features to the almost total exclusion of the positive Level 3/4 features of aging (such as growth, wisdom, love, and faith). Part of the beauty of aging is that the capacity for Levels 3 and 4 can grow in direct proportion to the decrease in the capacity for Levels 1 and 2. If one's view of life is restricted to Level 1 alone, this enhanced capacity and its intrinsic beauty will be lost altogether, leaving the aging process to seem quite undignified and even deprecating.

With respect to Level 2, if I identify my happiness and purpose in life with merely ego gratification and comparative advantage, then I will restrict my self-identity to my esteemable self. What will really matter about me are the number of achievements I have wrought, the awards and honors I have received, the recognition and admiration bestowed, and the power, promotion, and position obtained. These characteristics will become so important that they will likely overshadow both the likable self and the lovable self. I will, therefore, miss a whole host of intangible features that characterize my friendship (like the capacity to inspire others, to help and be there for others, for common cause and camaraderie, and the joy I can bring to others through my presence). I will also overlook the intangible features of the lovable self (such as the capacity for intimacy, deep concern, sharing of feelings, and mutual efficacy). Needless to say, this will not only inhibit my capacity for friendship and love; it will also narrow my view of myself to a fraction of my human potential.

As with Level 1 above, one can see the consequences of this on the view of suffering, ethics, and freedom. Suffering that does not lead to specific Level 2 goods (competitive advantage, admiration, and so on) will be viewed as essentially negative and meaningless. Ethics will be reduced to egoistic utilitarianism, and freedom will be viewed as an escape from the many threats of this world—threats that include most people.

The aging process will again be viewed in an essentially negative way. One will experience a decrease in one's capacity to achieve, gain comparative advantage, receive adulation, and obtain promotion and control. Since these are the only things that matter to a dominant Level 2 person, aging will be viewed as a complete loss of self and self-worth.

Inasmuch as one misses the enhancement of Level 3 and Level 4 capacities in the aging process, one restricts oneself to the essentially negative decrease in Level 1 and Level 2 capacities. Again, the aging process seems terrifying instead of a prospect for better self-communication, love, forgiveness, contribution, wisdom, self-transcendence, and faith.

With respect to Level 3, one begins to put the emphasis on the likable and lovable self. Though one does not give up the material and esteemable self, one's priorities have now shifted. The valuing of contribution, the recognition of the dignity of the other, and the consequent care that comes from this produces a care for oneself. As one begins to value the contributions one can make through one's talent, time, and energy, one begins to value those characteristics within oneself that will lead to such contributions.

Level 3 begins by noticing the contributions I can make and the way I can make my life valuable to a world that is much bigger than me. It begins with a recognition of how the five transcendentals lead to this kind of contribution. Eventually, I proceed to a recognition that some *inner work* must be done in order for this contribution (these five transcendentals) to burgeon within, through, and from me. I must tend to attitudes that will promote truth, fairness, goodness, love, and harmony. This means looking into authenticity, humility, honesty, courage, self-discipline, and the like. This transformation of ethical viewpoint also leads to a transformation of self-image. Interior characteristics that seemed in their intangibility to be so abstract and therefore ignorable (such as authenticity, sympathy, generative concern, and humility) now appear to be necessary means to the ends that I love and want to pursue (the transcendentals). When this occurs, I become aware of some deeper dimension within me, a dimension that is in tune to virtue, love, and character. When I was in Level 2, I had very little cognizance of this inner dimension, but now, as I struggle to incorporate the authenticity and virtue necessary for love and contribution, I see that I have almost missed this profound dimension of myself. The more I pursue self-transformation, the more I discover how real this domain of presence, love, and character really is. Eventually, it becomes bigger than life, and when it does, I find myself having so much to give. The quality of the gift (the truth, the love, the justice) is improved, and it seems as if I do not have enough time to give it all away and that people can't seem to get enough of it. I eventually discover that this interior dimension is so real and so powerful it transforms every relationship, action, and word that issues forth from me. It even transforms my internal words to myself. There is a breadth, depth, richness, wisdom, sensitivity, and completeness that infuses itself into what comes out of me and goes back into me.

This radical change in self-image produces an equally radical change in my view of self-worth. I now recognize and value my "likable self" (the self capable of authentic, other-oriented, generative, caring friendship) and even my "lovable self" (capable of the depth, intimacy, and commitment that make affection come alive). This new awareness cannot help but alter my view of love, ethics (virtue), and freedom, for everything is now moving out of me before it comes back to me.

My desire to be "on mission"; my desire to make a contribution in the areas of truth, justice, goodness, love, and beauty; my desire to use my creativity, energy, and talents to enhance the good of concrete individuals and even the systems that govern organizations and the world leads to care, friendship, and love. The desire to make a difference in the world does not stop at creating a better system, writing a book, or creating a structure; it finally grounds itself in concern for real people. The desire for a better world cannot be inconsistent with the good of concrete individuals in the world. That is why I noted earlier that the common good cannot be separated from rights theory (see Chapter One). When one really cares about a better world, one will be open to caring about the individuals in the world. If this hasn't occurred, then one's movement to Level 3 could be seriously undermined. If one cares about a structure more than the individuals affected by the structure, then one should look closely at one's motives, for it may be that the desire to leave a legacy or to be known as a great "pursuer of justice" is more important than achieving the good for a person. This thinking could be a sign of ego gratification (Level 2) more than a desire for contribution (Level 3). The error here is captured initially in the logical inconsistency of caring about the whole without caring about the parts. There is another more poignant sign of this error, namely, real people are really transcendental (having the desire for unconditional Truth, Love, Goodness/Justice, and Beauty). Structures are not. They are merely human fabrications that have constantly to be refigured, because they can collapse in the course of history. The importance of historical legacies can therefore be greatly exaggerated.

The progression of the development of Level 3 now begins to emerge. First, one begins either with a concern to contribute to the whole (for example, structures and systems) or to contribute to individual people. Though most people have a preference, some begin with caring about both equally.

Secondly, one begins to extend one's interests into the less developed domain. For example, if one was more concerned about structures, one begins to look for the good news in particular people and to develop concern for them. So also, if one began with a preference for individual people, one begins to concern oneself with the structures and the common good that affects them. This choice to move beyond one's preferential domain is integral to an authentic move to Level 3.

Thirdly, one's choice in steps one and two above begins to affect one's view of self-worth, for I now prize those powers, habits, and qualities of myself that promote contribution to individuals and to the whole. I am now much less interested in what people think of me and far more interested in the contribution I am really making. I am less interested in people acknowledging that I am making a contribution to the culture and more interested in actually making a contribution (whether or not that contribution appeals to popular sentiment). I am less interested in having people think I am a loving person and more interested in making sure that the people within my purview are being taken care of. I really see this contributory and caring part of myself to be the core of my being. My reputation, in contrast, begins to take a back seat.

I am not suggesting here that reputation is not important for credibility or that one should not rejoice in the good that one is really able to do, for clearly, credibility and real contribution are integral to my identity. I am here suggesting only that reputation cannot be focused on as an end in itself and, therefore, that it must be subordinated to the capacity for love and the desire for real contribution. It is now reputation *for the sake of* love and real contribution.

Fourthly, I begin to prize those means virtues that allow love and real contribution to emerge freely from them (such as humility, self-discipline, courage, authenticity, patience, kindness, and generosity). Prior to step three, these characteristics might have appeared to have been abstractions. One might have viewed them as being important because a particular psychologist, philosopher, or religious figure thought they were important, but one did not really believe that these constituted the real core, the important core of one's being. Now, as one moves progressively into step four, one begins to honor these means virtues as if they really mattered, indeed, as if the were the very entryway into the meaning of life itself.

This view of self-worth clearly changes one's perspective on the aging process. Instead of viewing aging as a decline in one's powers (in one's capacity to achieve, gain comparative advantage, receive adulation, and obtain promotion and control), one now sees aging as an increase in one's powers (the capacity for love grounded in patience, humility, generosity, authenticity, and breadth and depth of vision). This growth in the capacity for humble love can do more good for the next generation in six months than thirty years' worth of pursuing unmitigated winning, reputation, and achievement. Again, one can see how a decline in Level 2 powers can lead to a rapid increase in Level 3 powers *when one values those Level 3 powers.* Those Level 3 powers, in turn, will produce lasting, pervasive effects for many generations to come.

With respect to Level 4, one now begins to put the emphasis on the transcendent self. Though one does not give up the material, esteemable, likable, or lovable self, one sees them within the context of one's transcendental nature and mission. As Level 3 becomes progressively more awakened, one begins to see the intrinsic, unconditional nature of Love itself, Truth itself, Goodness itself, Justice itself, and Beauty itself. As I probe the depths of Love, for example, I begin to see that it has no intrinsic boundary, and that it really is the unity that transcends all boundaries between people. Again, as I probe the depths of Truth, I notice that it really has no intrinsic boundary, but that it is the unity connecting all finite and conditioned truths. Again, as I probe the depths of Justice, I notice that it has no intrinsic boundaries, but rather is the unity that overcomes the inequities and boundaries among people and groups. In short, I am introduced to realities that, by their nature, overcome boundaries instead of making them. One may not explicitly recognize that one is dealing with realities that "overcome boundaries", but one can strongly intuit that one is immersed in pervasive or enduring realities.

If one has faith, one would characterize the above transcendent realities as attributes of a *personal* God. One would not be living to promote the transcendent realities that, by their nature, overcome boundaries among people and groups, but rather for God *who* overcomes boundaries among people and groups. The difference here is quite significant because the first position suggests that one can do it oneself, whereas the second suggests that one *needs* God to promote these transcendental ideals, and that one is God's instrument in this mission. In the first position the onus for promoting the transcendentals within the world lies squarely on the person. In the second God is the source of the transcendentals, and the onus for their promotion is limited to what a person can do as an instrument, vehicle, or conduit. The first position is open to discouragement and even cynicism because one could discover that one can never fulfill the charge of directly promoting the transcendentals in the world. This could ultimately lead to the claim that "life is absurd". For if I reach Level 4 (thinking that the onus for its actualization rests squarely with me) and then subsequently discover that I can never carry out this mandate, I might conclude that my inner nature is contradictory (I desire as my ultimate purpose what I can never attain).

In any case, when one reaches Level 4, one associates one's self-worth with one's connection to God or to the eternal, the unconditional, and the universal. At this juncture, one begins to see oneself as having an intrinsic transcendental nature (which is normally referred to as a "soul"). This term is used both by people of faith and by those who approach the transcendentals from a purely philosophical or rational perspective. One has now moved from an awareness of one's intrinsic dignity (Level 3) to one's intrinsic *transcendental* dignity. One is now caught up in an eternal and universal destiny, and this awareness, in turn, affects the way that one looks at others. If Level 4 is consistent with authentic Level 3, one will automatically transfer the intrinsic transcendental dignity (of one's own "soul") to that of others. One seems to be aware of the equality of dignity among all human persons. Somehow one sees that it is repulsive to Justice itself, Love itself, and Truth itself for one human person to have a transcendental dignity and the other not to have it.

I noted a danger to Level 3, namely, that one could be concerned about changing structures or systems without being concerned about individuals (that is, social idealism without love). The same can apply to Level 4. If one is not careful to integrate love for concrete, individual persons with one's pursuit of the transcendent, one might again find oneself promoting the greatest common good by undermining the good of the individuals participating in it. In short, one might say, "I'm too busy promoting the faith to attend to the needs of Joe", or, "The demands of promoting the kingdom of God require that I spend only ten minutes per week with family and friends." Even worse, I might think that it's necessary to create boundaries or even to promote hatred among people in my zeal to help God. The error of this reasoning can be seen by considering the logical inconsistency between promoting the common good (the good of the whole), while ignoring or even undermining the dignity of, or the good for, the individuals constituting that whole. Therefore, the achievement of Level 4 depends on an authentic appropriation of Level 3. Promoting transcendent ends must be consistent with promoting the transcendent soul in individual people.

The more I recognize the intrinsic, transcendent dignity of others, and the more I promote this dignity through an authentic appropriation of Level 3, the more I recognize the intrinsic, transcendental dignity in myself. The more I use my powers to see and promote the transcendent, the more I see myself to be transcendent by my very nature. And the more I recognize my transcendent nature, the more capable I am of recognizing it in others. This recognition of the transcendental dignity of all human persons gives my life *universal purpose*. I now see my actions (even my little acts of love or "unlove") as having a universal significance. They are not restricted merely to a particular place in time; they seem to have an effect on the balance of good and evil in the world. I think of my life as affecting the kingdom of God or its emergence in human history. This intuition is generally not viewed in a narcissistic way ("My life is so great that it affects the whole of human history"). Rather, this universal destiny is attributed to *every* human being. Thus, all of our lives are tied up in a destiny that is universal and eternal. We all have the dignity of being able to affect the emergence of the kingdom of God through God's good grace. This eternal and universal dignity of all human beings, this capacity to contribute to, or negate what is universal and eternal, fills us with a sense of sublime purpose and awe for the mission we have *all* been given.

This awareness of transcendent, universal, and eternal nature, purpose, mission, and dignity seems to lie at the ground of all great cultural epics (such as *King Arthur*, *The Search for the Holy Grail*, *The Song of Roland*, and in contemporary times such stories as J. R. R. Tolkein's *The Lord of the Rings* or the movie series *Star Wars*). These epics see in all ordinary persons (like Frodo Baggins or Luke Skywalker) not simply a heroic destiny but a destiny coinvolved with the promotion of universal and eternal good. They point to a sublime purpose (filled with challenges, nobility, failures, and divine intervention) that shows each ordinary individual's existence to be an adventure capable of contributing to the transcendent good of all. If one has faith, one will conceive of this "good of all" as the kingdom of God. Some psychologists, philosophers, and writers believe that this awareness is intrinsic to human beings even as children (in an archetypal, symbolic story called "An Everyman's Odyssey"). They believe that they can see this awareness in the art and dreams of children from many diverse cultures. Perhaps this explains why epics like *King Arthur, Star Wars,* and *The Lord of the Rings* have had such amazingly popular, indeed, even universal appeal. Whether one subscribes to this theory or not, it still remains true that as one moves gradually into Level 4 one does have a greater sense of this sublime, universal, and eternal purpose of life, grounded in one's transcendental dignity. Furthermore, this awareness is grounded in and inextricably connected to an awareness of everyone else's sublime, universal, and eternal purpose of life. Thus, it seems that our awareness of our transcendent dignity is tied to our awareness of universal transcendent dignity. Transcendence and universality in the fourth level are inextricably related.

If the awareness of transcendent dignity is not accompanied by an awareness of the universality of this dignity, then one is not at Level 4. Rather, one is probably combining a belief in God or a belief in transcendent mystery with a Level 2 identity. These beliefs reflect an appreciation of a transcendent realm, but do not see this reality as affecting the dignity of individual human persons. Frequently, this manifests itself as a nonpersonal religion or even as superstition or magic. It sees the transcendent realm as something *fascinating* but not coinvolving love, justice, or goodness. The notion of "God", as a consequence, frequently becomes uncaring, depersonalized, and sometimes even unjust and capricious. This has two negative effects. First, one can use "God's will" to justify uncaring, impersonal, unjust, and even capricious acts. Secondly, one could think that "God" is less capable of compassion and justice than a human being, which, of course, can lead not only to unnecessary discouragement but even to unnecessary frustration and resentment. As a consequence, one can begin actually to spurn the transcendent end toward which one feels oneself called. "Why would I want to go there? It seems contrary to justice, love, and truth." As a consequence, one never pursues the transcendentals for which one's heart pines.

If, however, one's belief in God is accompanied by a Level 4 identity that is aware of the dignity of *all* human beings, and sees the transcendent connection among these dignified individuals, one's desire to purify one's pursuit of Love, Justice, Goodness, and Truth becomes considerably heightened. It was mentioned above with respect to Level 3 that a desire for Love could lead also to a desire for all those virtues that contribute to Love (such as humility, self-discipline, courage, authenticity, patience, kindness, and generosity). These virtues now take on a transcendent, universal, and sublime significance. One not only sees humility as a good and necessary virtue in the pursuit of Love (Level 3); one sees it as a sublime and necessary virtue for one's transcendent, universal purpose, and even for the good of the world and the kingdom of God. It now carries a weight, import, gravity, and dignity that it did not have in Level 3.

If one has faith, one will see humility as "the will of God". Hence, one can use the various spontaneous prayers mentioned in Chapter Three (section IV) to strive for this frequently elusive virtue. Certainly one identifies or connects one's transcendent self-worth to this virtue, and one bestows on this virtue a sublime dignity. By doing this, one does not become proud, for the pursuit of humility is done in conjunction with God. The objective, then, is not to master oneself (Level 2). The objective is to cultivate a habit with the help of God (the transcendent reality) for the good of all.

If one studies the lives of Jesus, Saint Francis, Mother Teresa, Mahatma Gandhi, Dietrich Bonhöffer, Martin Luther King, Martin Buber, Gabriel Marcel, Dag Hammarskjöld, C. S. Lewis, and so many others, one can see a similar pattern: an intimate awareness of the transcendent dignity of all human beings arising out of not only a belief in a loving God (transcendent reality) but also a deep care and commitment to *individual* human beings and the pursuit of good social structures and systems. This pattern not only indicates what they did, and the kind of life they led, but also what they prized in themselves (self-worth). They prized human dignity seen in the light of God and those attributes within themselves that made them free to recognize that dignity. They prized

Love itself (God) and Love's presence in others, in themselves, and in the connection between us all. This view of self-worth, caught up as it is in the Source and in everything grounded in the Source, gives rise to freedom to do the good for all, and each individual, as if it were the good for oneself. Evidently, this view of self-worth is intimately connected with one's view of quality of life and freedom.

This view of self-worth clearly changes one's perspective on the aging process. Instead of viewing aging as a decline in one's powers to pursue comparative advantage, admiration, and achievement, one now views aging as a fuller participation in one's sublime, universal, transcendent dignity. My aging well is not simply a good example for others; it is not simply a vehicle for imparting wisdom, love, and faith to the next generation. It has an eternal and universal significance beyond any beneficiary within my purview. It has a sublime dignity caught up in God's presence among us. Aging has a venerable quality *worthy* of compassion. Compassion is not extended to the aging simply out of the goodness of one's heart. Rather, it is given out of joy in being close to the venerable, close to those who exude a sublime dignity. Socrates' disciples did not extend compassion or sympathy to him because they thought of themselves as "nice people". They did it because they sensed his inherent transcendent dignity. They sensed the lovability in the sublimity of this man. This Level 4 dignity induced sublime love and life in *them*. Compassion was not only effortless; it was a joy.

This act of compassion is a two-way street, for it takes a Level 3 or 4 person to find joy in the venerability of a Level 3 or 4 person. Joyful compassion of this sort arises out of conaturality. Had Socrates' companions been in Level 2, his intrinsic venerability would have gone unnoticed as his disciples turned their attention to a more productive and "praiseworthy" mentor. Thus, Level 4 has its benefits not only in manifesting the venerability of the person but also in being able to see what is manifest.

III. Love

I noted previously that love of self and love of neighbor are inextricably related. It is difficult to love someone if one doesn't love oneself. The notion of self-worth will therefore have a considerable influence on the notion of love. The phrase "notion of love" does not refer simply to an idea that one carries about in one's mind. It refers to what one is *concretely* looking for in one's intimate relationships with others. I call it a "notion" because one may not be explicitly aware of it. Most human beings pursue some form of intimate relationship with others (for example, romantic friendships and committed or deep *nonromantic* friendships). When they pursue these relationships, they are looking to fulfill certain objectives. These could be objectives for oneself, for the other, for the relationship itself, and even for the transcendent domain. Whether these objectives be explicit or implicit, they have a profound effect on our dreams and hopes and on the way we conduct our friendships, view our identity, and actualize our goals. In view of the tremendous influence that this notion can have, it is imperative that people make explicit what they currently believe, what they want in their futures, and how they are going to move from the former to the latter.

The way we view "happiness" directly impacts the way we view both self-worth and love in our interrelationships with one another. The following briefly describes the way in which the various levels of happiness determine the notion of love (what we are looking for in friendship and relationship).

With respect to Level 1, the dominant concern is for what is external, tangible, immediately gratifying, physically stimulating, and pleasureful. This obviously affects what one is looking for in friendships. "Love" is identified with certain external phenomena and feelings. External beauty seems to be the dominant source of the feelings being sought and so becomes the dominant objective of friendship. If this external beauty is virtually the *only* objective of friendship, it compels one to possess it because this gives one control over one's "ultimate" fulfillment. In order to achieve this "divine" state, one has to treat the other as object. One cannot have perfect control over a free, self-conscious, transcendental being, because that very control would destroy free transcendentality. Obviously, turning the other into an object (a thing) not only diminishes the dignity of the other but also forecloses the possibility of intimate relationship. A person in Level 1, however, does not recognize either the value of intimate friendship or contribution to the common good. A beautiful possession is good enough, even if it immolates the dignity of that beautiful possession.

Physical gratification enhances the aesthetic sense and the feeling of control and is pursued as a means of bringing one's feelings to closure. If these elements are not accompanied by a recognition of the intrinsic dignity of the other (the other's likable or lovable self), one will reduce the other to a mere thing and eventually destroy the other's sense of freedom, self-efficacy, and dignity. This debilitates intimacy, commitment, and contributory behavior and even undermines the deeper sense of the romantic. It has devastating effects on the generative love needed for healthy family life and in the end makes it difficult for people to love anyone who falls short of certain standards of physical beauty.

I'm not suggesting here that physical beauty is not in some way related to romantic love, for many people experience a strong correlation between them. I am here noting only that if love is *reduced* to physical beauty and the feelings arising from it, it will result in a dehumanization of the other. This dehumanization could either be actively resisted (in which case the relationship will likely come to a bitter end) or accepted (in which case the other's freedom and individuality will be immolated and subsumed into the dominant party).

With respect to Level 2, if one's view is predominately ego oriented, then love as a *gift* of self will seem quite unintelligible. However, the ego orientation will immediately recognize the benefits of *being loved*.

Being loved is one of the most powerful Level 2 satisfactions. The other's outpouring of affection betokens my desirability (which is integral to my ego gratification). There is nothing wrong with the other finding me desirable. Indeed, this is an integral part of Level 3 and 4 love. However, in the Level 2 mind-set, ego orientation is so powerful that it tends to interpret "the other finding me desirable" as "love".

I do not recognize the radical incompleteness of this view of love, because I am looking at the world by looking at myself first. I am compelled to look at you with respect to me. This means I am constantly looking at you through my vision of myself. As Level 2 becomes more compulsive, my need to be desired follows in suit. Eventually, the other will not be able to satisfy my insatiable need. I have to turn to other people who are more acutely aware of my desirability. They are my true friends (particularly if they frequently acknowledge my desirability). I therefore progressively detach from the person who knows me too well or who does not have enough psychic energy to gratify my ego needs.

This attitude not only undermines even the possibility of commitment; it actually *compels* me to move from person to person. Each new person is (1) another verification of my desirability, (2) another occasion to possess the physically beautiful (Level 1), and (3) a convenient occasion to move on when previous persons are getting to know me too well. It never occurs to me that I am simply *using* the other to fulfill compulsive needs for ego gratification. The *other* may be acutely aware of this and could feel hurt, frustrated, or resentful by being treated as a mere instrument of ego gratification.

Sexuality in these relationships exacerbates the problem. While its intimate quality enhances the feelings of desirability (to the Level 2 person), it also enhances the feeling of "being used" to the "beloved" who is likely to be shortly abandoned. The feeling of abandonment and "being used" after sexual intimacy can be so profound that it can make the spurned person cynical about the romantic, can undermine trust in others, and can even do significant damage to self-esteem. If the second level of love becomes endemic to the culture, it could produce significant retardation in the ability to be generative, committed, intimate, and romantic. In other words, it could undermine the possibility of deep friendships, marital intimacy, and family life. These cultural problems are, of course, accompanied by significant emotional pain.

How can individuals and the culture protect themselves from the above problems? First, Level 3 and 4 individuals must protect themselves if they are attracted to compulsive Level 2 persons. They should think carefully about the impending consequences, for these consequences not only cause pain but also cause long-term damage to the psyche (such as a loss of trust, self-esteem, and a sense of the romantic). In short, it would probably be prudent for Level 3 or 4 people to seek intimate friendships with other Level 3 and 4 people.

Secondly, it is important for us as individuals to make every effort to move from Level 1 and 2 thinking to Level 3 or 4 thinking. Failure to do so will almost surely result in using and abandoning many intrinsically good, trusting human beings. If this is not attended to, it is likely that the inclination to "use and abandon" will grow progressively more compulsive, leading to a multiplication of victims.

Thirdly, the culture, for its own sake, must help the younger generation to move from Level 1 or 2 thinking to Level 3 or 4 thinking, for we cannot afford to lose the capacity for trust, intimacy, healthy self-love, and the romantic. It would constitute the virtual annihilation of interpersonal depth and marital commitment. Everyone from children to the elderly would suffer immensely.

With respect to Level 3, "love" moves from seeking affirmation of desirability to the joy of loving the lovable. It may do well to recall here that "love" is referring not simply to an idea but rather to "what I am seeking in a relationship". When a person moves to the third/fourth levels of happiness, ego gratification becomes contextualized by the desire to contribute. Normally, this desire to contribute manifests itself as a desire to contribute directly to a specific person and/or a desire to enter into common cause with the other to accomplish a good that is of concern to both. This desire to contribute to or with the other cannot be accomplished through infatuation or affection *alone* (Level 1 and 2 love). I must be able to reach deeper and recognize the intrinsic goodness of the other despite apparent weaknesses.

If the other is committed to Level 3 or 4, this project becomes immeasurably easier, for I can attend to the goodness of the other's ideals, commitments, love of others, kindness, and generosity. By seeing this, I am led quite profoundly to the intrinsic goodness lying at the other's intrinsic core. This incites a desire for committed friendship. A Level 3 person wants to support, help, build up, and connect with a person with this kind of goodness. I desire a connection with the other, not to elicit an affirmation of my desirability but rather to affirm the other's goodness and to affirm our common cause. If the other finds me desirable in this context, I would not interpret it narcissistically, for it is not the objective I am seeking; it is a result of seeking the good for, and common cause with, the other. Thus, the betokening of desirability is seen as a result of both my love and the other's love (my awareness of the other's goodness and the other's awareness of my goodness). It is a gift that I give because of the other's goodness, and a gift that the other gives to me for the same reason. In this context, then, the affirmation of desirability reinforces commitment instead of undermining it. It should be noted that this occurs not simply within romantic relationships but also in completely nonromantic, committed friendships.

When affirmation of desirability is subordinate to the affirmation of the goodness of, and common cause with, the other, ego sensitivity decreases substantially. I am not continually being hurt or angered by a lack of recognition. I no longer need to show off, exaggerate, or pander for attention. I am content to enjoy the other in common cause or to appreciate the goodness of the other. This not only decreases game playing, manipulation, and ego competitiveness; it also helps both individuals to see their self-worth in a different light (see above, section I). In Levels 3 and 4, my vision of my self-worth is conditioned by my vision of the goodness of, and common cause with, the other. I see myself through my friendship with, or love of, the other. Hence, I see myself as a contributor, a pursuer of common cause, a friend, and a generative, loving individual. This view of self-worth stands in stark contrast to the one that is grounded in ego gratification. When I see myself as friend, I become aware of many formerly intangible characteristics about myself (for example, the quality of my presence to others, the authenticity of my love, personal integrity, humility, patience, and kindness). Seeing these "new qualities" in myself changes my view of quality of life, others, and aging (see section I above).

In Level 3, commitment is not only easier; it's necessary. The only way I can enter into common cause with others and support and appreciate them is to allow them to share in part of my time and future. Commitment, of course, has many degrees.

A valued colleague with whom I share common cause may not at first want or require a significant commitment of my time and future; but as enjoyment and appreciation of the other grows with the passage of time, both I and the other could mutually decide to commit more of our time and future to each other. Such a growth in commitment requires mutual consent. I cannot desire greater commitment and then deliver an ultimatum to the other to follow suit. This would undermine the freedom and dignity of the other and eventually the friendship. If a free, mutual consent to deepen commitment occurs, then interdependence and care will increase.

If the friendship is romantic, this increase in interdependence and care will normally result in an increase in intimacy, affection, and attraction. These strong emotions support the unity and commitment of both parties. This intimate emotional bonding and interdependent unity can become so strong that it cannot be duplicated for another person. One simply cannot feel that strongly about a second person, nor does one want to, for thinking about another person in such a strong way seems to disturb the strong feelings that one had for the first person.

This extraordinarily strong commitment (which, as it were, makes the other a first priority) has a quality of exclusivity. This does not mean that the couple excludes others from their relationship, but only that they exclude others from the same level of commitment within the relationship. Indeed, when a couple is committed in this "exclusive" way, their capacity for common cause is substantially heightened, and hence they tend to allow many people to enter into and benefit from their relationship with one another. Level 3 and Level 4 love tends to move beyond itself.

Recall that love is "gift of self". It is evident that it is not only gift of *myself*, but also a gift of *ourselves*. Love not only goes beyond the self; it even goes beyond the intimate unity of ourselves and welcomes others into itself as a kind of "home".

It is easy to notice when a couple intends "exclusivity" in the wrong way. Instead of excluding others from the same level of commitment, they exclude others from their relationship and themselves. If you should visit their home, you feel like an outsider instead of feeling welcome. Indeed, the feeling can be so palpable that you will want to leave within five to ten minutes. Conversely, if the couple gives their relationship (their "us-ness") away, if they find common cause by serving others together, you will probably feel so much at home that the couple will have to ask you to leave at midnight. I am not suggesting that a couple needs to share all of their intimate moments with others. The couple will need and desire time alone for deep intimacy, and this deep intimacy, in turn, will provide the unity, the common cause, and the "home" that will welcome and help so many others.

Exclusive Level 3 love provides an appropriate context for the intimacy of sexuality. I noted above with respect to Level 2 that sexuality would exacerbate the problem of narcissism in a predominantly Level 2 relationship. It has precisely the opposite effect in the exclusive commitment of a Level 3 or 4 relationship. Sexuality now becomes part of both persons' gift of self to the other. As such, it lends considerable emotive support to the intimacy of exclusive commitment. It enhances the sense of unity, being at home, common cause, and deep appreciation of the other, which characterizes this intimate form of Level 3 love. This intimate Level 3 love also transforms sexuality, for one is frequently more concerned with the well-being of the other and family than with one's own well-being.

In a dominant Level 1 perspective, sexuality can become the aggressive pursuit and possession of the beautiful. In a dominant Level 2 perspective, it can become the aggressive pursuit of affirmation of desirability (which can become destructively narcissistic). In exclusive commitments with a Level 3 or 4 perspective sexuality finds its meaning through generative love and so enhances intimate gift of self rather than aggressive possession or pursuit of ego satisfaction. Just as there are Love 1, Love 2, and Love 3, so there are Sexuality 1, Sexuality 2, and Sexuality 3, where the third is the complete converse of the first two. In the third, sexuality is intimate, unifying, generative, and generating, whereas in Levels 1 and 2, despite the good feelings that can accompany sexuality, it frequently undermines the substance of generativity, romance, and committed love. It can even become aggressive, possessive, exploitative, and destructive.

At the end of the day, Level 3 rescues not only sexuality but also intimacy, trust, romantic friendship, nonromantic friendship, and interpersonal commitment. In short, it emancipates human depth and care and therefore conditions the very possibility of family life.

With respect to Level 4, love stems not merely from a recognition of the intrinsic dignity of human beings, but from the intrinsic *transcendental* dignity and lovability of *all* human beings. As was noted in section I (with respect to self-worth), transcendentality and universality go hand in hand. Hence, the more I recognize the transcendental nature of the other, the more I recognize that all human beings participate in it. Note that I am not speaking here of a love of humanity (which is a concept) but rather of a love of all concrete, individual human beings.

How does this love emerge? In a recognition of others' desire for unconditional, perfect, and eternal Love, Truth, Goodness, Beauty, and Being. This is accompanied by the concomitant recognition that I am incapable of fulfilling any human being. I further recognize that none of us is capable of fulfilling any of us, because none of us is Love itself, Truth itself, Goodness itself, Beauty itself, and Being itself. Love 4, then, begins with a corrective of Love 3. Left to itself, Love 3 is open to a fatal flaw, namely, that the deep, intimate, exclusive connection between friends seems to suggest that the *human* other can be the absolute fulfillment of the heart's desire. But the awareness of the transcendental dignity of the other calls this hyperromantic assumption into question. It makes me realize that if I am not God (unconditional Love), I cannot ultimately fulfill the beloved's ultimate desire, and furthermore, if the other is not God (unconditional Love), the other cannot ultimately fulfill my heart's desire. In short, we cannot ultimately fulfill one another even though our love is true, intimate, and exclusively committed. The other is too "big" for me to fulfill, and I am too "big" for the other to fulfill. The only thing that can fulfill any human other is a real, unconditional Transcendental (or God).

Now, Level 4 is not simply a recognition of what I am not. It is a recognition of who and what God is. As I noted in Chapter Three, section IV, human beings have not only an intuitive sense of their transcendental desire but also a sense that a reality exists that can satisfy this desire for the unconditional. Some, like Saint Augustine, tried to show that I couldn't experience a desire for the unconditional unless I had some awareness of it and that I couldn't have an awareness of it unless it came to me in my conditioned and imperfect nature. This is why Augustine claimed, "For Thou hast made us for Thyself, and our hearts are restless until they rest in Thee."

If one were to look at this from the perspective of faith, one could say that God dignified us with the desire for nothing less than the perfect and unconditional. He created this desire by simply being present to our self-consciousness. After sensing this presence, human beings could never be *ultimately* satisfied with anything short of the presence of God. This presence is responsible for all forms of human creativity, mysticism, and perfectionism. But God could not simply give us a desire for him without also giving us a strong intuition and awareness that that desire would be fulfilled. If God did not do this, we would simply collapse from despair. We would, in the end, proclaim in unison that life is absurd. We yearn ultimately for what we cannot have.

Coincident with the intuition of God's presence is the intuition of creation and Creator. When human beings conceive of ultimate fulfillment, they seem to link it back to an ultimate beginning. This could be due either to a rational judgment that past time requires a Creator[1] or to a simple intuition that one's ultimate end is linked to one's ultimate beginning. In either case, one has a sense that something ultimate, unconditional, perfect, and even eternal exists and that the whole of human destiny is linked to it. This awareness takes the notion of love to a new level.

---

[1] See Appendix 2.

The third and fourth levels of love in combination have another generative quality. Unlike Levels 1 and 2, they do not view the world as something to be possessed or dominated, but rather see others and the world as having immense value worthy of one's time, energy, and commitment. One sees others, the world, and even the kingdom of God as a good much bigger than the self, and every investment one makes to improve it enhances one's purpose and reason for being. One does not want to escape from or protect oneself from the outer world; one feels free, self-determined, and even self-fulfilled when one invests in and contributes to this outer world. Faith brings this second view of freedom to fulfillment in coresponsibility.

Those not having or wishing to pursue faith may want to skip the rest of this chapter and move to Chapter Five. The arguments made for personhood, inalienable rights, freedom, and the life issues in this book are not predicated upon the forthcoming description of faith. It is included in this volume only to help those possessing or interested in faith to integrate their faith into their personal and cultural philosophy.

Love and faith are inextricably related. As the reality of unconditional Love (God) is accepted and acted upon, love is transformed. It allows unconditional Love to touch one's concrete love of the other and allows this transformed love of the other to reveal the depth of unconditional Love. The relationship between faith and love may be described in four steps. The first concerns a belief in and an awareness of the unconditional Love of God. This step may be initiated by asking the following four questions. If these four questions are answered according to what follows, one will have embarked on the journey of both faith and the fourth level of love.

1. What Is the Most Positive and Creative Power or Capacity Within Me?

When one lives according to Level 3 principles, contribution becomes extraordinarily significant for purpose and identity in life. Hence, this first question, dealing with my most positive and creative power, is an attempt to find out the best means I have for making this contribution. Most people who have embraced a Level 3 perspective will probably answer "love", for as love has been defined with respect to Level 3 above, it cannot be negative or destructive. It builds up, generates, and creates. It is a pure force of positivity, unity, and common cause toward the common good. The more one detaches oneself from ego compulsiveness (Level 2), the more positive, life giving, and creative one's love becomes. This positivity and creativity in turn fill one's spirit through an intense awareness of higher purpose. If you answer this first question with "love" (from a Level 3 perspective), proceed to the second question.

2. If We (as Creatures) Are Made to Find Our Most Positive, Creative Purpose in Life Through Love, Could It Be That the Creator Is Devoid of Love?

Here, I am assuming that one is open to the possibility or the reality of a Creator. As noted above, this belief could be attributable to a rational proof for God's existence,[2] a mathematical proof of a beginning of time,[3] an Augustinian awareness of my desire for unconditional Love and its presence to me,[4] or a simple intuition of being loved by God that initiates

[2] Many such proofs have been written in the late 20th century. Some examples may be found in (1) Bernard Lonergan, *Insight: A Study of Human Understanding*, ed. Frederick E. Crowe and Robert M. Doran (Toronto, Canada: University of Toronto Press, 1992), pp. 692–708 (chap. 19); (2) Mortimer J. Adler, *How to Think About God* (New York: Macmillan, 1980), pp. 69–108; (3) James F. Ross, *Philosophical Theology* (New York: Bobbs-Merrill, 1969), pp. 140–94.

[3] The background for this was formalized by David Hilbert, the father of finite mathematics, in a seminal article on the distinction between actual and potential infinities: David Hilbert, "On the Infinite", in *Philosophy of Mathematics*, ed. Paul Benacerraf and Hilary Putnam (Englewood Cliffs, N.J.: Prentice-Hall, 1964), pp.141–51.

G. J. Whitrow, professor of mathematics at the University of London's Imperial College of Science and Technology, has formalized several arguments on the basis of Hilbert's distinction. See, for example, "The Age of the Universe", *British Journal for the Philosophy of Science* 5 (1954–55): 215–25, and *The Natural Philosophy of Time* (London: Thomas Nelson and Sons, 1961). Also "On the Impossibility of Infinite Past Time", *British Journal for the Philosophy of Science* 29 (1978): 39–45. William Lane Craig has written a more popular version of the proof in *The Existence of God and the Beginning of the Universe* (San Bernardino, Calif.: Here's Life Publishers, 1979).

Several noted physicists have also explored the boundaries of scientific knowledge and the possibility of a transuniversal creative force. One very interesting account may be found in Sir Arthur Eddington's *The Nature of the Physical World* (Ann Arbor, Mich.: University of Michigan Press, 1968). See especially chap. 15 ("Science and Mysticism"), pp. 316–42.

[4] Saint Augustine, *Confessions*, trans. R. S. Pine-Coffin (London, England: Penguin Books, 1961), bks. 9 and 10.

the desire to pray and give praise.[5] Whatever the source of one's belief in the Creator, one must reflectively consider that if one is made for the very purpose of love, could it be that the Creator is less loving than oneself? If this seems illogical or even vaguely nonsensical, one ought reflectively to affirm the love of the Creator and proceed to the third question.

3. If My *Desire* for Love Is Unconditional, Then Could It Be That the Creator of This Desire for Unconditional Love Is Not Himself Unconditional Love?

Level 4 is a recognition of the unconditional desire within ourselves for Love, Truth, Goodness, Beauty, and Being. If we assume that the

---

[5] In addition to the experience that many of us may recognize in our own lives, one of the key expositors in the 20th century of this natural, intrinsic awareness of God is Evelyn Underhill. See, for example, *Mysticism: A Study in the Nature and Development of Man's Spiritual Consciousness* (London: Methuen, 1930); *Practical Mysticism* (London: J. M. Dent & Sons; New York: E. P. Dutton, 1914); *Life as Prayer and Other Papers*, ed. Lucy Menzies (Harrisburg, Penn.: Morehouse, 1991); and *Man and the Supernatural* (New York: E. P. Dutton, 1928).

Benedict J. Groeschel has integrated psychology and spiritual development beginning with the call of God and proceeding through the three steps of the mystical life in *Spiritual Passages: The Psychology of Spiritual Development* (New York: Crossroad, 1989).

C. S. Lewis describes this initial experience of God as "stabs of joy" in the autobiography of his early life entitled, *Surprised by Joy: The Shape of My Early Life* (New York: Harcourt, Brace and World, 1955).

Rudolf Otto, "An Inquiry into the Non-Rational Factor in the Idea of the Divine and Its Relation to the Rational" in his classical work, *The Idea of the Holy* (New York: Oxford University Press, 1955).

Of course, descriptions of this fundamental spiritual experience go back to the earliest moments of the Old Testament (perhaps 1800 B.C.) and have been given sublime articulation by many spiritual writers throughout the centuries. For a brief explanation of 26 descriptions of this experience, see Elmer O'Brien, *Varieties of Mystic Experience* (New York: Mentor-Omega, 1964). Four of the best-known expositors include Bernard of Clairvaux (*Selected Works*, trans. and ed. G. R. Evans, in *The Classics of Western Spirituality* [New York: Mahwah, 1987]), Julian of Norwich (*A Book of Showings to the Anchoress* [Toronto: Pontifical Institute of Mediaeval Studies, 1978]), St. Teresa of Avila (*The Collected Works of St. Teresa of Avila*, vol. 1 [Washington, D.C.: ICS Publications, 1976]), and St. John of the Cross (*The Collected Works of St. John of the Cross*, trans. Kieran Kavanaugh and Otilio Rodriguez [Washington, D.C.: ICS Publications, 1979]).

There are literally thousands of books devoted to fundamental religious experience arising out of every religious tradition. A cursory search of the catalogues of virtually every library will reveal this.

Creator did not intend to frustrate this unconditional desire within all of us, it would seem that his very intention to fulfill it would indicate the presence of this quality within him, namely, would indicate within him the presence of unconditional Love, Truth, Goodness, Beauty, and Being. If the reader reflectively affirms this, proceed to the fourth question.

4. If the Creator Is Unconditional Love, Would He Want to Enter into A Relationship with Us of Intense Intimacy and Generativity, That Is, Would He Want to Be Emmanuel ("God with us")?

If one operates according to a Level 2 logic, this suggestion would be preposterous. Why would God (who is Creator and all-powerful) want to bother with creatures, let alone actually be among them and enter into intimate relationship with them? However, in the logic of love, or rather, in the logic of unconditional Love, such a suggestion seems quite consistent, for love is looking for the good news in the other, entering into a generative relationship with the other, entering into a unity with the other whereby doing the good for the other is just as easy as, if not easier than, doing the good for oneself. This kind of love has the non-egocentricity, humility, self-gift, deep affection, and care that would make infinite power into infinite gentleness. In other words, "Emmanuel" would be typical of God. This would characterize the way that unconditional Love would act, not being egocentrically conscious of the infinite distance between Creator and creature, but rather being infinitely desirous of bridging this gap in a unity opening upon pure joy. It would be just like God to be "God with us".

If the answer to this fourth question is correct, then our relationship with God, and surrender to God, will not be an eradication of freedom, but rather a fulfillment of it, for now Emmanuel will take our every action and bring it to completion for the good of every person. As a source of ultimate unity, God will allow our spatially and temporally conditioned actions to have a cosmological effect, to be somehow of immense importance to a world quite beyond our perception and imagination. If one's answers to the above questions resemble the ones given above, then one has effectively made the first step toward the unity of faith and love.

The second step in integrating faith and love (the acceptance of God's will) is a recognition that God's intentions for us cannot be separated from his being. If God is, possesses, or operates by unconditional Love, then his intention for us must be the same. Thus, God's will is for the optimum love, goodness, truth, and being to emerge from every act of human freedom manifested in the world. If God's will is to bring love even out of our malicious intentions, then his will should not be feared, but rather trusted in and prayed for.

We are frequently filled with childhood images of God that are inconsistent with unconditional Love. For example, we could conceive of God as being an exacting perfectionist who is tapping his foot impatiently, saying, "Spitzer, you have repeated this same mistake 1,322 times, and I've had it!" Or we could imagine the "payback God", saying, "Spitzer, the reason you have suffered this eye disease is attributable to an unloving act you did fifteen years ago, but I remembered it all these years and have been waiting to give you your just desserts." There is also the God of the comparison game, who wants only to prove how imbecilic I am by comparison with him. One can think of dozens of other viewpoints inconsistent with unconditional Love. The key to recognizing them is that they generally produce debilitating fear rather than trust, despair rather than hope, and therefore resentment and anger rather than love. They can frequently lead to silliness and superstition.

I recall when I was a child, I received a chain letter in the mail indicating that if I did not send ten letters like it to my friends, God would send me to hell. At the age of seven, I did not have enough money to comply with this demand. I was finally forced to ask my mother for ten stamps under pain of hell. My mother looked at me and said, "Do you really believe that God would send you to hell for not mailing out ten letters? I can't think of any more idiotic notion of 'God'." I, of course, didn't want to take any chances. I really would have rather had the stamps, just to be sure, but she wouldn't give them to me. And so I finally had to purge this "idiotic" notion of God from my mind and heart. We all have to do this as adults. If we do not, it is difficult to proceed in faith, for faith requires that we trust in the One who will make us truly free to love one another as he has loved us.

The third step integrating faith and love (surrender grounded in God's will) obviates the peculiar human tendency to want to achieve unconditional Love, Truth, Goodness, Beauty, and Being by oneself. There is a capacity for idealism in all of us. When we hear about absolute fairness and love, we would like to be the agents who bring it into the world. But we soon discover that we cannot do this for others, and others cannot do this for us (see the third crisis in Chapter Three). We have two options at this juncture: we can become frustrated or even dashed idealists and proclaim that life is absurd, or we can ask "God with us" to come to us (because we cannot bring ourselves to him by ourselves). If we trust in unconditional Love and believe in his unconditionally loving will, the second course of action (an act of surrender) becomes possible. We open ourselves to God to do for us what we cannot do for ourselves.

At this point, a radical transformation occurs in my meaning and purpose in life. I no longer live merely for love; I live for the intentions and purpose of *unconditional* Love. Since unconditional Love's viewpoint is frequently beyond our own, an act of surrender (radical trust) is required. Because the will of unconditional Love is eternal and unconditional, it is only *partially* visible. Hence, we must be led. There is a tradeoff here. If one wants to pursue what is truly loving, good, and just for everyone (God's will), one must walk through faith by means of a vision and power that is not one's own. The ultimate act of freedom is to *choose* to let unconditional Love do what I cannot do, think what I cannot think, and actualize what I cannot actualize on my own. The ultimate act of freedom is to make the most of my love by letting God bring it to its most profound fulfillment in his will. Ultimate freedom is choosing to let God lead me. The ultimate irony of faith is the discovery that freedom is not "being in control", but rather "being led".

The fourth step of integrating faith and love (humility grounded in surrender) is extraordinarily important in the purification of love. Most married people recognize that love requires humility (the capacity to detach oneself from one's ego perspective and egotistical desires). It may have occurred to the reader that the ideal of Level 3 love mentioned above seems almost impossible to live out on a day-to-day basis because it is quite difficult to be humble on one's own. One must be careful about thinking that humility can arise out of self-mastery (thinking, "I *will* be humble"), because self-mastery tends to orient us toward our ego. The reader may have theoretical objections to this proposal, but my experience has been whenever I try to master myself so as to bring about humility, I find myself in a worse state of pride than I was in before. This view of humility does not help the cause of love; it greatly hinders it.

I find a deep peace in saying, "Thy will be done." I can let all of my ego concerns go and say to myself, "There is only one thing that matters: what God wants." Thus, I do not have to be successful at a particular speech. I will be successful if I do my best and God wills it. And if God does not will it, I would prefer that I not be successful, for that success would be contrary to Love. Thus, I have detachment from all the "have-tos" in my life, detachment from all the "would-have-beens" and "could-have-beens" (unfulfilled dreams or disappointments). This does not lead to an attitude of "doing nothing, because God will take care of everything"; rather, it leads to an attitude of "do everything you can, because God will guide everything he wills to fruition". Surrender is enormously freeing. It brings with it a peace and a confidence, an assurance and a Love that unshackle human love from the fears, dashed expectations, and "have-tos" that compel us to protect ourselves before we can empathize with or care for the other.

In sum, faith brings love to fruition by letting God work through it in ways unseen by us and letting him deepen it in ways unimagined by us. With God, therefore, there is the power of love, and empowerment anchored in humility, gentleness, and surrender that opens upon a universal generativity and creativity constituting the most profound possible purpose if life. This, indeed, is the substance of things hoped for.

Chapter Five

Suffering Well

Introduction

One's view of success, self-worth, and love has a profound effect on the ability to suffer well. "Suffering well" may seem paradoxical at first because, from the vantage point of emotion, there does not seem to be anything "well" intrinsic to suffering. Human consciousness, of course, is more than emotional. It is constituted by beliefs and meanings, ideals, commitments, love, faith, interpersonal depth, and personal mystery. The "well" part of suffering is oriented toward these contents of consciousness. If one does not succumb to malaise, there is in suffering a very real possibility of growth in perspective, humility, self-understanding, courage, resilience, strength, enhanced purpose in life, creativity, wisdom, self-acceptance, and the capacity for justice, altruism, love, and faith. Growth in these attributes can also bring a host of positive *emotional* dividends: spirit, passion for life, energy, peace, deeper kinds of happiness (Levels 3 and 4), and even sublimity or joy.

How does one achieve these positive effects of suffering? How does one suffer well? It may do well to begin with what has now become a philosophical cliché: *if one does not find something positive in one's suffering, it will inevitably become malaise, and frequently depression or even despair.* Pain, weakness, or deprivation does not have to bring on depression or malaise. Depression or malaise occurs when nothing positive can be seen in the suffering. This produces a listlessness, a sense that it's not worth it to keep on going, a sense that life is more negative than positive; it sometimes produces a lack of hope, depletion of spirit, irresolvable self-pity, and the simple act of giving up.

Thus, if suffering is not to result in this negative state of being, it must be given meaning. One must be able to say that something good or positive is coming out of this suffering for oneself, others, or the community, for personal growth, wisdom, love, or some other quality. The key to suffering well, the key to transforming an extremely negative condition into an extremely positive one, is knowing where to look for meaning, where to look for the positive amidst the negative. From what has been said above, one might already have the idea that Levels 3 and 4 hold out the prospect for transforming the negative into a positive.

Before delving into this, it might be helpful to examine a few more clichés about suffering:

"Suffering is the occasion for the most poignant manifestation of human freedom."

"Suffering can either lead to the greatest openness of mind and heart or can close one off to the world and to other people."

"Suffering can lead to great gentleness and compassion or great bitterness and self-pity."

"Suffering can purify love or eradicate it."

"Suffering can lead to the most truthful self-assessment or to escapism and inauthenticity."

"Suffering can lead to great sympathy with others who are weak or deprived or secret hatred and arrogance toward them."

"Suffering can lead to universal wisdom and understanding or toward a perspective completely focused on oneself."

"Suffering can lead toward great faith or toward rejection of God."

All of these clichés reflect the seeming dichotomous nature of our response to suffering. But why do people have such different reactions to suffering? Because they *interpret* it differently.

The positive result of suffering generally comes from a Level 3/4 interpretation, while the negative result comes from a Level 1 or 2 interpretation. The broader one's view of happiness, success, self-worth, and love, the more likely one is to be transformed positively by the experience of suffering.

Inasmuch as a Level 3 or 4 interpretation is a matter of our choice, the first of the above clichés is true ("Suffering is the occasion for the most poignant manifestation of human freedom"). The choice we make at the moment of suffering (to see it in terms of openness of mind and heart, gentleness and compassion, love, truthful self-assessment, sympathy with others who are weak or deprived, universal wisdom and understanding, and faith; *or* their opposites) has the potential to change our outlook on life and others, our fundamental attitudes and emotive dispositions, our direction in life, our judgments about the value of life and community, and our ability to act on all the above. The choice we make in times of suffering can do more good or more harm, and have more lasting effects, than just about anything else that could ever befall us or be within our grasp.

Our interpretation of suffering, however, is not merely a matter of choice. It is also a matter of education. This is one of the primary reasons for the Life Principles project. If people do not have adequate information, they cannot make informed choices. If they do not know all the options available, they are likely to choose the ones that are most obvious (which, unfortunately, are generally most superficial). In short, without education people are likely to see suffering from a Level 1 or 2 viewpoint rather than from a Level 3 or 4 viewpoint. Why? Because it is the one that is most obvious, most encouraged by the culture, most advertised in the media, and least in need of explanation and reflection. The Life Principles project cannot make choices for people. We must do that with our friends, our community, our church, and/or our God. But the Life Principles project can open the horizon of options for the interpretation of suffering, which can lead to choices that are broadening, compassionate, life giving, spirit producing, and filled with personal and interpersonal love, growth, justice, and faith.

The positive effects of opening the horizon for the interpretation of suffering will touch the personal lives of individuals and the culture. Cultural effects may range from schoolchildren learning how to gain perspective from suffering to the elderly making choices about medical decisions. The latter effect is urgently needed in contemporary American culture.

When the elderly are admitted to nursing homes or hospitals, they are frequently presented with durable powers of attorney, living wills, and the like. Often they and their relatives are asked to make decisions about treatments they do not fully understand. As they embark on a new period of their lives, they are given very little preparation about how to contend with their new and frequently more limited circumstances. Some of these people find themselves flat on their backs in a hospital bed, having very little ambulatory ability or freedom of discretionary movement. Others are not quite this limited, but find themselves with more limited control, capacity, and acuity. Still others find themselves fighting bouts of chronic sickness. They all seem to share one thing in common: they have been given very little preparation for dealing with these new and even traumatic circumstances.

Most of the elderly have reflected much about poignant experiences in their lives. They can draw upon these reflections to center themselves on profound Level 3 and 4 viewpoints. When they do this they experience the above-mentioned positive aspects of suffering. Frequently they will find themselves moving between Level 3 and Level 2 perspectives, and between positive and negative effects of suffering. Nevertheless, it can be generally stated that the more one reflects on one's options for purpose and happiness in life, the more likely one is to have a positive and productive experience of suffering. This experience affects not only patients, but also the relatives, friends, and acquaintances who surround them in their illnesses.

After adapting this model of happiness and suffering to the needs of elderly patients and using it in clinical pastoral care and nursing homes, I am convinced that the vast majority of patients could improve their process of suffering and contribute far more to their family and friends by simply staying focused on Level 3 and 4 meanings. Sometimes all one needs to do is help an elderly person write and reflect about where he thinks he can contribute to his grandchildren or his children. Could he forgive someone against whom he has held a longstanding grudge? Could he accept an adult child from whom he might have distanced himself fourteen years ago? Could he just spend time with his little grandchildren, listening and manifesting his gentle, loving presence? Could he share a note of hope, wisdom, strength, courage, or even compassion for his children as he himself endures suffering? As one begins to move through these various questions and to make lists of family members, friends and acquaintances, it becomes readily apparent that so-called old age is really a new age, that there is much to do, much that cannot be overlooked, much that the so-called younger generation needs to benefit from in terms of time, compassion, gentleness, forgiveness, acceptance, commitment, quiet courage, wisdom, and faith.

It might be objected that the younger generation doesn't want any of this. They are too busy; they don't have time; they have to get on with their lives. This objection misses the whole point, because this program is for everybody. If the younger generation had a sense of Level 3/4 meaning, if they valued love, commitment, forgiveness, and faith, then spending the time with their elderly counterparts would reinforce the positivity of life and even suffering. But the fact that the elderly can be so easily dismissed by the quip "I don't have time" indicates that Levels 3 and 4 are somehow eclipsed by Levels 1 and 2 in this culture, and at the end of the day, this will not bode well for self-worth, love, suffering, and above all, for the common good. The very fact that we say, "We don't have time", manifests precisely why we must make the time.

These points having been made, let us proceed to an examination of how we can broaden our options for interpreting suffering for the most positive personal and interpersonal effects. Diagram 6 indicates three avenues of interpretation of suffering, which, when chosen in the situation, can transform suffering from a negative to a positive experience:

1. seeing the good in suffering

2. believing that there is a good in suffering even though it is not seen

3. trusting in God

The first two avenues are more concerned with a Level 3 interpretation of suffering, while the third is concerned with a Level 4 interpretation.

It must be emphasized that it is not enough to believe in a Level 3 interpretation of suffering. If one is to transform suffering from a negative to a positive experience, one must also (1) identify *specific* Level 3

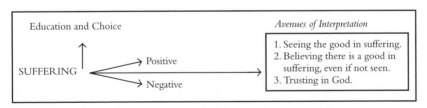

Diagram 6.

goods in the suffering and (2) *act* out of this specific vision of the good. The remainder of this chapter is devoted to these two points.

I. Transforming Suffering from a Negative to a Positive Experience (Moving from a Level 2 to a Level 3 Interpretation of Suffering)

A Level 2 view of suffering is not completely negative in its results. Inasmuch as it promotes autonomy, comparative advantage, and achievement, it can have the result of helping people to face suffering with greater personal strength and courage. Inasmuch as Level 2 can help people to delay gratification or to tolerate an unpleasant situation for the sake of overcoming adversity, it could be construed as positive. But Level 2 does not produce enduring positive effects. It does not transform a person's viewpoint or attitude toward life or others. It merely helps people to tolerate an unpleasant condition with strength and courage. This can be positive as an initial reaction, but it is very short lived, for it does not integrate a positive future outcome into the experience of suffering. It merely says, "Bear up under it. Courage! Hang in there. Don't let the bad times get you down." It is not the same thing to say, "Don't let the bad times get you down", as to say, "There are positivity and good in these bad times." The former is effective only for the short term. The latter is life transforming in the long term.

Closer examination of Level 2 reveals that it has extraordinarily negative long term consequences. Why? Because it grounds happiness, success, self-worth, quality of life, and love in comparative advantage, that is, in achieving more, winning more, being more popular, and having more control. When people are suffering, they generally do not have any of these. Indeed, it may be expected that they will be achieving less, winning less, and feeling much less self-esteem, popularity, and control. In short, if one is suffering, one can be virtually certain that a Level 2 perspective will exacerbate it and produce several negative effects, namely, closing one off to the world and to other people, bitterness, self-pity, hatred, escapism, hardness toward others, a self-focused perspective, and a rejection of God. Whatever short-term positive effects a Level 2 perspective will bring, they are generally counteracted by the negative long-term ones. A Level 3 perspective therefore, is needed not only for success, self-worth, and love; it is a requirement for dealing with suffering, deprivation, and loss.

It was said above that the first avenue for transforming suffering from a negative to a positive experience was to see the good in it. Given what was said above about how Level 2 exacerbates suffering, it is clear that this good must be located in either Level 3 or Level 4. Level 3 provides many such opportunities. The following are but a few:

1. growth in humility (detachment from ego)

2. greater awareness of the intrinsic dignity, goodness, and mystery of the other resulting in greater compassion (the capacity to "suffer with")

3. growth in forgiveness (the ability to let go of past harm)

4. growth in the ability to make contributions

5. growth in wisdom about what really matters

6. a greater ability for Love 3 (as described in the previous chapter)

7. growth in leadership toward the common good

The sixth and seventh points are clearly the result of the other five.

As noted in Chapter Three, our fundamental attitudes are constituted by what we are *looking for*. What we are looking for is generally what we are living for, and what we are living for is generally what we are looking for. If you have personally affirmed Level 3, you may want to copy the above list to use as a basis for daily reflection and for reflection during times of suffering. It is not necessary to reflect on these points alone. Indeed, it is much better to talk about them with your spouse or friends. The more you reflect on these points prior to the moment of suffering, the easier it will be to adjust your perspective on them in the moment of suffering. The more you know these perspectives to be true and to embrace the deepest meanings of human existence and love, the more easily you will be able to make recourse to them to provide meaning at the moment of suffering.

A brief elucidation of the above seven points will help you to reflect on what you are looking for.

With respect to the *first point (growth in humility)*, it was noted above that the purification of love occurs through progressive detachment from one's ego interest. I am not here implying that one should want to ignore one's ego interests, but only to be detached enough to see the bigger, more positive, more enduring picture. The experience of suffering can help to produce this detachment by breaking down the absolute way in which ego interests can frequently be treated. It is so easy for young people to assert, "I can't possibly be happy unless I have . . .", or to say, "The world really should treat me with perfect fairness", or "I deserve X, and I intend to get it at *all* costs." These very glaring blocks to love in the younger person can turn into much more subtle and devious blocks to love in the adult (see Chapters Three and Four). When suffering occurs, these blocks can be effectively challenged, and sometimes completely overcome.

When things are going well, one has very little reason to challenge one's current philosophy. If asked, "Am I a loving person?" I would generally respond, "Of course. I can't think of any real way in which I can improve. I think of myself as a rather generative, humble, contributory, patient, and kind person." I really do believe this when things are going well. The trouble is that I am missing whole encyclopedic volumes about myself that I have no desire to study until such time as my view of myself is thrown into question. *Suffering tends to throw one's current identity into question, allowing for the consideration of new data.* We tend to screen out data, even very important data, when we do not see a need for it or when we find it unpleasant. This data may be extremely important in detaching oneself from one's ego interests, or even in knowing the extent and depth of one's ego interests. It could therefore be extremely important in one's pursuit of love, compassion, and the common good.

The experience of suffering throws all assumptions into question. It compels people to ask, "How can I make sense out of this? What am I missing? Why is this happening?" or even, "What is the meaning of life *now*?" At this juncture, a Level 3 person must attend, in an act of contemplation, to data that may have previously been ignored. One might want to attend to the suffering of others, to the feelings of others, to unfairness in the world, to the good things in the community hitherto unnoticed. One may want to attend to one's values, to virtues held dear. One might want to take a look at values, ideals, and virtues from the past that may have been forgotten. One may want to converse with others on these topics or purchase some inspirational books. It is important to write down thoughts, insights, experiences, hopes, and directions as these take on more depth. It is also important to review and discuss this data frequently so that it can become part of one's conscious and subconscious makeup.

As one studies the new data, one is likely to find that it gives a very penetrating insight into the intrinsic dignity and mystery of the other, the vastness of the world and its people, one's inability to be in perfect control of one's own life let alone the life of others, one's need to be in interdependent interrelationship with others, and the falsity of being at the center of one's own universe let alone everyone else's. Such insights should not be merely considered, but seized upon and acted upon as if they were they very fabric of love, and therefore of life. They will be difficult to hold onto when more stable and peaceful times reoccur. Nevertheless, they are the ingredients of humility that deepen and authenticate delight, affection, intimacy, charity, commitment, and every other form of interpersonal unity. They also deepen joy because joy is never greater than when it is based upon an authentic vision of the truth of oneself, others, the world, and, in the case of faith, God.

Suffering can also open one to the *second of the above-mentioned points (greater awareness of the intrinsic dignity, goodness, and mystery of the other resulting in greater compassion)*. It throws one's unreflective assumptions into question. When times are good, it is easier for me to look at others as they appear, as they speak, or as they manifest talent. When times get hard, the reflective Level 3 person might ask, "What really makes a person to be a friend? What makes friends stick by me when I am vulnerable and moody? What is it that produces loyalty and depth? Why is it that some people do not judge me on the basis of criteria from the comparison game? What is it about people that allows them to be generous without counting the cost? What spark of goodness allows them to serve rather than ignore the vulnerable? Why is it that people naturally seek to be contributive if they are not caught in the throes of the comparison game?" These questions and many like them give rise to an insight of the heart about the goodness and mystery of individual human beings.

Recall what was said in Chapter Two about the meaning of "heart". The heart is the power to intuit directly intrinsic goodness, lovability, beauty, and mystery. It is not like the mind's grasp of reality, which is relational (for example, the relationship between genus and specific difference, among numbers in numeric systems, among locations on maps, or causes to effects). Direct intuition of mystery touches a person, awakens a sense of truth and certitude, fills one with depth and spirit, and has the capacity to change one's life. The reasons of the heart are frequently harder to obtain than those of the mind, but suffering allows it. It allows us to remove the screens of prejudice, bias, historical resentments, jealousies, fears, and simple ignorance. Suffering uses its vulnerability to cut through the superficial screens, giving one's power of intuition a quick moment to apprehend directly the mystery and goodness of the other. From the vantage point of faith, this is like a glimpse of God's vision of us, which carries with it a profound awareness of the other's transcendental soul. This awareness of the other leads to a deep respect, which opens the way for compassion and forgiveness.

Compassion is a difficult virtue to comprehend in today's world. It means to "suffer with". But why would anybody want to suffer with somebody? It seems like nothing's getting done. It would make much more sense to heal them, get them some food, or do something about their condition. These things are certainly important, but what's the point of *compassion*? Compassion begins with a profound awareness of the intrinsic dignity of the other. That awareness allows us to be present to that other when all earthly appearances seem to be fading. Lucy, an elderly woman to whom compassion is given, at first feels uncomfortable. She would like to have something more, be something more, be more "worthy" (in the Level 2 sense) of the other's time and attention. But eventually she begins to see, sometimes out of pure need, that the other isn't looking for any of that. The other is serving out of a vision that is much deeper, a vision that sees mystery, a vision that is capable of an almost pure form of empathy, a vision that sees worthiness without the benefit of earthly appearances. In this vision, weakness is not abhorrent; it is the opportunity to be present in a more profound way to the human mystery manifest in the deep glow of eyes betokening helplessness.

Eventually, Lucy, the Level 3 recipient of compassion accepts the compassion, knows love, and knows her own lovability. It is never a perfect experience. Frequently this experience is mixed with feelings of inferiority, renewed desire to be independent, and worries about domination or inauthentic love; but generally, somewhere in the mix, there is the sense of being loved for oneself, and therefore, of having a self to be loved. It was noted in Chapter Three that our self-image is composed of both the esteemable self and the lovable self. The recipient of compassion is well assured that it is not the esteemable self that is being "suffered with", but rather the intrinsically dignified, mysterious, lovable self, which God and some others see beyond all appearances. Suffering, therefore, initiates a kind of magic, a radical transformation of both the giver and the recipient of compassion. When Mother Teresa found herself basking in the joy of a man who had his six-inch fingernails clipped as he lay dying in her house, she revealed the great lesson that suffering, though a negative in itself, provides the occasion for human mystery, unity, and love to be manifest fully. According to her faith, this is what God preordained for humanity from all eternity.

With respect to the *third point (growth in forgiveness)*, suffering has a way of putting all human hurts into context. When things are going well, it is easy to believe that life is neat and clean, that people's histories are pristine, disciplined, and even elegant. One can be assured that people's reflective grasp of their meaning is nearly perfect, and therefore, they shouldn't be subject to pettiness, egocentricity, and compulsion. When things are going well, one does not have to suffer fools gladly. But suffering produces a curious turn of consciousness. It makes life messy and makes thinking murky. It reveals one's own vulnerability and therefore the potential vulnerability of others. It shows how frustration, anger, and self-pity can completely take over one's consciousness and therefore might actually do the same in others. Suffering's messy world again throws off the assumptions about the would-be perfection of people.

There is a deeper meaning to suffering. It makes one confront one's own weakness. Either one can hate it and therefore fight it, or one can accept it and, by implication, begin to accept the weakness of others. Those who hate weakness in themselves, of course, generally tend to hate weakness in others. But the continual presence of suffering in these individuals makes life an almost intolerable burden. Therefore, it is incumbent upon those who are suffering to keep the whole Level 3 viewpoint on self-worth and love at the forefront of their minds. If they do, the dividends will be remarkable, for then they will be able to accept weakness in themselves not because they are settling for second best, but because they are judging themselves according to a higher standard than that of the comparison game. Once they have accepted weakness in themselves according to this higher standard of self-worth and love, they will begin, by sheer consistency, to apply it to others. The intrinsic dignity and mystery of the other will call forth this consistency from them. The moment this weakness is judged aright, empathy—true empathy—can occur; and once true empathy occurs, forgiveness follows in its wake.

Empathy is a process of the heart, a deeply intuitive process that culminates in understanding and radical acceptance of the other in both the other's mystery and fallibility. Mystery betokens the transcendent, while fallibility points to a fall. But when weakness is judged aright (Level 3), fallibility is not so easily characterized. It begins also to denote helplessness and need, compulsiveness, vulnerability, inferiority, insecurity, and moments of being insulted, disrespected, and rejected. I am not saying here that people are not in some sense responsible for their actions, that their vulnerability, insecurity, or history completely *excuses* them from their misconduct. What I am saying is that people are frequently not as responsible as might at first appear, that consciousness and intentionality are messy and ambiguous, and that our response to them should likewise have enough gray to see the mystery shining through the fallibility.

Empathy produces a connection with the other. It allows the intrinsic mystery and dignity spoken of above to shine through fallibility. It understands the complexity through which the human mystery is manifest, and it, therefore, recognizes that although a pure standard of justice may be necessary for a legal system, it cannot be so with families, friends, or even ordinary personal relationships. Therefore, when weakness is judged aright and empathy binds me to the fallible other, I have the possibility of forgiving.

Forgiveness here means intending to let go of a just claim against the other. The other may have insulted me or undermined me, taken what belongs to me; he crossed a line or transgressed the boundaries of fairness. This gives rise to my *just* claim against the other. If I hold onto this claim, two consequences will likely occur: (1) my resentment will grow, and (2) violence will beget violence, and vengeance will beget vengeance. The other will eventually resent me for resenting him for resenting me for resenting him . . . The only way for the cycle of violence and vengeance to end is forgiveness. One of the parties must at least *intend* to let go. It is often said that, given human fallibility, forgiveness is the most important condition necessary for the possibility of love. It may well also be the hardest condition necessary for love.

Forgiveness is not excuse. If one has a valid claim against another, then the other has quite probably perpetrated something which is inexcusable. But forgiveness is not asking for some rational explanation or validation of the injustice that occurred. Rather, for the sake of the other, for the sake of allowing the other to be free to start again, for the sake of interrupting the cycle of vengeance begetting vengeance, one chooses, in a moment of empathy (recognizing the goodness of the other), to let go of a just claim.

Forgiveness is not forgetting. Forgetting lags behind the intention to let go by months or even years. Even though there will never be a coincidence between forgiving and forgetting, one can generalize as follows:

First, if one forgives (intends to let go of a just claim), then the course of time will bring forgetting. But if one does not forgive, then one will not forget. Indeed, one's resentment will only grow, and one's memories will become more skewed.

A second distinction is also relevant. Forgiveness does not mean enduring continual abuse. We all have a right, indeed, a responsibility to protect the integrity of our physical, mental, and spiritual personhood. Hence, we have the right and responsibility to take any evasive action that is required to prevent the continuation of abuse.

With the above distinctions in mind, we can now make the following generalization: suffering provides the occasion for judging weakness aright (Level 3). It therefore enables me to empathize with others in their fallibility (allowing me to see the mystery through even provocative, intentional fallibility). This empathy, this deep connection, this care amidst the messiness of human consciousness, enables me to let go of an inexcusable offense in order to allow that mysterious other to proceed with life and to allow me to proceed with my own. If suffering, which is negative in itself, is allowed to work its mysterious transformation through the logic of Level 3, it could produce more forgiveness, and therefore more healing, peace, restoration, and unity, than could be imagined.

With regard to the *fourth point (growth in the ability to make contributions)*, it will now be evident that detachment from one's ego interests provokes engagement and even excitement in contributing to others. We saw in Chapter Three that living for contribution could alleviate the compulsiveness of living for comparisons. Suffering has a way of making this transition a necessity. It incisively reveals the inadequacy of the Level 2 perspective. Unfortunately, suffering of its own accord does not effect the transition from Level 2 to Level 3. As was noted above, this can be done only by education and choice. If one is aware of the potential of the Level 3 perspective to provide healing and enhanced purpose in life, then the occasion of suffering becomes a crucial turning point in one's life where one can incisively move from Level 2 to Level 3. This occurrence will increase the depth and breadth of one's contribution to individual others and the common good. A complete explanation of this may be found in Chapter Three (section III).

With regard to the *fifth point (growth in wisdom)*, we might begin with the familiar cliché that there is no cheap wisdom. Perhaps this means that an awareness of what really matters, of what lies at the foundation of reality, and what gives my life direction and purpose can be so easily obscured that it requires a lifetime of discipline to remove the obstacles to my vision. As has been made clear above, suffering provides the occasion for removing such obstacles. It throws assumptions into question, opens me to new data, forces me to go beyond the superficial, and encourages me to empathize. As such, suffering provides the occasion to help myself and others move toward the depth of authenticity and love that help us to become fully alive.

Inasmuch as suffering helps us to reexamine our presuppositions about others and life, it moves us into a *contemplative* state. Contemplation is extraordinarily important because it gives the time and the space necessary to gain greater depth of the heart. This kind of deep contemplation can, for example, give rise to spontaneous insights like "vengeful thoughts are hypocritical" or "humility does transform the quality of every action I perform" or "even the most gratuitous insults cannot make me undermine my purpose or hate another". An act of contemplation in a moment of suffering can make such insights so lucid and transparent that they can become a permanent part of one's conscious and subconscious condition. They can become one's most important personal truths.

Contemplation is not valued much in today's "action-packed" society because it doesn't seem to *do* anything. But inasmuch as contemplation helps us to achieve deeper "understanding of the heart", it has the potential to transform the quality and even the quantity of our actions in the world. Contemplation during times of suffering is much more poignant than contemplation outside of suffering. The vulnerability, openness, and acuity that suffering brings in its wake allow for greater depth and lucidity of the truths of the heart. But it must be remembered that this vulnerability will have these positive effects only if one is looking for them within a Level 3 or 4 context. In a Level 1 or 2 context such vulnerability will be viewed as essentially negative, and contemplation will probably result in self-pity and torturous solitude.

As has been stated above, suffering alone cannot bring wisdom of the heart. It must occur within the context of education and choice. Without a culture and community that support these two components, suffering can become the agent for antiwisdom, that is, for excessive narrowness, caution, and shallowness. Suffering can make me fearful, sceptical, and even cynical when viewed through the eyes of Level 2. It may be concluded from this that suffering needs wisdom in order to bring wisdom out of itself. Wisdom begins with education and awareness, and suffering provides the depth, breadth, feeling, and heart that transform mere generalizations into actual acts of humility, compassion, forgiveness, and love.

With regard to the *sixth point (the ability to grow in the third level of love)*, it must now be clear that the previous five outcomes open upon the capacity to commit oneself to another through good and hard times, for the benefit not only of the relationship but also beyond it. As explained in Chapter Four, the capacity to love leads not only to contributory behavior but also to the acceptance of the other and to a friendship or relationship grounded in the finite but self-transcendent truth of ourselves. The emotional dividends for both parties in the relationship are Level 3 meaning and happiness, an equanimity and peace about life, a capacity for intimacy and commitment beyond mere affection, and a subtle yet constant joy that results from this. The joy one feels is not ecstatic, though on occasion it could be. Rather, it is more like a sense of harmony with one's surroundings (and certainly with God, if one has faith). It produces the kind of peace that leads to good judgment, connection with others, and, above all, patient endurance in hard times. For the sake of simplicity, let us term this complex, subtle emotion "joy/harmony". The subtlety of this emotion makes it difficult to grasp directly.

However, it might be easier to see it through its absence. When a radio is on in the background throughout the day, it becomes so subtle one barely notices it. Yet when one turns off the radio, it suddenly becomes apparent how much the radio was contributing to one's sense of well-being. There are three psychic manifestations arising out of the *absence* of the above-mentioned subtle joy/harmony:

1. A sense of being out of kilter with the totality, not being at home within the cosmos: not belonging, or being alienated from one's surroundings.

2. An increase in ego sensitivity: enhanced needs for admiration, compliments, and control; extreme sensitivity to "being in second place"; hypersensitivity to failure; assessment of the world in terms of how it affects me; and the destructive emotions of the comparison game (jealousy, suspicion, fear, contempt, and so on).

3. Decreased capacity for genuine intimacy, compassion, care and concern. It is harder to find the internal reserves to look for the good news in the other and to respond with the desire to do good for the other. Bad news in the other is more difficult to tolerate.

As Level 3 love returns, these emotions begin to dissipate.

How does suffering enhance this level of love and its consequent subtle emotions? As implied above, one has a fundamental *choice* at the moment of suffering. One can choose either to empathize more with the sufferings of others or to isolate oneself more from others by moving ever more deeply into one's own privacy. The first option is always available because suffering produces vulnerability, which, in turn, enables one to empathize with the vulnerability and weakness of others. This moment of empathy (compassion) produces freedom. It is a choice to move *out* to the other at the very moment when one wants to move more *into* one's self. This choice begins permanently to transform one's psyche, making one more aware of the needs of others, of the potential for contribution, and of the needs of the community and culture. But it is more than mere awareness. It is a desire, or even a restlessness to *do* something about these needs. If one gives way to this desire, one will find new meaning, intimacy, compassion, and subtle joy/harmony. Thus, suffering alone does not lead to love. Suffering plus *choice* leads to the third level of love.

It must not be thought that choosing to interpret suffering positively in one or two instances will lead to the capacity for deep and lasting commitment. The latter requires many such choices. However, each and every choice leads to greater meaning, compassion, intimacy, and subtle joy/harmony, which in turn produce a positive change in one's psyche (that is, enhance one's capacity for deep and lasting commitment). Eventually the compounded layering results in a remarkable detachment from ego and a capacity for self-sacrifice, which is imbued with subtle joy/harmony. From the vantage point of Levels 1 and 2, this is nonsensical, for ego detachment and self-sacrifice in this view seem quite unpleasant. Indeed, they *are* unpleasant when one does not have the freedom that comes through suffering, that is, the freedom to love. As one continually chooses to empathize with the need and vulnerability of others through one's own suffering and vulnerability, one acquires the capacity to feel joy/harmony through detachment and self-sacrifice. As one develops in this capacity, the third level of love becomes easier, and sometimes even effortless. Hence, the subtle joy/harmony of love increases in depth and pervasiveness and, in its turn, seems to touch and affect family, friends, community, and even the culture.

With regard to the *seventh point (growth in leadership toward the common good)*, it is a small leap from the third level of love to genuine concern for the culture. As noted above, the third level of love is not oriented only toward the inwardness of a friendship or relationship. As meaning, compassion, intimacy, and joy/harmony increase, so does the capacity for outwardness (that is, beyond the relationship). The outwardness of love has a *continual* quality. It not only seeks to manifest itself in individual friends but also seeks to take that friendship into ever-wider contexts (that is, less intimate groups of family and friends and the community and culture as well). If a friendship is truly grounded in Level 3, it will constitute a *"we"* that wants to be contributory. This gives *us* greater meaning, compassion, intimacy, and joy/harmony, which in turn deepens the relationship. The more *we* are energized by doing something positive beyond *our* selves, the more we have the capacity to deepen our friendship; and the more we deepen our friendship, the more we become energized by doing something beyond ourselves. There is a natural propensity for such friendships to expand. We naturally invite others in. Indeed, we can even invite other groups of friends into our friend-ships, which produces a community of Level 3 love. If the capacity for ego detachment and self-sacrifice can be maintained in the larger group, it will become true *koinonia*—a community dedicated to the culture and society. This is the community out of which leaders are born, lead-ers who do not seek power for themselves but share their vision, gifts, and energy for the good of others, leaders who are genuinely detached from ego and therefore detached from the obsessions and compulsions of political and cultural power. The humility and love that come from choosing empathy in the moment of suffering undermine the seeming inevitability of Lord Acton's famous phrase, "Power corrupts, and ab-solute power corrupts absolutely." Power need not corrupt. Power plus love leads to infectious, charismatic momentum toward the common good. This quality will be specifically addressed in Chapter Seven.

In sum, there are four choices that can help us to suffer well:

1. Prior to suffering, *choose* to move toward Level 3 by embracing the six fundamental attitudes mentioned in Chapter Three. This will open one to the above-mentioned Level 3 "benefits" of suffering when it occurs.

2. At the moment of suffering, *choose* to interpret the suffering positively by looking for the seven outcomes mentioned in the above list.

3. At the moment of suffering, *choose* to use your vulnerability to empathize with the need and vulnerability of others (instead of going inward into isolation).

4. After the first three choices, *choose* to use the qualities of Level 3 love (such as humility, detachment, forgiveness, compassion, wisdom, intimacy, vision, capacity for self-sacrifice, and its con-comitant joy/harmony) to transform power, prestige, and priv-ilege in your life into infectious, charismatic leadership for the common good.

These four choices turn suffering into a gift. They empower us to love, they impart the freedom of permanent commitment, they trans-form our capacity for organizational and cultural leadership, and they enhance our family life. Beyond this they give us a different view of others by revealing their intrinsic, self-transcendent, and mysterious dignity at the very moment of their weakness. They tell us of the mystery and joy/harmony in compassion and self-sacrifice. They speak of a whole new arena of hope and a whole new vision, which has the capacity to transform human culture, and hence, they express the deepest philosophical foundations of the pro-life movement.

II. Moving from a Level 3 to a Level 4 Interpretation of Suffering

Just as the vulnerability of suffering opens one to new levels of empathy, meaning, and love, it also opens one to unconditional Love. Vulnerability helps us to accept help not only from others (detaching us from the myth of self-sufficiency implicit in an exaggerated Level 2 outlook) but also from a higher, loving Power. As one allows this unconditional Love to touch our sense of personal dignity, worth, and lovability, the seven outcomes of suffering mentioned above become more deeply and permanently manifest.

This subsection presumes either faith, an interest in pursuing faith, or a desire to inquire into faith. If you are not engaged by one of these dispositions, you may want to skip to the next chapter. I include this section of the book for this more restricted audience, because it can offer substantial assistance in times of suffering.

So how does faith affect love and suffering? It brings trust, hope, and loving grace into the seven qualities mentioned above with respect to Level 3. The following exposition will address each of the outcomes from this perspective.

Before embarking on this project, it might be recalled that faith is not surrendering one's ability to choose; it is choosing to surrender. In the previous chapter (section III), I mentioned four questions that lead directly to faith in an unconditionally loving God, who desires to come among us. I noted that human beings cannot bring themselves to the natural transcendent fulfillment they desire (perfect Truth, Love, Goodness/Justice, Beauty, and Being). Even though human beings have an intrinsic *desire* for these transcendental qualities, we do not *possess* these qualities by nature and therefore cannot bring ourselves to them by ourselves. Unconditional Love has to come to us (Emmanuel) because we cannot bring ourselves to what we are not. This is the critical choice of faith. If we do not invite "God with us" into us, we will have to bring ourselves to what we cannot get to by ourselves. As was noted above, the second option leads to nihilism or absurdism, for it betokens a life of continuous frustration.

The choice to invite the unconditionally loving God into our lives resembles, in some respects, the initiation of a friendship. It leads to dialogue, self-revelation, and journey, and above all, one begins to feel more and more at home with one's friends. But here the analogy stops, for as one comes to be at home with the unconditionally loving God, one begins to experience a level of peace that is quite new and unique. It is a peace filled with hope and confidence, a soothing assurance that everything will make sense in the whole divine order. The moment one feels this soothing assurance, one knows it is not arising out of one's own cognition or power. It must be stressed that this peace is not a manifestation of "convincing yourself". The reader will know how much attention, effort, focus, and energy are required to keep mindless optimism going. The peace of which I speak is almost effortless. Though it is subtle, it makes for good judgment in everyday life. It makes life an adventure instead of a problem. It enables one to experience empathy in the most difficult situations. Though one cannot directly feel peace most of the time, one can know it by all the above effects. Through the choice to be in relationship with God (who would never *force* such a relationship on us), we find a peace that enables us to give a most profound interpretation to suffering, which, in its turn, helps us to achieve the seven positive outcomes of suffering.

With respect to the *first outcome of suffering (detachment and humility)*, it should be noted that fear is perhaps the most frequent inducer of pride. When one is scared of humiliation, failure, what others might think, being thought worse, scoring less, being less, or achieving less, one is most likely to insist upon one's worthiness (even aggressively), to act pretentiously, to be more sensitive to criticism, to exaggerate, or even to lie. By now it must be clear that this irrational fear arises out of an exaggeration of the second level of happiness.

Faith can be extraordinarily helpful in overcoming these fears. It helps to solidify Level 3 thinking and takes a person far beyond it. I mentioned the most essential of all prayers in Chapter Three (section V): "Thy will be done." This prayer has the capacity of transforming fear into peace. When one gives over the success or failure of a particular project to God, the above-mentioned peace begins to manifest itself. Again, it is not a peace based on self-insistence, requiring substantial energy and focus. Rather, this peace manifests itself in detachment: "If it is your will, then let it succeed; if not, let it fail. I will do my best and leave the rest up to you." Notice that the detachment is grounded in a Reality other than oneself. That is why it is not exhausting, insistent, or even neurotic (obsessive compulsive). I might initiate the prayer "Thy will be done", but God's will brings the peace that I cannot give myself. I know only too well from my own life that if I were the source of this peace, I would be not only exhausted but also unable to sleep thinking that the peace would go away when I could no longer hold the world together. It is God's love and energy that ground this effortless detachment, this peace-filled detachment that breaks the chains of exaggeration, pretense, bravado, and lies.

But pride is deeper than fear. It manifests itself not only in times of failure or potential failure but also, perhaps especially, in times of success. It is here that one begins (albeit only implicitly) to start thinking about oneself as the center of the universe, to believe that one can be one's own fulfillment or even others' fulfillment. This temptation to take over divine prerogative is a subtle, though not inconsequential, form of self-idolatry. Self-idolatry first manifests itself in a paradoxical "joy" of pure autonomy. For a fleeting moment one believes in the illusion of complete independence and self-sufficiency, but eventually it begins to manifest itself as acute loneliness because one recognizes that one really doesn't have control over the people on whom one depends. Indeed, one doesn't even have control over oneself. This short-term "joy" begins to turn into anger, rage, isolation, cynicism, and incipient despair.

Again, the prayer "Thy will be done" can be very helpful in overcoming this ironic propensity, which uses success to ruin love. This prayer prioritizes God's will above one's own will because it recognizes that God's will is unconditional love, while one's own human will seems to fall short of this. One can still desire that unconditional love become a reality for the world, but in Level 4 thinking, one recognizes that one cannot do this oneself, and therefore, the only way it can be done is through the unconditionally loving God. Thus, this prayer represents the only realistic way that the perfect ideal of Level 3 (contribution/love) can be actualized. At this point, faith's "surrender" becomes intelligible. One recognizes the need for surrender in order to achieve the perfect ideal of love for the world and for oneself. Thus, this surrender is the fullest use of one's freedom. One becomes an instrument of a love that is not only bigger than one's own but also perfect by its very nature. "Thy will be done" is therefore at once a prayer of freedom through surrender and a prayer of being fully actualized while letting go. When one comes to understand through experience the truth of this declaration, one will experience the peace mentioned above, the peace that does not require my energy, focus, and insistence.

"Thy will be done" is not a prayer of passivity. It does not somehow replace my effort, education, and good judgment. Rather, it places the "best I can do" within the larger framework of an unconditionally loving Providence, which can overcome, in its own time, all acts of pride and "unlove".

What does all of this have to do with suffering? Suffering helps to develop this empowering surrender, while this empowering surrender helps to transform suffering into love. How does suffering lead to empowering surrender? As noted above, suffering is a lack of control. If one does not choose to give it a positive meaning, its intrinsic negativity will become its meaning. If one does not orient it to growth in love, then it will likely lead to growth in bitterness and isolation. However, if one *chooses* to orient suffering toward love, it can purify every attitude and transform every action into the optimum of contribution and love. "Thy will be done" is the prayer of choosing to prioritize the will of the unconditionally loving God over one's own will. Hence, the moment of suffering, that is, the moment of powerlessness, can become a poignant invitation to surrender one's will to the will of God for the sake of love in the world. The powerlessness intrinsic to the moment of suffering elicits, like no other experience, "Thy will be done" from the suffering person. If one knows this prayer, understands that it intends unconditional love for the world, and prays for this intention, the prayer will work its miracle of peace in the midst of suffering. It will give the fullest possible purpose to suffering. It will be a conduit for the unconditionally loving God to become manifest not only in the world but also in the depths of one's own heart. Hence, suffering calls forth the very act of empowering surrender, which transforms it into the ideal of love. This "empowering surrender" may seem paradoxical until one chooses it, at which time the experience of peace, purpose, and love coming through suf-

fering will provide more than adequate confirmation of the unconditionally loving God's positivity amidst what at first appeared to be
mere negativity.

The above makes clear how important it is that people who understand this empowering surrender communicate it to those who are suffering. If the suffering person does not know this prayer, or does not
understand what it intends (unconditional love), or does not remember
to pray for this at the time of suffering, that person will not be able to
benefit from the peace, purpose, transformation, and love for the world
that comes through the will of the One who honors it.

A similar reciprocal action can be seen between "Thy will be done"
and the *second outcome of suffering (greater awareness of the intrinsic dignity,
goodness, and mystery of the other)*. As noted above, the vulnerability and
powerlessness intrinsic to suffering elicit empathy for the same vulnerability and weakness in others. They thereby enable us to put this weakness in perspective, allowing the true mystery and goodness of the other
to emerge above and beyond these negative attributes. "Thy will be
done" will invariably bring about this result. The will of God perme-
ates the experience of vulnerability with the awareness of the transcendental ideal of love to which we are called. When one prays "Thy will
be done", it is virtually impossible to focus solely on the feelings of
vulnerability and powerlessness, for it ushers in the perspective of God,
which illuminates the purpose and intended result of all suffering, namely,
growth in love, for self and the world. This has the effect of revealing
the transcendent, loving ideal for every human being. It reveals mystery, soul, and the transcendent reality beyond the merely material and
apparent. "Thy will be done" transforms weakness and vulnerability
into the vision of true mystery and transcendence.

"Thy will be done" also brings about the *third outcome of suffering,
namely, forgiveness*. When suffering is caused by another through insensitivity, insult, or injury, a large part of the psychic pain of this experience comes from the ruptured relationship. Attributing intentionality
or bad will to the perpetrator of the hurt enhances the pain. The more
intimate one's relationship with the perpetrator, the greater the pain.
As noted above, holding on to the hurt only serves to exacerbate it, and
therefore forgiveness is the only way out. Even though forgiveness is
not forgetting, it does, in the long run, lead to forgetting, and therefore, the alleviation of pain. But forgiveness does more than simply

alleviate pain. It deepens our love and understanding of others, which in turn deepens our love and understanding of ourselves, which in its turn opens upon an even greater love of others, and so on.

Unfortunately, ego concerns undermine the acquisition of these most precious benefits of forgiveness. When we hurt, we want to keep the claim that we have on others as if it were our most prized possession. We want to hold that claim over that other person, saying, as it were, "You owe me for what you have done to me", or more precisely, "You will *always* owe me for what you have done to me; your continual acknowledgment of this is the only way of alleviating the hurt you have caused." There is something in our nature that wants to say, "I want you to undo the harm you have done, every day of your life. That is what I need, and therefore that is what you owe me." In the logic of strict justice, this position is not without merit. However, in the logic of human frailty and misunderstanding, it is both unrealistic and destructive. Human beings have to be given the chance to start anew. They can be called to responsibility, but they cannot be made to pay again and again.

"Thy will be done" makes forgiveness a possibility, for one does not have to let go in a void, as if the hurt would never be redressed. One lets go into the hands of God to redress the matter in whatever way would optimize love in the world. By using the prayer "Thy will be done", one overcomes the need for blame, continual recognition of the hurt, and consequent debt, through a more powerful desire for God to prevail in the world. The desire for love achieves its power over the desire for vengeance through the awareness of the peaceful presence of God in the relationship. As noted above, "Thy will be done" brings peace, which, in its turn, brings empathy (toward love) and detachment (from vengeance).

There is another dimension to this. As one prays "Thy will be done", intending that God prevail in the world, one begins progressively to recognize one's own shortcomings. One sees more clearly how far short of the ideal one truly is. One begins to see greater manifestations of the pride that undermines love in one's own life. This awareness does not lead to discouragement or despair, for "Thy will be done" again reveals God's intention toward one's own weakness. One becomes certain of the forgiving and healing touch of God. This restores what was negated, brings back home what was alienated, and enhances the empowerment of surrender. When one has been forgiven much, one is led to forgive much. Inasmuch as "Thy will be done" opens the way to a recognition of one's own shortcomings and to an even more powerful recognition of God's forgiving and loving intention directed toward one, it leads toward greater forgiveness and love of others. Thus, "Thy will be done" allows forgiveness to bring together the three loves: love of God, leading to love of self, leading to love of neighbor, back to love of God, self, and so on. Human suffering, accompanied by this prayer, is positively transformative not only for self but also for every love relationship that forms and constitutes that self.

By now it must be clear that if "Thy will be done" can actualize and enhance humility, empathy, awareness of the intrinsic dignity of others, and forgiveness, it will also enhance the other four positive outcomes of suffering (*contribution to others, wisdom, Level 3 love, and leadership toward the common good*). Suffice it to say that suffering presents an invitation to say this most important prayer, which in turn invites God into our hearts. The presence of God is at once an awareness of our dignity and destiny, empathy and peace, and the transformation of suffering into the transcendent loving mystery we were created to be.

In the previous section, I concluded by listing four choices that could transform suffering from a negative to a positive experience. I have found the following choices to be quite helpful in making full use of faith to effect this transition from suffering to love:

1. Prior to suffering, direct prayer to the actualization of the six fundamental attitudes of Level 3 (contributory identity, looking for the good news in others, and so on).

2. During the suffering, pray "Thy will be done" for each of the seven positive outcomes of suffering mentioned above.

3. At the moment of suffering, pray specifically for empathy with others' vulnerability in order to become more aware of the true mystery of others (grounded not in self-sufficiency but in transcendent love).

4. Use the love arising out of the surrender to God (steps 1 through 3 above) to transform power, prestige, and privilege into infectious, charismatic leadership for the common good.

By making these four choices, I have noticed through experience and inner conviction a truth that has transformed my life:

The unconditionally loving God would never permit suffering or evil to happen that would not, in the end, lead to greater good or love for me, others, and the world.

The reader might now be asking, "When I am suffering, how can I possibly remember all these qualities of suffering and the choices that allow faith to actualize them?" This is a very good question because one's memory, concentration, and horizon of thought are severely restricted by pain, fear, pride, anger, depression, and the like. The reader might also be thinking that the prayer "Thy will be done", rich as it is, is too abstract in a situation of suffering. In order to simplify the above advice in times of suffering, and in order to make "Thy will be done" more specific and concrete, I would recommend the following six spontaneous prayers to the reader. Their poignancy and simplicity will help to galvanize the above material while providing a conduit for God' grace to effect peace, even at the greatest moments of tragedy.

1. "Help!"

2. "Lord, do not waste one scintilla of this suffering."

3. "Lord, snatch victory from the jaws of defeat."

4. "I give up, Lord. You take care of it."

5. "Lord, you are the just Judge. You take care of this person."

6. "Lord, make good come out of whatever harm I might have caused."

1. "Help!" This very simple prayer is extraordinarily efficacious because it is God's will always to help us in our suffering. His help sometimes brings a halt to or alleviates the suffering. Sometimes it does not, but God's help *always* brings greater good (and therefore, greater love) out of suffering for anyone who is open to that goodness or love. God's help will always advance goodness in the world if the human community will allow this to occur. It will always advance the cause of love if human pride does not get in the way. Therefore, we must pray this prayer as if God wants to help and is helping, for indeed, he does want to help, and he is helping at all moments. The reader might be thinking, "But if God wants to help and is helping whenever we ask, why doesn't he help a little more quickly? Why do we have to wait and live in ambiguity? Isn't this view just a little bit naïve?"

The above view is not naïve, if one considers that unconditional love (which is God's will) requires that four objectives be actualized in every situation of suffering:

1. that suffering be *eventually* alleviated

2. that human freedom be respected

3. that love and goodness be optimized for the individual

4. that love and goodness be optimized for the world

If the unconditionally loving God is going to achieve these four objectives in a *finite and conditioned* humanity living in a *finite and conditioned* world, he will not be able to actualize the first objective instantaneously (that is why the word "eventually" was used).

The second objective frequently conflicts with the first objective of suffering. For example, if God sees a person getting ready to insult another person, he could instantly alleviate the pain by muting the insulting party. If he did not want to destroy the insulting party's freedom by so doing, he might be able instantly to alleviate the pain of the insult in the receiving party by bestowing his divinely loving perspective on the receiving party. Of course, this would obliterate the receiving party's own freedom to interpret the insult. One can now begin to see the difficulties in trying to balance human freedom (objective 2) with the alleviation of suffering (objective 1).

To make matters even worse, objective 3 also comes into conflict with objective 1, because God could perceive that short-term suffering might alleviate a much more severe, longer term suffering. For example, a student could receive a C− on an exam, which could cause him to attend more to studies, which could become a lifelong benefit. God could also allow suffering to engender a questioning process about life's meaning in a person living a Level 2 (comparison game) lifestyle. This questioning process might open this person (with the help and advice of others) to consider a contributory identity, leading toward a more pervasive, enduring, and deep life. By doing this, God would allow one form of pain and deprivation to advance the cause of love, which in turn would alleviate deeper and more prolonged forms of suffering arising out of the comparison game.

Finally, objective 4 also comes into conflict with objective 1, for family members, friends, employees, and even the community, can significantly benefit from one's growth in humility, forgiveness, wisdom, and/or peace. God can allow suffering in a particular person to optimize love and goodness in the world.

I do not mean to oversimplify God's perspective here. I mean only to show that the instantaneous alleviation of pain may not be the most loving thing to do. Indeed, it could be completely counterproductive to freedom and love. Therefore, if God's purpose is not only to optimize love and goodness in the world but also to actualize love and goodness in his kingdom, one cannot say, "A loving God would instantaneously alleviate suffering." One can only say, "A loving God will optimize love in the world." The timing of the alleviation of suffering, therefore, must be left up to his unconditionally loving providence.

When we pray the prayer "Help!" we are asking God to optimize love according to his timetable. If it helps, think of God as the most loving parent one could imagine. Feel, for a moment, the dilemma of that loving parent, who would rather suffer in the place of his child but also simultaneously realizes that his child must make his own decisions, acquire the virtue to stand up on his own feet, and have the option of "unlove" if he is to have the option of love. Recall from above that God did not design us with a "love microchip" that would produce optimally loving behaviors. Obviously, this would have been the creation not of a loving person but only of a loving marionette. God had to create a creature with the option to choose "unlove" in order to allow love to be chosen by the creature and therefore for love to arise not out of programming but out of the creature's own decision and action. In the same way, a loving parent cannot do the loving for his child; he has to let go, even if it means letting the child choose poorly, in order for the child's love to be his own.

But God has more in mind than this hypothetical parent, because he is also trying to optimize freedom and love for all of his beloved children (billions of them) simultaneously. Some have more need than others, some have suffered more deprivation, and some have more resources with which to cope with suffering. The unconditionally loving God is trying to optimize love at every moment for all of them, in the midst of their freedom to perpetrate "unlove". It is, therefore, best to entrust God with the timing and to say, "Thy will be done", or, in its shortened form, "Help!"

A rather famous poem entitled "Footprints" sums this point up rather poignantly. A man is standing on the beach with God, reviewing his life. At each moment in his life, he sees his footprints next to God's in the sand. But at the times he was experiencing the most difficulty, he noticed only one pair of footprints. He asks God why, when he was most in need, did God abandon him. God's answer was that in those times of suffering the footprints in the sand were not the man's but God's, who had been carrying him all along. My view of suffering is quite similar. God is not only carrying us in our suffering but also carrying every one of us in our freedom. Frequently, we have difficulty seeing him in his loving activity, but he is there, poignantly there, in peace, inspiration, meaning, and above all, love. If we keep praying the vital prayer, "Help!" (the shortened form of "Thy will be done") and look for his guiding hand in the most loving perspective we can muster, we will not only grow to the point of consummate joy with him, we will also be instruments of the actualization of his unconditionally loving kingdom. What could be better?

2. *"Lord, do not waste one scintilla of this suffering."* This second prayer gets to the heart of "Help!" It is really asking that the Lord optimize freedom, goodness, and love in a situation of pain and deprivation.[1] Again, it must be remembered that God does not want us to suffer, but rather allows suffering to actualize freedom and love within the world as a whole. It was noted above with respect to the previous prayer that God might delay the alleviation of suffering to meet one or more of three other objectives. But now, a slightly different question arises, namely, "Why would God allow any suffering at all? Is it really necessary in order for freedom and love to be optimized?"

---

[1]This prayer is integral to Christian theology and could be restated as follows: "Lord, make the Resurrection come out of this Cross." It asks that, inasmuch as the Cross is necessary for the sake of love, the Lord use it for that purpose and bring Resurrection out of it. It is perfectly legitimate to pray, as Jesus did, that the cross pass us by (e.g., "Father, if it is your will, take this cup from me; yet not my will but yours be done" (Lk 22:42), or "subject us not to the trial" (Lk 11:4), or, "Lead us not into temptation, but deliver us from evil"). After all, God does not want us to suffer. God allows suffering in the world only to respect human freedom and optimize love.

In my view, suffering is integral to freedom and love. First, with respect to freedom, love cannot exist unless human beings have the choice not to love (see the previous subsection). Otherwise God would have made mere marionettes performing preprogrammed loving behaviors. The choice not to love introduces into the world the possibility of suffering caused by free agents. God, therefore, had to allow the possibility of suffering in order to create the possibility of love in free agents who were imperfect, conditioned, and bound to make mistakes.

But what about suffering that is not caused or preventable by free human agents? The following parable might help to illustrate in a very simple way this most complex question.

Once upon a time, God created a world of people seated at a large banquet table. He laid a sumptuous feast before them all, but had seemingly neglected to create these beings (who looked much like humans) with elbows and wrists. Hence, they were not able to partake of the banquet. As most free and loving creatures do, these began to speculate about why God would have allowed this obvious deprivation to occur. People were beginning to die of starvation while seated before a sumptuous feast.

One group of creatures seated at one end of the table speculated that God could not possibly be all powerful or all knowing, for if he were all knowing, he would have seen his mistake, and if he were all powerful, he would have been able to rectify it. It was clear that God was merely an Olympian figurehead.

Another group began to speculate, "If God exists, he is certainly all powerful. Therefore, it is clear that he is not all loving. If he were all loving, he would have noticed and corrected this mistake. Therefore, he must be something akin to a sadist who enjoys seeing us squirm in an impossible pursuit of self-preservation."

Another group, the nihilists, began to speculate that if God existed, he would have to be both all powerful and all loving. After all, love is an essentially positive characteristic, and if an all-powerful being exists, it would have to possess this pure manifestation of positivity. Therefore, it seemed that God did not exist. Furthermore, since we ultimately desire unconditional Truth, Love, Goodness, Fairness, Beauty, and Being, and God does not exist to fulfill what we cannot give ourselves, our existence must be absurd.

Finally, a fourth group deferred their speculation momentarily to take note of the creatures sitting directly across the table from them. They noticed their neighbors suffering first, and in an act of empathy and compassion, they felt that it was easier to do the good for the other than to do the good for themselves. At that very moment of compassion, they used their elbowless arms to feed the creatures across the table from them and so discovered how to feed and be fed in an act of compassionate love. This group discovered a contributory identity. They began to see the good news in the other and began to be moved by the desire to help the other, which led, paradoxically, to being fed themselves. The God who had created this world was not so much concerned about the ingestion of food as about the method of feeding. He had allowed suffering to manifest love amidst the more tangible and immediately gratifying desire for Levels 1 and 2. He had broken down the barriers of autonomous personhood in favor of interpersonal personhood and allowed the joy of love to emerge simultaneously with the happiness of having one's appetite satiated. Cessation of hunger was his objective, but not merely the cessation of physical hunger. His ultimate objective was to fulfill the yearning to be compassionate and to receive compassion, to become interpersonal persons, to form a human community around the common good, and to find our peace in giving ourselves away.

I do not mean to devalue the suffering of people by such a simple illustration. I know the depth of pain that can be caused by suffering arising out of so-called natural causes. I here mean only to suggest the following: if God's purpose is to teach us how to love, then it is likely that the purpose of all suffering arising out of natural causes should be precisely that. Therefore, if we are *looking* for love in our suffering and trusting the all-loving God, love will arise out of our suffering both for ourselves and for the human community around us. Irrespective of whether we can see this love becoming manifest, we must trust in the unconditionally loving God, for it is in trusting in him that we will find the freedom to look for love and, in that freedom, find a way of actualizing love in suffering.

How can we call this trusting attitude to mind in the midst of suffering? Through the prayer "Lord, do not waste one scintilla of this suffering; make good come out of it for me, the community, and your kingdom of love." The more general form of this prayer is "Thy will be done", for bringing love out of suffering is precisely his will.

3. *"Lord, snatch victory from the jaws of defeat."* Sometimes we get to a point in our lives where we are sliding fast down a slippery slope, and we cannot see a way of even slowing our momentum, let alone stopping

ourselves before we hit the bottom. We have to endure multiple problems simultaneously, and we do not have control over any of them in
their individuality, let alone in their conglomeration. I have always found
this prayer to be particularly useful in those times. I ask God literally to
take control of this vast array of chaos. I put myself in his hands and ask
that he might allow me to escape from what seems to be an impending
crash. Throughout my life, I can honestly say that God has done this. I
never cease to be amazed at how situations start resolving themselves,
and the ones that don't resolve themselves lead to a new and previously
unknown horizon of human relationship and opportunity. The more
general form of this prayer is, as might be expected, "Thy will be done",
for it is precisely his will to snatch us out of the jaws of impending
disaster and bring new life, new love, and new opportunity for the good
out of the "near miss".

4. *"I give up, Lord. You take care of it."* As noted in Chapter Three
(section V), this is not giving up *on* life, but giving up *to* God. When
you turn yourself over to the all-loving God (who brings peace beyond
all understanding), God takes over as the ground of your identity and
destiny, and you will likely feel an immediate relief from not having to
do this for yourself.

I experienced this quite poignantly while studying theology in Rome.
I had approximately six weeks to learn Italian in order to take all my
classes in that language. I felt quite confident going into my first class
on the Synoptic Gospels. As the professor began to speak (quite rapidly!), I found that I wasn't able to understand anything he was saying. I
began to think, "I'm going to flunk this course! How am I going to
explain this to my family and friends?" The more I began to panic at
the prospect, the less I understood from the professor. Finally, I had
reached a state of complete confusion and fear. Naturally, I tried to
figure out how I had gotten into this mess and what I could do to bring
myself out of it. The answer was too big and too confusing, which only
led to my increased anxiety. Finally I decided to pray the prayer, "Lord,
I give up. You take care of it." As I let God take over as the ground of
my identity and destiny, I began to calm down. The calm was so significant, it was like steam coming out of my ears. This peace arising out
of trust in God allowed me to understand the professor more and more.
After about two weeks, I found myself understanding him almost completely. Everything turned out just fine in the end.

The more general form of this prayer is, as usual, "Thy will be done", for it is God's will to "take care of it" without doing it all for us. He wants to be the ground of our destiny, to satisfy our desire, and to help us in our time of need. He is not asking to take over our identity or to absorb us in his infinity. He wants our individual and interpersonal personhood to be grounded in his unconditional love and to be fulfilled through his unconditional love. Nothing could make us freer or happier. Nothing could help us to make more good come out of our lives. Nothing could make us reach our individual, interpersonal destinies more quickly.

5. *"Lord, you are the just Judge. You take care of this person."* As was explained above, forgiveness of others can be quite difficult because it is not *excusing* others (who have reasons for their actions), but rather letting go of a just claim (an offense for which there seems to be virtually no reasonable explanation). When forgiveness is called for, hurt from another's insensitivity or cruelty can be quite deep. If one attempts to let go of this just claim by oneself, it can be very difficult. As one tries to "forget about it", one finds oneself remembering it all the more. As one begins to try and push the offense out of one's mind, one plays the tape with even more ferocity. Instead of stewing and brewing for weeks, use your faith and try this prayer, "Lord, you are the just Judge. You take care of this person." You are asking God to use his divine perspective on justice to judge the person who has offended you, and in so doing, you are allowing him to be the ground of the act of forgiveness. If I have to be the ground of this act, I will want to take control of what this person knows about the offense caused and about how that offense will have to be redressed in the future, and about how this person will relate to others, and so on. Since I cannot do this, I may as well let the just Judge take care of it by putting this problematic development in his hands. In my life, this has been the one and only way I have been able truly to let go of offenses that I felt required forgiveness. The more general form of this prayer is, as usual, "Thy will be done", for it is God's unconditionally loving will that we forgive one another and use his providence and love to ground this act of forgiveness. In this way, the cycle of vengeance begetting vengeance, and violence begetting violence, will be interrupted and transcended by God's purpose of love.

6. *"Lord, make good come out of whatever harm I might have caused."* This prayer is particularly useful for situations opposite the one mentioned

immediately above. Have you ever had the experience of intentionally or unintentionally saying something that you subsequently discovered could have hurt a person quite deeply? If you are anything like me, you will severely regret the action. Sometimes it is possible to ask for forgiveness of this person immediately, but not always. When I cannot do so, I tend to take my offense home with me, toss about in my bed till three o'clock in the morning, and exaggerate the amount of depression and harm the other person is experiencing from my uncaring act. I want to call up the person at three in the morning and explain what I really meant, but of course this could exacerbate the problem.

Why not use faith in these moments of powerlessness, by using the prayer, "Lord, make good come out of whatever harm I might have caused"? God, who works in the hearts of human beings in ways unbeknownst to us, will oblige this prayer immediately. He can inspire others with deep understanding, compassion, patience, and forgiveness. I have had hundreds of experiences where I said something that I later thought would be misinterpreted or taken hurtfully. After saying this prayer, I have frequently experienced the offended party coming up to me days later and saying, "Father Spitzer, when you first said this, I took it the wrong way, and I was hurt, but subsequently, I saw your true motives for saying it." All I could think was, "Whew!" It is almost as if God just led me and this other person out of an impending collision at the very last moment. The general form of this prayer is, as usual, "Thy will be done", because it is God's unconditionally loving will to make good come out of whatever harm we might have caused. Indeed, it is his will to do everything possible to bring greater good and greater love out of potential and real harm.

There are many other similar prayers that I have not mentioned here. The above have been particularly helpful to myself and to people whom I have served in the past. Eventually, each specific prayer melds into "Thy will be done", allowing God's unconditionally loving will to bring good out of suffering, peace out of anxiety, and his unconditionally loving kingdom out of a world fraught with frailty and imperfection. In the end, he will incite free compassion out of deprivation, love out of vulnerability, and light out of darkness.

Chapter Six

Ethics and Freedom

Introduction

It may be wondered why the discussion of freedom comes after the discussion of ethics. As will be seen, the third and fourth levels of freedom are oriented toward ethical objectives. Hence, an understanding of them requires an antecedent understanding of basic ethics. The subject matter of both topics will be divided into Level 1 and 2 on the one hand and Level 3 and 4 on the other. Recall that Level 1 and 2 finds its happiness in bringing the outer world under the control of the inner world (by possession, mastery, winning, admiration, and other forms of comparison). Levels 3 and 4, in contrast, are oriented toward investing the inner world (thoughts, words, actions, and creativity) in the outer world, to make it a better place. These opposed dynamics have the same radical effect on ethics and freedom as on success, self-worth, love, and suffering. Let us begin with ethics.

I. Ethics

In general, ethics is dedicated to right conduct. It seeks to establish criteria that will help orient human behavior toward what is true and good. Some ethicists view the good as that which has beneficial consequences for a particular individual or group (utilitarians/consequentialists), while others view the good as a quality intrinsic to human actions and intentions, independent of particular consequences (deontologists). In any case, all groups are interested in discovering a set of guidelines that will allow human beings to actualize optimally the good in their lives. In view of this, ethics may be considered an essentially Level 3 or 4 (contributory) enterprise. I do not want to imply here that people living on Levels 1 and 2 are unethical. As will be seen, they make, and try to live out, certain ethical assumptions, but frequently do not make them explicit. As a consequence, their ethical thought patterns are less clear and systematic.

As noted in Chapter Four (section III), all human beings, whether they be on Level 1 or Level 4, struggle with ethics. Fear, ego, jealousy, suspicion, contempt, and pride seem to manifest themselves very suddenly and with great impact. Nevertheless, it can be said in the same breath that clarity and systematization of one's intentions and thoughts help in actualizing the good. When one becomes more aware of what one wants and why one wants it, it becomes easier to recognize urges that are contrary to or even destructive of it. Even though one might indulge such urges, one might more quickly turn from them in the midst of indulgence. Levels 3 and 4 support ethics (the actualization of the good), while ethics supports the actualization of Levels 3 and 4. Before explaining this, it would do well to give a brief description of how ethics manifests itself in Level 1 and 2 personalities.

A. Ethics on the First and Second Levels of Happiness

First, it must be stated that most people on the first and second levels are interested in living out the first and most fundamental rule of ethics: the Silver Rule. It may be recalled that the Silver Rule states, "Do *not* do unto others what you would *not* have them do unto you." In other words, try to avoid harming others, and if you cannot avoid it, at least try to minimize the harm. This rule is far more restrictive than its counterpart, the Golden Rule, which states, "Do unto others as you would have them do unto you." This might be roughly translated as "Optimize the good for others." This "good" goes far beyond the avoidance of harm, though of course it includes avoiding harm. It could be an act of kindness, mercy, or patience; or it could be a gift of time, energy, creativity, or love, which go beyond mere avoidance of harm.

Most Level 1 and 2 people would say, "I don't want to harm anyone." They may say this out of a sense of conscience, love, cultural training, family training, societal expectation, and/or a self-appropriated principle. However, the emotions of the comparison game can very easily get in the way of this good intention. Jealousy, inferiority, fear, suspicion, contempt, emptiness, and ego sensitivity all have a way of short-circuiting even the most well-intentioned people. Furthermore, Level 1 and 2 people have difficulty understanding the Golden Rule because it is essentially contributory (Level 3 and 4). They may make statements like, "I am not responsible for doing anything more than avoiding harm. I carry my weight, they should too." Some Level 1 and 2 people, however, are very much enamored by the Golden Rule, but allow the emotions of the comparison game to be so dominant in their lives that their love for the Golden Rule becomes merely sentimental.

By merely sentimental, I mean believing that when one *feels* good about doing an action, one has, in fact, really *actualized* "the good" in that action. This one-to-one correspondence need not be the case, and therefore the good feeling could be quite misleading. For example, someone can have a good feeling that an act of genocide has "cleaned up the gene pool". Naturally, most people run up against the need to define "the good". This begins the process of cognitive ethics, or good thinking. Regrettably, good thinking and clear definitions do not necessarily instigate *desire*, and without desire, good thinking cannot be actualized.

As was noted in Chapter Two, each of the four levels of happiness represents a level of desire; and further, every person possesses each of these levels of desire. Hence, it cannot be said that dominant Level 1 or 2 personalities are devoid of contributory or ethical desire. But it can be said that this contributory desire is rendered ineffectual by the extremely strong manifestations of Level 1 and 2 desires, which are both pleasant (in times of acquisition and success) and unpleasant (the emotions of the comparison game). This emotional overwhelming of the contributory desire makes ethics less clear, less focused, less dynamic, and therefore, less efficacious. The suppression of Level 3 desire can turn the ethical enterprise into a kind of mind game, where ethical dilemmas force the abandonment of certain principles until there are no principles left except tolerance. When this point is "achieved" ethical relativism seems to be the only sensible solution. One may have the impression that there is something wrong with genocide (because it harms others), but one is not willing to risk making it a principle, because principles seem to have an unwavering quality. At the end of the day, some of our best minds will have dedicated themselves to the ardent defense of relativism, while believing that they were really trying to safeguard ethics.

This has the peculiar effect of making the prevention of harm *essentially* a matter of law (exterior controls) instead of a matter of ethics (interior controls). Law, necessary as it is, can never *replace* ethics. Law cannot be zealous for the good; it does not go the extra mile. It does not help one to move toward one's highest end. It acts as a barrier to those who lack all of these qualities. It tries to control from without (very expensively) what does not arise from within. If ethics is a healthy quality within the human spirit, law would be much less necessary, less expensive, and less cumbersome. Perhaps more importantly, culture attempts to orient people toward their highest potential, whereas law is in the business of settling disputes. It moves toward lowest common denominators and arbitration. Therefore, ethics, not the law, must be the basis of culture. We must use the legal system to protect the rights of individuals from those lacking interior principle (see Chapter Seven), but we cannot stop at the law. We must reach for the principles and virtues that will help the culture to help our people achieve their highest purpose amidst the common good.

Why do we then need a philosophy of the pro-life movement? Why not just settle for a law? Because even though a law would serve to protect the rights of the preborn and vulnerable, it would not impart the interior desire impelling us, as individuals and as a people, to transform our lives, our families, and our culture toward an essentially contributory community of love and the common good. The law is indispensable so long as there are people who would ignore the Silver Rule. Ethics is indispensable so long as there is a desire to bring our culture to the optimum of love and the common good manifest in the Golden Rule.

In my view, the more quickly one breaks away from the emotions of the comparison game, the clearer will be one's *need* for ethics. The clearer one's need for ethics, the stronger one's desire for it. And the stronger the desire for ethics, the more interested one will be in the truth of ethics where it may be found. The more interested one is in the truth of ethics, the more one is likely to give the benefit of the doubt to belief in *principles* instead of *relativism*. I am not trying to prove a case to anyone here, but only attempting to follow the pattern of reasoning that has led real people in my research to move from a position of relativism to a reasonable belief in principles. I appreciate the work of those who have committed themselves to cognitive ethics, but

I would ask them to test the above line of reasoning in their own courses and seminars. Can people be budged from an essentially relativistic position (even for their own good or the good of their families) if there is not some antecedent choice to move from the emotions of the comparison game to a contributory view of life? If my thinking is correct in this regard, it would do well to devote the lion's share of this section to looking at ethics from Level 3 and 4 perspectives.

B. Ethics on the Third Level of Happiness

You may have noticed upon completing Chapter Three that it is far more difficult to live the six fundamental attitudes than you might at first have thought. For example, you might have looked for the good news in a spouse or friend immediately upon completing the chapter. However, the next day, this fruitful endeavor could have been completely forgotten. It is difficult to remember Level 3 attitudes because they are not our "default attitudes". Other readers may have noticed that they were able to remember this change in attitude, but found it very difficult to maintain without expending a good deal of energy. The reason for this (explained in section II below) is that the new attitude has not yet achieved the status of a habit (an integral part of one's subconscious self-image and reflex responsiveness). Indeed, one's habit might well be to look for the bad news in the other. Therefore, one might find a part of oneself (the conscious volition) *trying* to look for the good news in the other, while another part of oneself (the subconscious reflex response) is looking for the bad news. The harder one tries to look for the good news, the more one winds up fighting oneself. This internal conflict, in turn, consumes energy and produces a variety of responses ranging from "giving up" to anger and resentment toward the new attitude.

For this reason, Eastern and Western philosophers and psychologists have, for over three thousand years, advocated the necessity of forming a habit in addition to making a choice about a new attitude. Choice is the conscious part of changing attitudes; building habits is the subconscious part. Freedom, therefore, cannot be reduced to choice alone; it must encompass the longer and more arduous enterprise of forming subconscious reflex responses (that is, habits).

It is absolutely essential, therefore, not only to choose the ideal of Level 3 and 4 as the *end* and purpose of one's life, but to locate the *means* of getting to this end, which can be turned into habits. Two kinds of habits must be attended to:

1. those pertaining to inner attitudes (virtues and vices)

2. those pertaining to outward actions (norms about right and wrong conduct)

The project of ethics must first identify any means that will very likely lead to or away from Level 3 or 4 ends. I do not intend to reinvent the wheel here. The last three thousand years of written history in both the East and the West have given rise to a distilled wisdom about the attitudes and actions that lead toward or away from a Level 3 or 4 end.

1. Virtues and Vices

My reading of history reveals seven major virtues and concomitant vices, which have been linked with the achievement of Level 3 and 4 ends, as shown in diagram 7.

The reader undoubtedly has both a conscious and subconscious awareness of the lived meaning of the above virtues and vices. Therefore, I do not intend to address them in great detail. Rather, I will examine them only as examples of one of the most important principles of ethical behavior: *it is not enough to know virtue; one must love it.* Love stands at the

Virtue	vs.	Vice
1. Self-control		Sensuality
2. Courage		Fear
3. Generosity and equity		Greed
4. Hard work/commitment		Sloth
5. Patience/peace of mind		Anger
6. Magnanimity		Jealousy/envy
7. Humility		Pride

Diagram 7.

core of desire, and desire is what translates knowledge into action. Love is more than mere appreciation. It directs the whole human psyche toward its objective. The more one loves someone or something, the more one is inclined to direct one's attention and action toward its good or actualization. Thus, if we are to promote virtue within the culture, it is not enough to make children or students aware of what traditional or contemporary wisdom says is virtuous. We must stimulate, provoke and promote the love within the student. How do we stimulate and provoke such love? By first provoking a love of the end that virtue helps to actualize (namely, love and the common good). How, in turn, can we stimulate a love of love? By the three steps mentioned in Chapter Three:

1. identifying the crises of the comparison game while pointing to their remedy (that is, contributory attitudes and looking for the good news in others)

2. taking explicit recognition of how contributory attitudes produce peace of mind, trust, and optimally meaningful and loving lives

3. noting how "looking for the good news in the other" promotes the possibility of love and the common good

It is not enough to be aware of these three steps. One must *live* them, *reflect* on this lived experience by oneself and with others, and, if one has faith, integrate it into one's life of *prayer*.

We live in a society that tends to think (at least implicitly) that knowledge is sufficient. Once I have a kind of "mental control" over material, once I have it organized or placed within a larger context, I become satisfied to the point of virtual complacency. I know it, I tuck it away, and therefore I've "got" it. Unfortunately, when it comes to virtue, one hasn't "got" much of anything by mere knowing. One needs the hard lessons of the heart, the trials, successes, and failures of attempting to live for contributory ends when life is not perfect, people are not perfect, and above all, I am not perfect. Love of others that transcends trials and imperfections becomes a love of love, a desire for love to be the end and purpose of life, a heart on fire for a purpose that is truly worthy.

The above point may be summarized as follows: living a Level 3 or 4 life leads to love of others, and love of others leads to love of love as the true end and purpose of life. Once one desires this love as an end, one must now attend to the means of achieving it. Most individuals recognize vices (attitudes that undermine love) before virtues. When we love children, it is frequently easier to see what endangers them than what promotes their good. One doesn't even have to think about such dangers. When dangers are present a mother immediately recognizes and acts against them. The same holds true for the love of love: one can feel and sense the attitudes that are antagonistic to it. Hence, when children learn ethics, it is frequently easier to show them what undermines love than what promotes it. They can then see the virtuous attitude in light of the vice and hence grow to love it.

This can be seen by looking at the above-mentioned list of vices. With respect to the first of the above-mentioned vices (sensuality), if one loves love as the end and purpose of life, one will feel an alienation toward sensuality that undermines a contributory attitude, a recognition of dignity and mystery in others, and the ability to commit oneself to others. Needless to say, drunkenness and lust do not promote a recognition of the dignity and mystery of others. But it is not enough to recognize this. One must *feel* an alienation from one's purpose, and therefore from oneself, when one is tempted to move in such a direction. This feeling of alienation should not be construed as an unhealthy or neurotic guilt feeling. On the contrary, it is the most healthy feeling one can have if one is attempting to live a life of love and high purpose. Yes, such feelings of alienation are painful, inconvenient, and sometimes debilitating, but nevertheless they provide counterfeelings to the ones that drive one to undermine one's higher self. *Knowledge* alone cannot combat *feelings* and *desires*. As Aristotle noticed long ago, one needs rational *desire* and, I would hasten to add, feelings of love and alienation to counteract the very powerful feelings of sensuality.

Please do not think that I am against the pleasures of food, drink, and appropriate sexuality. Obviously, these are integral to a complete life. Level 1 desires are not bad in themselves. Indeed, they lead to the good of the individual (to the satiation of hunger, to family life, and to growth in love). However, if Level 1 desires become ends in themselves, they not only limit the pursuit of the second, third, and fourth levels but also tend to undermine these higher levels.

When one experiences alienation from inappropriate sensuality (sensuality that undermines love), it becomes easier to love the virtue that counteracts this vice, namely, self-control. If one were to say to an adolescent, "Love the virtue of self-control, the virtue of self-discipline", he might well respond, "Why do I have to impose more discipline, more energy, more effort on this abstract pursuit? I have enough troubles in my life. Anyway, it's boring." Love of this virtue is not likely to arise out of a mere admonition to do so. However, adolescents can very much appreciate the love of contributory behavior, the benefits of looking for the good news, the mystery and the dignity of others, and so they can appreciate the love of love in others as the end and purpose of their lives. The deeper their experience of this love, the more poignant will be the alienation they experience from conduct that separates them from this love. And the more poignant their alienation, the deeper will be their love of the counteracting virtue. Adolescents need not experience such love and alienation in their own lives. They can appropriate it through empathy with others' life stories or from good books or films. They can experience it from religious stories, cultural myths, heroes, and sports figures.

The second of the above-mentioned vices (fear) provokes a similar response. To the degree that one loves love as the end and purpose of life, one will feel alienated from fears that prevent one from pursuing such love. If I fail to defend or promote my family, friends, community, and ideals in public because I am afraid of what others might think, I will feel alienated from my purpose and myself and even feel a sense of disgust with my behavior. When "fear of embarrassment" occurs, I experience a counteracting feeling of disgust at giving way to the fear. Now I must choose to act either toward the fear or away from it (toward my life's purpose and away from my disgust at betraying it). The choice is, of course, painful, and one could think that it is much easier to give way to the fear than to have to choose to act against it again and again. But in the end, repeatedly choosing to act against the fear is worth all the effort, for to give way is to betray one's highest meaning, friends, family, community, ideals, indeed, oneself. The harder path is clearly the more meaningful path. Hence, one should not despise the feelings of alienation and disgust in the hard choices of life; one ought to appreciate and even revel in them. They are the frontline defense of love and a life well lived.

When one is confronted by conflicting feelings in an ethical situation, it seems like one has two selves, that is, two faculties of consciousness.

I am reminded of Saint Paul's observation, "Why do I do what I don't want to do? I do the evil that I would not do, and I do not do the good that I would do" (Rom 7:15). Obviously Saint Paul feels passionate about conduct that undermines love, while at the same moment feels a disgust and bewilderment at those feelings. It bifurcates his personality. But he discovers that through love and faith, he has a "fighting chance" of doing the virtuous thing. If virtue is not easy for saints (who possess both love and faith), imagine what it would be like for someone possessing mere knowledge. Is the culture putting our adolescents in this position? Are we expecting them to be virtuous by arming them only with knowledge? Are we taking the proper steps to cultivate love within them? Are we giving them the experience of Levels 3 and 4 to cultivate that love? Do they have enough Level 3 and 4 heroes, stories, and examples? If they don't, the culture will likely allow its view of love to become more superficial until it is finally synonymous with the passions that undermine this love.

When one feels alienation and disgust at fear that undermines love as one's highest purpose, it becomes quite easy to love courage. In my view, courage is one of the easiest virtues to love. When I was a child all of my heroes displayed great courage, and I hoped that I would one day be equally courageous. I loved courage, or so I thought. Today as I reflect on it, I don't believe I loved "courage", but rather bravado and heroism directed solely at self-promotion. I loved the "courage" of a child. Mature courage sees that this false courage undermines love. Blind ambition and the pursuit of heroic self-promotion rarely promote an awareness of the intrinsic dignity and mystery of others. Thus, seeing a virtue in terms of the love of one's end and purpose (that is, love of others) is important to facilitate not only the *practice* of the virtue but also the *understanding* of the virtue. If I understand courage in light of love, I will immediately know that bravado, macho, and self-promoting heroism are not healthy "courage". The same holds true for self-discipline. One could, living out of one's self-discipline, be very tyrannical and judgmental of others who do not possess the same capacity. But if I understand self-discipline within the context of the love it serves, it will be obvious that such tyranny falls outside the bounds of healthy self-discipline.

We can, therefore, make a distinction between two kinds of virtue: (1) virtues that can be ends in themselves (ends virtues, such as love) and

(2) virtues that cannot be ends in themselves, but are necessary means to the end of love (means virtues). The seven virtues in diagram 7 are means virtues. They are necessary for love, but if turned into ends in themselves can act contrary to love. Self-control and courage are obviously necessary for love, but if they do not serve the purposes of love they can become quite judgmental, self-promoting, and even tyrannical.

The same characteristics may be noticed with respect to the third of the above-mentioned vices (greed). When one pursues a Level 3 lifestyle to the point where one desires love as the meaning and purpose in life, exaggerating the importance of material wealth produces feelings of alienation. A feeling of emptiness frequently arises out of trying to ground one's identity in mere things. These "things" are simply not enough. They're not worthy of being my primary purpose and focus in life. When one acts like they are, one feels empty. Again, these alienation feelings open the way to a love of the virtues of generosity and equity. These virtues are obviously consistent with Level 3 and require little additional explanation.

The reader will be able to see how a Level 3 lifestyle can also engender feelings of alienation with respect to sloth, anger, jealousy, and pride and how these feelings of alienation can open the way to a love of hard work/commitment, patience, magnanimity, and humility. Pride and humility, however, merit some special consideration. As noted above, pride exacerbates all the other vices. When one's whole ego, identity, goals in life, feeling of self-worth, and feeling of progress are anchored almost exclusively in a comparison (the "better than"), sensuality can now be exaggerated by the ego needs connected with it. Similarly, fear can be exaggerated if one's whole self-worth is on the line. Issues of ego control can certainly exacerbate greed, anger, and jealousy. But how does pride exacerbate sloth? When one cares only about how the world affects *me*, everything that does not affect me seems boring, uninteresting, and deserving of little energy.

Pride can also be quite insidious. It has the quality of being at times almost unnoticeable. It creeps up on a person and then pounces. Suddenly one finds oneself needing lots of praise, feeling overly sensitive about ego issues, filled with jealous rage or contempt, and if one is lucky enough to catch it, says, "Where is this coming from?" Frequently, many don't catch it at all, and it just keeps on going until friends and family members call it to one's attention.

By now it must be clear that a Level 3 lifestyle is antithetical to pride. The more one looks for contribution and the good news in the other, the more pride will produce feelings of alienation. Indeed, the longer one lives a Level 3 lifestyle, the more quickly one will notice pride when it arises. As mentioned above, these feelings of alienation pave the way for a love of humility, which carries with it the peace of an ego that is content with itself, the peace of an ego that does not have to pursue "the more" compulsively. This humility, in turn, becomes the means for even greater love.

In sum, it should be noted that one cannot simply embrace virtue; one must love it. To the extent that one loves others, one will also love the ends virtue and means virtues that will bring it about. The more one strives to live authentically out of these loves, the more habitual these virtues will become.

2. Norms Pertaining to Right and Wrong Conduct

Let us now turn to external conduct. Virtue and norms promote the same end: love. Virtues are interior means, while norms are exterior means to this end. Therefore, virtues are focused on attitudes, while norms are focused on actions.

As with the seven virtues mentioned in diagram 7, traditional wisdom has consistently pointed to five norms of conduct that will promote a meaningful or loving life, as shown in diagram 8.

These norms are undoubtedly quite familiar and intelligible to the reader. It will suffice to give a few observations about their relationship

Rules of Right Conduct vs.	Rules of Wrong Conduct
1. Respect for life	Harming life
2. Respect for person of others	Domination/servitude
3. Respect for property of others	Harming another's property (stealing, vandalism)
4. Truth and honesty	Lying
5. Fairness	Cheating

Diagram 8.

to each other and to the ends virtue (love). It should be clear that harming life and livelihood, domination and involuntary servitude, harming another's property, lying, and cheating are generally not in the best interests of love. Furthermore, the corresponding norm of right conduct can be seen to promote directly the cause of love (for example, respect for the life, person, and property of others, truth, and fairness).

These norms are an integral part of the legitimate expectations we have of others at home, in the workplace, and in our society. Indeed, they are so much a part of our expectations that we do not believe anyone can truly be ignorant of them and therefore use ignorance as a legitimate excuse. If someone were to go to court and say, "I didn't know assaulting him was wrong", or "I was really surprised to find out that I shouldn't have stolen that computer", we would probably laugh. These norms, therefore, constitute the implicit promises that we make to each other for the sake of good order. Therefore, they are the foundation of our laws and our beliefs about rights. As will be noted in the next chapter, the foundation of the law and rights is not the Constitution. Rather, it is the common expectation that all human beings know and are obligated by the above five norms. Thus, these norms do not simply apply to people living in the third and fourth levels, but also to people living in the first and second levels. People living in the first two levels are obligated by common expectation, implicit promises, and social contract. People on the third level are similarly obligated, but also see these norms as protecting and promoting love as their meaning and purpose in life. Thus, people living on the third level are *interiorly* motivated to *pursue* these norms for the sake of love, whereas people living on the first two levels are *exteriorly* motivated to *hold* to these values for the sake of order. Notice how different these two perspectives feel. People living in Levels 1 and 2 *have to* pursue them, whereas people living in Levels 3 and 4 *want to* pursue them. The first group could view the norms as constraining, while the second group could well view them as liberating. The first group might view them as something *to be observed*, while the second group views them as something *to love*.

I return once again to the point made in the previous subsection, namely, that love of virtue or the norm helps one adhere to the norm without external constraint. If I love the norm of respecting life, I do not need an external constraint or the threat of a penalty to carry it out. One might think that it really doesn't matter what one's motives are for living according to the five norms (that is, because one loves the norm, or because one fears an external penalty). So long as the norm is carried out, the interior reason for so doing seems irrelevant. But this is surely not the case. For if one reacts only to an external threat or constraint, what would happen if that constraint were not evident? What would happen if the threat were not severe? Wouldn't one be inclined to "take a chance"? These negative societal consequences are not the only reason for thinking that Level 2 ethical motivations are inferior to those of Level 3.

When Level 3 people act contrary to the norms of right conduct, they feel self-alienated. This was explained with respect to virtue in the previous subsection. People living in Levels 1 and 2, however, may not experience such feelings of alienation. They may not feel qualms about undermining love, because Level 3 love may still seem like an abstraction. Without these feelings of alienation, the temptation to lie or cheat for the sake of expediency may be quite overwhelming. One might begin to make ethical decisions on the basis of whether one is likely to get caught instead of on the basis of what is right or wrong. Indeed, the terms "right" and "wrong" may seem quite subjective, abstract, or even vague. Level 3 people, in contrast, will see "right" as being in conformity with love as their end or purpose and "wrong" as conduct contrary to love. They will not only understand this; they will feel it, desire it, and frequently actualize it.

There is yet another reason why a Level 3 approach to ethics is preferable to the Level 1 or 2 approach. Inasmuch as Level 1 or 2 individuals have no real love of the norm, they tend to relativize it. When they come up against an ethical choice, their instinct is not to hold firm to it, but rather to check out whether it is really applicable, to assess the degree of exposure, or, as usually occurs, to call a lawyer. Though these instincts can keep a person out of jail, they often do not arrive at the most responsible solutions. They frequently go contrary to the purposes of love and common good and can initiate cycles of hurt, vengeance, and even violence. They can undermine trust so severely that the courtroom replaces conversation, and governmental structures replace community. The "neighborliness" intrinsic to love, which forms the basis of community, is eclipsed by the boundaries, structures, and protections of a legal system gone too far. If the normal communication intrinsic to a healthy community gives way to unending legal intervention, the common cause that holds that community together will be replaced with fear and suspicion.

I am not here suggesting that we don't need boundaries and protections from people with criminal intent or psychotic delusions. I lament only the fact that many people think this is sufficient for the common good. Without neighborliness, community, and the societal expression of Level 3 love, the quality of our life and culture will substantially decrease. Yes, there will always be friendships, but society will never be the same.

To sum up, then, a Level 3 lifestyle promotes not only the love of others but also the love of love as the end of life. This, in turn, produces feelings of alienation when the above five norms are violated. These feelings of alienation not only help to combat temptation but also open the way to love of respect, truth, and fairness, which underlie the neighborliness, rights, common cause, and community that truly make life worth living.

C. Ethics on the Fourth Level of Happiness [1]

If one believes in an unconditionally loving God, and that God calls us to participate in this unconditional love, then one is likely to believe also that God has revealed the path leading to that love. One is also likely to believe that God will assist us in pursuing this path of love (that is, provide us with inspiration and grace).

How does the unconditionally loving God do this? In two ways: (1) by granting us the outer word (revelation through Scriptures and other means) and (2) by granting us the inner word (the peace that is beyond all understanding).

With respect to the outer word (revelation), it cannot be thought that an unconditionally loving God would not provide vehicles through which his unconditionally loving will would be made known in the world. Hence, it is reasonable to believe that God would send prophets,

---

[1] This next section concerns faith. Readers who do not have faith or are not interested in pursuing faith might want to skip to the next section. As noted before, this section is written specifically for those who do have faith and will want to integrate their faith into their personal and cultural philosophy.

inspiration, his Spirit, and, for Christians, even his Son into the world sublimely, yet concretely, to reveal the meaning and path to this love.

Much of what has been called revelation by the world's major religions includes the list of virtues and norms mentioned above. The New Testament, Old Testament, the Koran, and the Wisdom literature of the East address in great detail the meaning of these virtues and norms. But these texts do not simply treat these virtues as mere means to the end of love; they infuse these virtues with divine will and spirit. Humility, then, is not merely a prudent means to the end of love; it is a virtue loved by God and given by God to human beings to reach the end of Love. Humility, therefore, is not merely a human attitude; it is a gift of God to facilitate love.

It was noted above that understanding virtue was not enough. Love of the virtue makes it effortless and efficacious. Therefore, a person who loves God will love humility because it is a gift of the God he loves. This person does not love humility simply because it leads to love in the world; he loves humility because it is of the essence of God and is the gift of God. His love of God strengthens and increases his love of humility beyond any natural capacity. Thus, virtue, *as revealed by God*, is virtue more loved and desired, that is, virtue capable of being more lived.

With respect to the second way in which God is involved in virtue, that is, the inner word (the peace beyond all understanding), this peace comes through abandonment to his unconditionally loving will. I return once again to the central prayer of faith: "Thy will be done." When this prayer is said with confidence in the affection, goodness, forgiveness, kindness, and patience of God, God's response (at least in my faith life) is peace. This prayer and God's peace can transform fear into gentle courage, addiction into gentle fortitude, pride into peace and humility, expediency into respect.

How does this occur? As noted above, this peace is a feeling of being at home with God and the totality of all that is. The absence of such peace is a profound emptiness or alienation from that totality. The feeling of "being at home" accompanies and reinforces the various virtues and norms mentioned above, while the feeling of alienation accompanies the above-mentioned vices.

When I pray, "Thy will be done", I do not need tighter control to be virtuous. It is quite the opposite. Virtue comes from letting go into God's hands. This act of surrender gives a tremendous ethical freedom.

Ironically, this freedom comes not from trying harder, but from trusting more and trying less. One's psychic focus is not on what I am going to do or have to do, but on trusting in and entering into God's domain, being aware of God's home and love all around me, which in turn makes the temptation seem to slacken.

Being aware of God's home and love (and the peace it brings) does not guarantee that one will not succumb to temptation. The problem lies not in God's peace, but rather in *my* capacity to attend to that peace at any given time. I might be quite tired or might shift my intentional focus from being with him to the temptation. I might also be distracted or disturbed by memories, habits, compulsions, and addictions. Temptation can be extraordinarily complex. Despite the complexity and difficulty of maintaining attention to God's home and peace, there can be no doubt that "Thy will be done" is an essential aid in the pursuit of virtue; not a stoic virtue, but a gentle, loving virtue betokening the home from which it comes.

II. Freedom

In Levels 3 and 4, the notion and actualization of freedom follow directly from one's love and capacity for virtue. This is not the case for Levels 1 and 2, because their notion of freedom is quite different. I will therefore begin by differentiating the Level 1 and 2 notion of freedom from the Level 3 and 4 notion of freedom. The rest of the chapter will then be devoted to nuancing the Level 3 and 4 view of freedom.

A. "Freedom From" Versus "Freedom For"

In the Level 1 and 2 perspectives, freedom is viewed essentially as "freedom from", that is, escaping from present constraints, future constraints, demands of others, duties, and any other form of imposition. It may be recalled that getting and maintaining control is one of the primary objectives of a dominant Level 2 perspective. Relationships are frequently reduced to "comparison games" and "control games" instead of friendship and community in the pursuit of common cause. This perspective finds its way into one's feelings about freedom. One *feels* free when one is getting out of something, that is, getting relief or release from a potential obligation or constraint. Conversely, one *feels* unfree, hemmed in, or even enslaved when new responsibilities are "imposed", or when one is forced to focus on one course of action rather than another. These feelings creep into one's use of the words "freedom" or "choice".

Levels 3 and 4, in contrast, view freedom as "freedom for". Freedom is not so much getting out of something as pursuing and actualizing the fullness of one's potential. Since love represents this full potential, one feels free when one is *capable* of acting for the sake of others and the common good. "Freedom for" is concerned with building the capacity to actualize what is worthy of oneself. Therefore, unlike "freedom from", it seeks to focus, to discipline itself, constrain itself in the pursuit of that discipline, commit its future, and even obligate itself. It does not view these activities as "impositions", but rather as essential ingredients to the actualization of one's highest meaning and purpose.

Inasmuch as "freedom for" seeks to actualize what is truly worthy of oneself, and love is inherent to this full actualization, "freedom for" is essentially *commitment* to love. On the surface, commitment is a continued dedication, a capacity to pursue objectives through the difficult, boring, and adverse times. Such commitments are based on love, for merely conceiving, dreaming, or feeling good about ideals is not enough to get them actualized in times of adversity or emotional lows. One must want the ideal almost as much as life itself. In other words, the ideal must be so integral to a life well lived that one feels like a part of oneself is missing when the ideal is not being actualized. In many ways this is not like love of a person, who constitutes a transcendental mystery and can respond in creative, caring ways. But it does have one thing in common with love of a person, namely, that life seems radically incomplete without it. It is this feature that carries one through the most difficult times.

"Freedom for" is filled with love of its objectives and the persons involved in it; but as was seen in the previous subsection, this love, this desire to see the objective actualized through even the hardest of times, requires *means virtues*. It was noted above that love of persons (gift of self for the good of the other) would not be possible in hard times without self-control, courage, equity, patience, magnanimity, and above all, humility. The same can be said for commitment. What would commitment be without self-control, courage, equity, and patience? Without these means virtues, commitments to ideals would be mere dreams. Norms of right conduct are likewise integral to the pursuit of love, and so are also integral to commitment. Long-term commitments cannot be predicated on cheating, lying, harming life, domination, servitude, and harming property. Without truth, fairness, and respect, one's ideals and loves will be torn apart by inconsistency and self-destruction. Hence, "freedom for" and love, virtue, and the norms of right conduct go hand in hand. They are integral parts of the same weave. Such is certainly not the case for "freedom from".

It cannot be said that "freedom for" is completely distinct from "freedom from". Obviously, if I am pursuing a particular ideal, I may have to foreclose other pursuits in order to make time, energy, or psychic space available for my primary pursuit. This could be viewed as escaping constraint, "getting out of something", or "freedom from". This overlapping of the two "freedoms" should not obscure the answer to the key question of this section, namely, what is my *dominant* view of freedom, escape or commitment? When do I really feel free—when I view "freedom from" as an end in itself, or when I view it as a means to the greater end of "freedom for"?

One must be careful not to confuse one's personal view of freedom with a political view of freedom. Political interpretations of freedom are not meant to describe commitments or one's potential for an optimally lived life. They are concerned only with the very narrow range of problems surrounding the protection of citizens from undue constraint by hostile parties. Political freedom, then, is concerned with protection and so limits itself to the domain of "freedom from". Personal freedom goes far beyond protection to the domain of actualizing the fullness of one's potential. The government's job is to protect citizens from *abuse*. The individual person's job is to *optimize* potential. It is therefore incumbent upon civics teachers and philosophers alike to make students aware of this crucial distinction. If they do not, those same students might see their own personal freedom in terms of only the narrow range of political freedoms ("freedom from") instead of the optimization of their full potential ("freedom for").

It was said in Chapter Three (section IIIA) that Level 2 tends to view life as a problem, whereas Levels 3 and 4 lead to viewing life as an adventure and opportunity. If, for example, I have a comparative view of myself, I feel more easily threatened. I more easily view people as problems instead of mysteries. I see relationships as requiring control instead of seeking common cause. I can even view myself as a problem instead of a mystery. If life is a problem, and people are problems, and even I am a problem, my fundamental desire will be to *escape*. Hence, "freedom from" is an inevitable ingredient of Level 2's problematic view of life. In contrast to this, Level 3 views life in terms of contributions, love, and potentiality for this love. It looks for the good news in others and therefore tries to see the mystery in others. As a result, it elicits hope, love, and therefore *commitment*. "Freedom for" is, therefore, an inevitable ingredient of Level 3's orientation toward love.

"Freedom from" has several negative consequences for family, community, and culture. First, it shifts the focus of young people away from "goals that are worthy of me" to "what I don't want to do". It shifts the inner dialogue of choice within a young person from an essentially positive and proactive tone to a negative and reactive tone. This obviously stifles forward thinking, creativity, love, and all of the means virtues. It makes young people insular, self-protective, and even self-absorbed and self-pitying. It causes overreactions to rather small impositions and commitments and undermines long-term commitments (such as intimate friendships and marriage). It provokes the need for immediate gratification and immediate solutions to problems and leaves dormant the capacity for perseverance, determination, and dedication. If "freedom from" becomes the dominant way in which the culture collectively *feels* freedom, it will severely hamper the future of the family, ethics, love, and therefore, rights and the common good. It is therefore incumbent upon the pro-life movement and any other Level 3 organization to use every educational means at its disposal to move the culture from a dominant notion of "freedom from" to "freedom for".

B. Defining "Want" and "Choice"

One's beliefs about freedom are connected with what one wants. Unfortunately, we do not define the word "want" very carefully, and so we become confused about the true objective of our choice. My little niece said something like the following recently: "I really want that candy bar, but I should not eat it because I'll gain weight. Therefore, I can't have what I want." When one looks at this statement, one might say that my niece thinks she is unfree or that she is unable to get to her objective. But further scrutiny reveals that she is getting to what she really does want, namely, to remain slender. Thus, she is really exercising her freedom, but is convinced that she is not. My niece is not the only one to fall into this trap. The majority of Americans have, at some time in their lives, confused the intensity of desire with what they really want. This has caused them either to choose only the most intense desires or, like my niece, to choose what they really want, but believed that they did not. In either case, this misconception is likely to lead to greater discontent and superficiality within our culture.

If people believe that their most intense desire is what they really want, they will always move toward Level 1 and Level 2. As I noted in Chapter Two (section III), the lower level desires tend to be more intense, tangible, and immediately gratifying. In contrast to this, the higher level desires tend to be more pervasive, enduring, and deep. In order to move toward the higher level desires, one must *choose* the greater goodness intrinsic to what is more pervasive, enduring, and deep over what is more intense, tangible, and immediately gratifying. One must *choose* the greater intrinsic goodness of the objective over the greater intensity of desire, choose to delay gratification, and sometimes even choose to embark on a long and subtle search for the greater objective. If one confuses what one really wants with the intensity of desire, one will rarely choose what is more pervasive, enduring, and deep; one will miss a lifetime of opportunities to pursue what is intrinsically good, noble, and worthy of oneself. One may even miss the opportunity for love and virtue. This one "little" confusion could lead one to underlive one's life and underestimate one's potential. One may not even know what to look for in the area of happiness, contribution, common cause, love, and the common good. One may think that the satiation of intense desire is all there is to life.

A second negative consequence arises out of this misconception. If, somehow, like my niece, one manages to do what one really wants, but believes that it is not what one really wants, each act of "freedom for", each act that moves toward what is pervasive, enduring, and deep, will result in a dissatisfaction with one's life. One will constantly be fighting oneself to do what one really wants. Evidently, this can lead to bifurcation of personality, and dissociative behavior.

If the culture is to avoid both of the consequences of this misconception of "want", we will first have to correct it on an intellectual level. This can be easily done by making the distinction given in Chapter Two, section III, namely, there are two kinds of wants: (1) those that are intense and tangible, but not pervasive and enduring, and (2) those that are pervasive and enduring, but not intense and tangible. People will tend to *choose* what they think they really *want*. Whenever we are confronted by such dilemmas, we have to make reality by choosing either what is enduring and deep or what is intensive and tangible.

It must now be apparent that the above misconception also obscures the notion of choice. If I believe that the intensity of desire is what I really want, then choice is nothing more than simply letting the strongest stimulus prevail. I thereby become an implicit determinist. I am simply a stimulus-response machine that does nothing more than respond to the strongest stimulus. Freedom, therefore, seems to be an illusion.

However, if I am cognizant of the fact that I must choose between the intense/tangible and the pervasive/enduring in order to determine what I really want, then I am likely to use this power of choice in a way that does not always correspond to the strongest stimulus (the most intense feeling). Rather, I may choose an objective that has virtually no intensity of feeling but seems noble and good in itself. *After* choosing it, I could feel ennobled by the choice.

The second step in averting the two consequences of the above misconception is to use the power of choice. The more one uses it, the more one will recognize it and be inclined to use it in the future. If the culture, therefore, is to become truly free, it must make the distinction between the two kinds of wants and then use the power of choice to determine what one really wants. Anything short of this will likely result in a hedonistic, implicitly deterministic view of "choice" that will grossly debilitate the culture's potential for growth in love and the common good.

Once one intellectually recognizes the power of choice and makes use of it, it remains only to keep it informed. The more I know about the world, others, love, and virtue, the more I will be able to identify precisely the path I must follow to pursue that love. Thus, the fruitful actualization of what I really want depends on educating myself in the humanities, the sciences, the ways of commerce, and if one has faith, in theology and revealed truth.

C. Freedom on the Third Level of Happiness

"Freedom for" is connected to the development of habits. The love that makes commitment possible becomes permanent and continuous when one transforms it into a habitual response. The ancients referred to such habits as "second nature". First nature consists of the qualities with which one is born. Second nature consists of the permanent qualities that we bestow upon ourselves. We can bestow these qualities on ourselves by turning them into reflex responses, that is, responses that are so ingrained in our subconscious patterns that we no longer consciously have to will them into action. For example, when one has developed good study habits, one no longer has to fight oneself or exert great concentration to sit at the desk and open the book. If one is not exhausted, one very *naturally* and unthinkingly opens the book and proceeds to study. Clearly, the more habitual one makes the means virtues and the norms of right conduct, the more committed—the more *free*— one is to actualize one's highest purpose in life. Thus, any treatment of "freedom for" will have to explore ways of making virtue, norms, and love more habitual.

When one begins the process of change, one generally feels an internal tension that can last for two or more weeks. If I decide, for example, that I'm going to turn over a new leaf and study for two hours every evening after being in the habit of watching television, I will run up against almost immediate psychic conflict. It will feel like I'm fighting myself, like I have to exert tremendous energy and concentration to overcome the other habit. But after I get into it for approximately ten minutes, the internal conflict begins to subside. If I love my goal (for example, becoming a good attorney) enough and therefore continue to move through this threshold of inner conflict day after day, I will eventually find that it becomes quite natural to open the book and study. I don't have to fight myself any longer. I am free to do what was once so difficult.

The more emotionally complex a habit, the more difficult it is to form. Why? Because there are so many emotional avenues through which the old habit can fight or block the new one. There are five proven techniques that can help a person to form new habits in very emotionally complex areas.

The *first technique* concerns loving the objective of one's commitments. As mentioned above, the more one loves the objective of one's commitments, the more one's whole psyche is involved in moving toward this objective. This means that failure to achieve the objective will give rise to feelings of radical incompleteness. This provides the desire and emotional power required to move one through difficult or boring times. Such love is cultivated by reflecting on the goodness of the objective, or the good that can come from it, and attaching one's meaning or purpose in life to this particular good (Level 3). If, for example, one would want to be more self-controlled in one's passions, one would first turn to the goodness of love, that is, a life filled with contribution, common cause, looking for the good news in the other, and so on. When one *feels* and knows the goodness of such a life, one also will begin to feel alienation arising out of exaggerated sensuality, which is not commensurate with this goodness. This alienation, in turn, will reflect positively on the virtue that helps to overcome the alienation, namely, self-control.

The *second technique* of habit formation concerns awareness of what I will term "the threshold period". As one begins to actualize a new habit, one immediately encounters a period of maximum resistance. This period of maximum resistance generally lasts at least ten minutes, but is quite finite in duration. Love of one's objective (for example, the virtue of self-control) provides the emotional power to get through this threshold period. But love is frequently not enough, for one must also be aware that the threshold of resistance will eventually diminish and that the new habit will start taking on a momentum of its own. Without this awareness, one might believe that the period of maximum resistance will last forever. No one could stand such a thought without simply giving up. This, by the way, is why most New Year's resolutions fail.

The above can be summarized by the following equation:

1. strong love of a particular objective, *plus*

2. awareness of the finite time of the threshold period, *equals*

3. the emotional power to get a new habit off the ground.

Inattentiveness to either one of these techniques will result in yet another failed resolution.

The *third technique* concerns changing one's self-image to correspond to the new habit. If one has a conscious or subconscious self-image that is incommensurate with the new habit, it will be virtually impossible to move toward that new habit. If, for example, I subconsciously believe that I am not a self-controlled person, or that there is something about my personality that makes it too hard for me to be self-controlled, I will not be able to change. My subconscious self-image, which sets up my comfort zone, will make me feel like I am far outside that comfort zone when I pursue self-control. This feeling of discomfort will make me subconsciously correct my behavior until I am back in my comfort zone. If I am out on the golf course and I begin to score a seventy-five, my subconscious might well say, "That's not like me. I never score a seventy-five." I can be sure that I will not score seventy-five by the end of the game, because my subconscious will correct my behavior until I'm back where I am "supposed to be".

Our self-image is derived from a variety of sources in our childhood, adolescence, and adulthood. We pick up comments from our parents, teachers, bosses, friends, and family members and transform them into beliefs about ourselves. A teacher might say, "You can't draw." If I give that teacher sufficient credibility, I will believe the statement and transform it into a belief about myself. In the future, whenever I am asked to draw something, I will become nervous and even display not only psychological resistance but also physical symptoms of discomfort, which will assure that the product of my hand looks like it was done by an infant.

Some people mistakenly believe that change is a matter of stoic self-discipline. "All I have to do is force myself to be a community leader, and eventually I will get used to it, and the habit will be formed." Nothing could be further from the truth. If being a community leader lies outside of, or is contrary to, my self image, then forcing myself to stay outside that self-image (outside my comfort zone) will do nothing more than make me experience a panoply of negative emotions (boredom, anger, fear, alienation, and even panic). These emotions will become so burdensome that I will eventually feel compelled to return to my comfort zone and abandon the process of change. I will probably also be too scared to pursue that change again: "I don't want to feel those emotions again. That was too hard. That confirms it. Being a community leader is not like me." Therefore, forcing myself past the threshold period without first checking that a new habit is commensurate with my self-image will serve no purpose other than frustration and retreat. If I want to appropriate good habits, I must first check my beliefs about myself.

There are many techniques for changing self-image in order to appropriate new habits. The most common ones involve *visualization*. When I visualize or picture myself being a self-controlled or courageous person and love myself in these visualizations, I will, over the course of time, accept and appropriate that new self-image in my subconscious. At this point, I will have expanded my comfort zone. Once I feel comfortable with the new habit as part of myself, I can then implement the first two techniques and begin the process of habit formation.[2]

The *fourth technique* concerns reinforcing one's new self-image. As noted above, one's subconscious self-image can take the form of a voice saying, "You're not good enough to do that." In order to facilitate visualizing the contrary, one needs to hear one's own voice, or the voice of a mentor, repeatedly saying that one *is* good enough to do that. One can write this down on a daily basis, say it to oneself, and listen to one's mentors. The repeated voice eases the process of visualization, which in turn expands the comfort zone and allows one to pursue the new habit.

Obviously, one must also pursue the skills and education necessary to be good enough to accomplish the objective. It is not good enough to *say* that one is good enough when the reality is not there. But it is also the case that many people do have the skills and education to do something that they tell themselves they cannot do. Both reality and self-image must be engaged if appropriate new habits are to be formed.

The *fifth technique* concerns the use of prayer. If one has faith, one will clearly want to bring the power of prayer and grace into the process of change. As I have made clear above, faith gives rise to a peace and humility that I cannot bring about for myself. These two qualities give rise to a detachment from old habits that greatly facilitates the process of change. This peace and humility can cut through the tension at the beginning of change and make possible what might otherwise have been an insurmountable obstacle. This will be discussed in the next subsection.

---

[2] Lou Tice, *Smart Talk for Achieving Your Potential: Five Steps to Get You from Here to There* (Seattle, Wash.: Pacific Institute, 1995).

D. Freedom on the Fourth Level of Happiness[3]

The fourth level of freedom is quite different from the other three in that it is grounded in an act of surrender rather than an act of emotional power or will. Even though the third level of freedom ("freedom for") is quite open to prayer and grace in its orientation toward love, it is based upon moving through the threshold period by an expenditure of emotional energy and a correction of self-image. The fourth level of freedom can be quite compatible with this, but it begins first and foremost with surrendering to God's will. Once I have abandoned myself to divine providence, once I have *chosen* to let God's will be the all-important reality in my life, I can then situate the above-mentioned five techniques within the peace and home that this providence brings. The deeper the surrender to God's unconditional love, the greater the peace and detachment from passions and old habits, which, in turn, eases the way through the threshold period and any changes in self-image that may be required.

Surrender to God's love not only eases the way to change; it also gives guidance along the way. The only difficulty with the third level of freedom is that it relies so heavily on *my* perception of the good or noble objective. The problem is that my perception is partial, filled with scotomas, and weakened by pride and self-interest. What if I have a radically incomplete view of love or virtue? What if I could not properly apply a good definition of love and virtue to my life? What if I have an incomplete or misconceived self-perception? What if I pursue the wrong order of objectives leading to love and virtue in my life? I could prolong or even undermine the very desire to move toward love and virtue that lies at the heart of God's will. At this juncture I need more than an act of surrender to be free. I need God's self-revelation in the world (in Scriptures, the church community, and worship). I need to surrender to a specifically applicable manifestation of God's unconditional love so that I might be able specifically to conform to his loving will in my life. When "freedom for" is seen only through the third level, one can never be sure that one is moving

---

[3] This next section concerns faith. Readers who do not have faith or are not interested in pursuing faith might want to skip to the next section. As noted above, this section is written specifically for those who do have faith and will want to integrate their faith into their personal and cultural philosophy.

toward optimal love. The only way of assuring this is to try to conform oneself to the will of unconditional love in every way one can. God is not only peace; he is truth. He is the peace and truth of unconditional love. Surrender to him alone will bring this truth. Everything short of it leaves me waylaid with doubts about the incompleteness of my ability to grasp the depth and breadth of the destiny that he has prepared for us all. But if we surrender and open ourselves to the multiple manifestations of his reality in the world, then he will be our companion on the journey. His truth will be our light, and his peace will be the staff that supports us.

E. Freedom and Abortion

At the moment a woman is confronted with the "choice" to abort her preborn child, there can be no doubt that she feels the pressure of multiple constraints. Why would she take the life of the fruit of her womb unless she feels a greater anxiety if she does not? How can she reject what is intrinsically lovable and integral to her being unless it is provoked by fear or some other equivalent anxiety? Rejection of one's preborn infant is not natural. If this be the case, it seems almost inevitable that a woman who "chooses" abortion is reacting to the very strong and intense emotions of the moment. I am not in any way undervaluing the deep anxiety she must feel as she confronts this decision. On the contrary, her anxiety could be nothing other than intense in order for her to make the decision to abort.

If this "decision" is not to be an unreflective manifestation of "freedom from" (an immediate accommodation to the strongest stimulus—Levels 1 and 2), and if this decision is, therefore, to be made within the context of "freedom for" (Levels 3 and 4), then it would seem essential to offer some form of counseling where this mother could again become cognizant of the ideals of Level 3 (love, virtue, and commitment) so that she would be able to choose between what is intensive/tangible and what is pervasive, enduring, and deep. As noted above, "choice" is not merely exercising the option of the most intense emotion, but rather choosing what is less intense but more intrinsically ennobling. The vast majority of mothers would certainly view the birth of their child to be far more intrinsically ennobling than an abortion. Yet, the intensity of the moment could push a mother away from this noble objective.

If people are sincerely "pro-choice", why would they be against a prospective mother examining her meaning, purpose, and happiness in life before she made her so-called choice? Why would they be against her rekindling a Level 3 view of self-worth and love in her attitude toward herself? What would be wrong with reawakening her love of love as the highest purpose in life? Should we not at least try to support and comfort her Level 3 identity as well as the intensity of her emotion at a given moment?

Does "comfort and support" really mean letting a person choose according to the momentary intensity of her emotions? Does "comfort and support" mean allowing a person to run from what is most pervasive, enduring, and deep? Jesus, Gandhi, Socrates, Moses, and Mohammed all comforted their disciples, but never like that. The great philosophers and leaders who built up the possibility of economic justice and the common good sought to comfort the citizens of this world, but never like that. They preferred a comfort and support that may not have been the easiest, but nevertheless made accommodation for what was most pervasive, enduring, and deep. They knew that the comfort they sought for the people they loved would, in the end, be undermined by their failure to announce the whole truth about purpose, self-worth, love, virtue, and freedom. They knew also that the whole truth would not always be the easiest, but would certainly promote the highest dignity for the human mysteries who so touched their hearts.

Since this matter is of such significance to the future of our culture, since the use of the word "choice" in this hotly debated political arena will so keenly influence how our culture will view itself and its potential, it would seem incumbent upon the "pro-choice" movement to define its view of "freedom" and "choice". Once defined, we can together examine how it affects the interpretation of the other nine categories of cultural discourse (happiness, success, self-worth, love, suffering, ethics, personhood, rights, and the common good). Then, as citizens, we can decide which set of definitions is preferable for the future of our culture. We can decide with informed choice which definitions are most complete, most respectful of the multifaceted dimensions of the human person, and most likely to lead to a flourishing of love and of our culture.

F. Freedom and Euthanasia

Euthanasia can have similar negative effects on the view of freedom which, in its turn, would negatively impact the view of commitment, virtue, love, person, and rights. The direct negative impact of euthanasia will be taken up in Chapter Ten. This section will be limited to a brief exploration of how euthanasia erodes the notion of freedom.

"Freedom" in the Level 3 or 4 perspective is the key to a pervasive, enduring, and deep life. It is the vehicle through which *commitment* to these goals, which may not necessarily be tangible, immediately gratifying, and emotionally intense, can be actualized. Thus, "freedom" in this perspective must be rational, detached from the intensity of momentary emotion, and open to what is pervasive and enduring. The rhetoric underlying euthanasia necessarily views freedom in a different way. To begin with, euthanasia necessarily views death as better than life. Therefore, it can never be oriented toward what is "enduring". Secondly, euthanasia is necessarily a voluntary cessation of contact with the human community; therefore, it cannot be oriented toward what is pervasive. Thirdly, euthanasia is the antithesis of commitment, because commitment requires both a future and a connection with somebody or something beyond myself. Thus, euthanasia may be a "choice" or an "option", but it is certainly not "freedom" in the Level 3 or 4 perspective.

This points to a much deeper problem within the culture, namely, that "freedom" is viewed as an end in itself instead of as a vehicle to what is most pervasive, enduring, and deep (for example, optimizing love, justice, good beyond self, and faith—Level 4). If "freedom" were to be viewed as an end in itself, then the most we could do in life is to have many options and make many choices, but we would be going nowhere in particular. Multiplicity of choice would replace direction toward a worthy goal. This would be the most pitiable of legacies to leave for our youth. It would truly create not only a lost generation but also a superficial one. In order to leave our youth with something worthy of their time, energy, and struggle, we must again help them to focus on what is the deepest possible meaning of their lives. *After this,* we can focus on the choices and freedom they have to get there. It cannot be thought that the rhetoric of "death as ultimate choice" will *not* affect our youth. They pick up cultural cues more readily than we can possibly realize. They will convert this rhetoric of euthanasia into a

mantra about "'freedom' as *mere* choice" before we see the implicit
implications of our slogans. Indeed, many of our youth are already full-
fledged believers in this mantra and are doing everything that they can
to live up to our "highest expectations" of them.

Actions speak louder than words, and euthanasia speaks most loudly
because it concerns death with which youth have a continual fascination. If death really is a solution, and choice of death is really the "ultimate choice", then goals, commitments, relationships, virtue, and love
simply slip off our youths' mental radar screens. Perhaps our young people won't buy the rhetoric. Perhaps they'll see the inherent flaws in the
rhetoric of "death as ultimate choice", but if they don't replace it with
what is pervasive, enduring, and deep, if they don't rise above it with
ideals, discipline, and virtue that is truly worthy of themselves, they are
likely cynically or passively to disregard the cultural legacy we have left
them. In either case, the result is at best pitiable.

It is not simply youth who are adversely affected by the rhetoric of
euthanasia. The elderly are most severely affected. Anyone who has visited a nursing home can tell you that when the residents first arrive,
they are bewildered and lost. They feel disconnected from family and
friends as they move into a new community of people who are still
strangers to them. This is the point at which they need desperately to
define "quality of life" and "self-worth". If they define these two identity categories from a Level 2 point of view, their experience in the
nursing facility is likely to be miserable. As their physical powers diminish, so too do their capacities for achievement, winning, admiration, control, and the other objectives of Level 2. Thus, their view of
themselves and the worthiness of their lives will likely decline to the
point of incipient despair. If, however, they define their self-worth in
the perspectives of Level 3 and/or 4, the diminishing of their physical
powers could be a means of enhancing their capacity for wisdom, virtue, love, forgiveness, and faith (see Chapter Five). This enhanced love
could be communicated to the future generations who surround the
elderly in their time of need. The effects of such love and the compassion of the next generation could last in families (and also in the culture) for decades. The last years of life could be, therefore, the most
poignant.

Ironically, at the very moment our elderly people need the most help
to bring their later years into focus for this important and poignant life

mission, they receive the least. Very few nursing homes or enhanced care facilities explain the possible options for defining quality of life, for either their residents or their families. Instead, they may be given several legal documents with various medical procedures to choose. Many have no idea why they would choose one rather than another. Now, add to this confusion a brand new "option": euthanasia. What does this say to the elderly about the worthiness of their lives? "Instead of seeking treatment for pain and depression so that you might pursue your poignant mission, you have the option of committing assisted suicide." No matter how much we attempt to "gussy up" the assisted-suicide option, our elderly people will read the message about "no self-worth" into it. They are, after all, sensitive, intelligent, and filled with life experience. In the quiet moments of reflection after the option has been presented, they will get the message. This message has two devastating effects. First, it could prematurely terminate the most poignant part of their lives, and second, it will bias their life interpretation toward Level 2. It will compel them to regress in their most mature years. This message will, in turn, be communicated to all the younger generations surrounding this elderly person, and hence they will absorb the same Level 2 meaning in life.

If freedom is informed choice, if it is rational and detached from the emotions of the moment, if it is open to what is most pervasive, enduring, and deep, then euthanasia is contra freedom, for euthanasia does not promote informed choice. It is not oriented toward looking at the various options for meaning and purpose in life. It does not patiently educate and elicit the deepest parts of the human personality. It does not seek a profound view of freedom or love. It simply suggests that death is better than life and that death is the ultimate choice. We do an incredible disservice to our elderly with this option. They are persuaded to throw away what could possibly be the most poignant part of their lives, to diminish their self-worth, and to view their greatest gift to the next generation as "final exit".

There is yet another, perhaps more serious tension between euthanasia and freedom. This concerns the imposition of a *duty* to die. At first glance, euthanasia may seem like a new option or freedom, but we must probe more deeply into the psychology and sociology of such an "option". When the medical profession offers this option to an elderly or terminally ill person, an implicit pressure can be created to make use of it, even when that person is of a mind *not* to do so. This might occur because of explicit or implicit pressure from a family member, a friend, a doctor, a lawyer, or even an insurance company. It could also occur in far more subtle ways: the tone of voice or the facial expression of a family member or physician who explains the "option" to the elderly person. A misconception may surface that pain control or hospice care is expensive or unduly burdensome to family or friends. The elderly patient might believe that hospice care is not covered by insurance or that pain and depression are untreatable.[4]

One can imagine thousands of scenarios in which an elderly or terminally ill person might begin to feel a completely *unwarranted pressure* to make use of the new "option" to die. Such pressures are well documented in the Remmelink Report[5] and in the literature of death and dying. In 1998, Derek Humphry, founder of the Hemlock Society, suggested that many of the elderly may have an explicit "duty to die—a responsibility within the family unit—that should remain voluntary but expected nonetheless". He justified that, "Medical expenditures at the end of life are disproportionately high, while the elderly consume a disproportionate amount of health care resources", and added, "economics, not the quest for broadened individual liberties or increased autonomy, will drive assisted suicide to the plateau of acceptable practice".[6] Needless to say, all "options" are not "freeing". Some impose

---

[4] To the contrary, medical professionals have long known that "ninety to ninety-nine percent of terminal cancer pain can be controlled with the use of hospice and palliative care units" (Martin L. Smith, M.D., et al., "A Good Death: Is Euthanasia the Answer?" *Cleveland Clinic Journal of Medicine* 59 (1992):99–109. See also Michael H. Levy, "Medical Management of Cancer Pain", in *Principles and Practice of Pain Management*, Carol A. Warfield, ed., (New York: McGraw Hill, 1993), p. 235. In a personal communication to Carlos Gomez, M.D., Dr. Pieter Admiraal (a Dutch anesthesiologist, clinical pharmacologist, and leading advocate of legalized euthanasia) has been quoted to the effect that pain control and alertness can be achieved in practically all cases—given sufficient effort and sophistication on the part of all involved. The World Health Organization also affirms similar statistics with respect to pain control for the terminally ill (*Cancer Pain*, World Health Organization, Geneva, 1990). Even Derek Humphry (the founder of the Hemlock Society and author of *Final Exit*, a controversial "self-help" book) admits that "only a small percentage of terminal physical pain cannot be controlled today" (*Let Me Die Before I Wake: Hemlock's Book of Self-Deliverance for the Dying* [Los Angeles: Hemlock Society, 1984]), p. 76.

[5] *Medische Beslissingen Rond Het Levenseinde (Medical Decisions about the End of Life)*, 2 vols. Vol. 1, Report of the Committee to Study the Practice concerning Euthanasia; vol. 2, The Study for the Committee on Medical Practice concerning Euthanasia. (The Hague, 1991).

[6] Derek Humphry and Mary Clement, *Freedom to Die* (New York: St. Martin's Press, 1998), pp. 313–15.

implicit and explicit duties on large populations of people. In the case of euthanasia, we have an option that imposes the most *unfreeing* duty on one of the largest populations within our culture, namely, the duty to die. If we allow this movement to continue, it will not only bias our view of freedom toward Level 2; it will also annihilate our freedom altogether in an unwanted duty to die.

It might be objected that somebody really might "want" to die. So I return to the question that animated the above discussion on freedom, namely, is "wanting" succumbing to the strongest emotion of the moment, or is "wanting" the informed, rational pursuit of what is most pervasive, enduring, and deep? If we do not have this latter definition of "want" before us at the moment of our decision, we would not be acting in freedom, but only out of impulse (strong, momentary emotion). We would believe ourselves to be acting in freedom, but would be as far from freedom as we could possibly be.

An example of this can be found in the case of "Louise J". Louise was a terminally ill young woman who committed suicide in 1993 with assistance from Ralph Mero of the Seattle-based suicide organization "Compassion in Dying". In a lengthy article for the *New York Times*,[7] the author, who was granted permission by the family to be present at the suicide, recounts Louise's serious hesitations just days before she died:

> Louise became silent. All her calm words about being certain, of wanting to die, masked the real point. Everyone—Mero, the mother, the doctor, the friend, and, most significant, Louise herself—had described suicide as something Louise wanted, a poetic expression of control, a triumph over the indignities of disease. But what Louise really wanted, it now became clear, was simply to not be sick any more. If she couldn't have that, then suicide was a second choice. Suicide was not a victory, but rather a nightmarish end to a nightmare.... Earlier in our conversation Louise had denied feeling frightened. But now, lying ashen-faced, less than a foot away, she looked terrified.
>
> "It's O.K. to be afraid", her mother said.
>
> "I'm not afraid. I just feel as if everyone is ganging up on me, pressuring me", Louise said. "I just want some time."

From the article, it's not clear whether Louise received adequate treatment for depression. But it is clear that her friends and family assumed

---

[7] Lisa Belkin, "There's No Simple Suicide", *The New York Times*, Nov. 14, 1993, pp. 48–75.

her strongest emotions were an indication of what she really wanted and that she was therefore engaging in an act of self-determination. If we, as a culture, believe in this illusory freedom, we will never bother to pursue what we really need in order to live our lives to the full. We should deeply consider the devastating effect this could have on our youth. It is therefore incumbent upon us as a culture to challenge one another to define "want" in the moment of decision. If we do not, we will reduce ourselves to mere creatures of impulse.

In sum, the incomplete and even illusory view of choice/freedom implicit in the abortion and euthanasia issues have the potential for undermining commitment, virtue, and love, not to mention life principles that are pervasive, enduring, and deep. If we collectively subscribe to them, they are sure to lead not only to superficiality but also to an undermining of the rights of human beings. This will be discussed in the next chapter.

Chapter Seven

Person, Rights, and the Common Good

Introduction: The Relationship Between Person, Rights, and the Common Good

In the introduction to the book I noted that our view of "person" influences our view of rights, which in turn influences our view of the common good, which in turn influences the development (or decline) of the culture. First, it must be stressed that our view of rights is meaningless without our view of "person", for everything we believe about rights turns on this view of "person". Rights belong to persons. Therefore, if a culture were to declare a class of human beings to be nonpersons, those human beings would be systematically deprived of rights. This is the logic behind every form of prejudice and removal of rights. Society may proclaim, "All persons are endowed with inalienable rights of life and liberty." But if it subsequently claims that a certain class does not qualify as persons, it can, of course, refuse to acknowledge their inalienable rights. One can now see how dangerous a subjective view of "person" is (see Chapter One). If the majority within a society were, in the absence of an *objective* definition, to declare persons to be those with excellent tans, a fair-sized minority from northern climates would be in trouble. Therefore, we need not only an objective definition of "person", but as complete an objective definition as possible.

Secondly, our view of the "common good" is dependent on our view of rights. The "common good" can be a very precarious concept, for it can be interpreted in a totalitarian way that disregards harm to particular individuals. For example, I might initiate a new cultural revolution that could enhance the income of all citizens by $5,000. One could hardly deny that this would be *a* common good. However, in order to accomplish this, approximately one million people will have to starve to death. In view of the fact that 200 million people will benefit, a large number of unaffected citizens might consider this "unfortunate" loss to be tolerable. Therefore, for the good of the "whole" (totality) we might decide as a group to pursue this objective. We might, then, resoundingly pass an initiative despite the fact that the unfortunate one million are screaming that it is a "tyranny of the majority".

This little example is not as farfetched as it might seem. Consider the totalitarian excesses of Stalinism, the Khmer Rouge, Nazi Germany, and the Cultural Revolution in China, to mention just a few. What is the problem? Is it that the common good is dangerous? No. Rather, the common good *without rights* is dangerous. Rights acknowledge not only the intrinsic goodness of the individual but also the qualities required to maintain the life and humanity of this intrinsically good individual. These qualities cannot be removed even for the sake of the "whole". Hence, rights contain a prohibition to society, namely, that the good of the whole cannot lead to the removal of those qualities necessary for the individual to survive as a human being. Notice that the protection of society can supersede the inviolability of a person's rights when that person is violating the equal or greater rights of another, but it cannot violate rights merely for the good of the whole. In brief, rights theory is a protection against the concept of the common good becoming a totalitarian tyranny of the majority. There are certain things that the good of the whole cannot supersede. The two most widely acknowledged of those are life and liberty.

Thirdly, the common good (with its accompanying recognition of rights dependent on a complete, objective definition of "person") is responsible for the development (or decline) of the culture. A culture is not merely a set of common values or an impetus for common welfare and progress. It is a living expression of these values and this impetus toward the future. As such, what we believe about the common good will determine our view of common cause and common direction. If that view of the common "*good*" is totalitarian, then our common cause and common direction could support prejudice, injustice, and even the elimination of a significant part of our population. Therefore, our notion of the "common good" could lead to cultural decline. Fortunately, the opposite is also the case. If our view of "person" is rich, our view of rights and the common good will also be expansive and deep, and this in turn could lead toward substantial cultural development.

Therefore, the above definition of "person" is more than a mental exercise. It is more than a philosophical inquiry. It is the real determining force of rights, the common good, and the development of culture. Nothing could be more important. This is not "book learning". This is not a "language game". It is a concerted attempt to discover, in the most complete and objective way, what a human person is so that those persons might be protected and their rights acknowledged. But more than this, the expansive definition of "person" will lead to an expansive definition of the common good, which will in turn lead to the development, rather than to the decline, of culture. We owe it to the culture, to our children, and to ourselves not only to come to as complete an objective definition as possible, but also to set our *hearts free*—to care about this definition and its cultural implications.

Up to this point in the book, I have attempted to set out an objective definition of "person" (Chapter One) and to show its implications for happiness, success, quality of life, self-worth, love, suffering, ethics, and freedom (Chapters Two through Six). It now remains to connect this view of "person" to a view of rights that will protect all "persons" and therefore the common good. In order to do this, it might be best to restate the three conclusions to Chapter One (section V).

A. Definition of "Person"

A "person" is a being possessing a guiding impetus toward fulfillment through unconditional, perfect, unrestricted, and absolute Truth, Love, Goodness/Justice, Beauty, and Being. This definition will be considered valid irrespective of whether the above-mentioned "guiding impetus" originates from merely genetic sources, a spiritual source (such as a soul), or both. We have seen how these unconditional qualities manifested themselves in our pursuit of happiness, success, self-worth, love, ethics, and freedom. Together, they betoken an intrinsic, unconditional dignity inherent in human individuals and their interpersonal interaction and unity.

B. The Critical Principle

Inasmuch as *any* being should be treated with a dignity commensurate with its nature, persons should be treated with an *unconditional* dignity commensurate with their guiding impetus toward fulfillment in *unconditional* Truth, Love, Goodness/Justice, and Beauty. Such a dignity acknowledges not only the intrinsic worth of a human being but also the intrinsic *unconditional* worth of the person. This unconditional dignity is, in the last resort, the ground of inalienable rights, which acknowledges a universal duty to protect and promote this unconditional dignity. More than this merely political consequence, the acknowledgment of this unconditional dignity grounds a *desire* for the common good and *care* for the other and so frees the heart to pursue friendship and love, and a culture worthy of both.

C. The Critical Assumption

In view of the intrinsic, unconditional dignity of the human person, we *cannot* in any way risk destroying it, for this dignity does not belong to us. It is *intrinsic* to the person. Furthermore, the harm done would be unconditional and absolute in its proportion (commensurate with the nature of the person). Hence, we cannot risk violating the Silver Rule (do no harm), for a harm here would constitute the destruction of unconditional dignity. In order to prevent such an unconditional harm, we must, as a culture, make a critical assumption:

> *Every being of human origin is a "person" (as defined above) with an intrinsic, unconditional dignity.*

Perhaps the greatest harm done in human history has been to assume that a being of human origin was *not* a person (not possessing an unconditional dignity). We can see this with respect to slavery in ancient and recent times, genocide, and totalitarian political persecutions of every kind.

Doubt about personhood should never be considered a warrant for denying it. This could lead to pervasive, unconditional harm, based not on certainty but on doubt. Given these consequences, I must restate the critical assumption in even bolder terms:

> *When in doubt, err on the side of assuming and according personhood to every being of human origin, whether or not the activities of that being manifest the above unconditional qualities of personhood.*

Failure to do this will simply cause us to repeat the errors of history.

I have presented one approach, which I consider to be most capable of manifesting the nature of the human person and therefore the real presence of human personhood. Many other approaches have been tried. I consider these approaches to be incomplete or essentially subjective. These approaches fail to grasp the complete essence of the human being and leave themselves open to excluding real persons from social and legal personhood and therefore from just protection under the law. Any approach to personhood that does not recognize the full essence of humanity runs the risk not only of being elitist, but of actually taking away inalienable rights that properly belong to the person and not to the agent removing them. Hence, I am here writing not as an academic, but as a concerned citizen and human being. I feel myself to be coresponsible for other fellowmen and hold myself accountable to their inalienable rights. As such, I criticize others' views of "person" not because I think I'm right, but because I think that these alternative views of "person" are hurting both individuals and our culture.

I. Inalienable Rights

Abortion and euthanasia are clearly human rights issues. The pro-life movement calls itself the right to life movement. "Pro-choice" advocates talk about abortion rights, privacy rights, and the right to die. Neither side explains what they mean by the word "right". People claim to have rights, states protect or "create" rights, but rarely does anyone define rights. Before we can sort out the competing claims made by both ends of the political spectrum, we must define rights in as complete, objective, and rigorous a way as possible.

Human "persons" by definition possess those inalienable rights because they have an unconditional dignity commensurate with their impetus toward fulfillment in unconditional Truth, Love, Goodness, Beauty, and Being. As noted above, we must assume that every being of human origin is a "person" (possessing an unconditional dignity). Otherwise, we risk doing unconditional harm (destroying the unconditional dignity) to both individuals and the culture. "Unconditional harm" means either the destruction of unconditional dignity or undermining the very *possibility* of exercising the powers of one's personhood (the pursuit of unconditional Truth, Love, Goodness/Justice, Beauty, and faith). The possibility of doing unconditional harm obligates us to unconditional respect. No government or state obligates us to respect human beings. The unconditional dignity of human beings (which makes possible unconditional harm) obligates us to unconditional respect. This *obligation*, which all human beings by virtue of their unconditional nature elicit from all other human beings, is an *inalienable right*.

A. The General Notion of a Right

The concept of "rights" refers to legal conditions that are either necessary or desirable for the fulfillment of human personhood within a society or state. Rights are obligations of the state or other individuals toward the individual person. They may be *inalienable*, which means they belong to the individual by nature and can neither be taken away nor surrendered (see above), or *extrinsic*, which means they are established by law and may be removed by law (for example, the right to free press or to bear arms). Prior to 1400, political theory focused mostly on the state's obligation to protect and provide for the common good of its citizens. However, devaluation of human personhood, capricious rule, and the eclipsing of the good of the individual by the good of the group produced an abusive climate that led many political thinkers to conclude that the common good and individual good had to be addressed simultaneously.

The notion of "rights" arises out of this need to address both interests. "Rights" must be acknowledged to mediate between the common good and individual good. A right is a good of an individual, which, if protected, will contribute to the common good. A right is an individual good that cannot come into conflict with the common good and without which the common good cannot be achieved. This balance between the common good and the individual good alleviated much governmental abuse. Rulers could no longer automatically crush individual good by invoking the common good or allege that serving the interests of government sufficiently protected individual interests.

The reality of inalienable rights is recognized by Thomas Jefferson in the Declaration of Independence. Inalienable rights are intrinsic, natural possessions of the person because persons have an unconditional dignity eliciting unconditional respect from others. At the very least, this unconditional dignity obligates others not to commit an unconditional harm to fellow human beings (that is, to destroy unconditional dignity or undermine the very *possibility* of exercising the powers of one's personhood).

Just as individuals are obligated to refrain from unconditionally harming beings of human origin, so also is the state, for the state's purpose cannot be contrary to the unconditional obligations of the individuals who constitute it. Hence, the state's primary duty is to protect the inalienable rights of its citizens. Note that this is an intrinsic duty of the state. Citizens of the state don't give its government a mandate to protect inalienable rights; rather, a state by its very nature is obligated to protect inalienable rights. Otherwise, it opposes the very individuals who constitute it. It would be, as it were, an intrinsic contradiction. Any state that does not protect the inalienable rights of its citizens loses its raison d'être and thereby becomes illegitimate.

There is, of course, an exception to this logic, which is the person who has become a threat to the inalienable rights of other citizens or has actually infringed on those rights. Part of the state's role in protecting the inalienable rights of citizens is defending them against foreign or domestic aggressors. Any person who persists in threatening or infringing upon the inalienable rights of others must be prevented from doing so. This is the ground of the state's power to police.

Hence, the *inviolability* of inalienable rights does not extend to persons who violate the rights of others. Such persons may be incarcerated—a *violation* of their inalienable rights to liberty and the pursuit of happiness—but they still *retain* their inalienable rights. Inalienable rights may be violated, their exercise may be limited for just cause, but they cannot be taken away. Violation of the rights of aggressors contributes to the common good by protecting the rights of their potential victims.

Extrinsic rights (or "positive rights", also called "alienable rights") must be distinguished from inalienable ones. Extrinsic rights do not belong to human beings by nature. Violating them does not cause unconditional harm (as do killing and slavery). Rather, they are generally connected with the fulfillment of a specific function, such as free speech or freedom of the press, and they are important for the existence of a democratic government (which acquires legitimacy through the will of the governed and through protection of the inalienable rights of all).

Because extrinsic rights are given by the state, they can be taken away by the state. For the more important extrinsic rights, this could be done by a constitutional amendment, which would require a two-thirds majority vote of Congress and the state legislatures. If a majority in a democratic polity declare certain liberties to be rights of citizens, these liberties become extrinsic rights until such time as the majority of citizens decides they no longer want them to be rights. This may, of course, never happen, but it is, in theory, possible. (A Constitutional amendment eliminating freedom of the press or freedom to bear arms is theoretically possible.)

Inalienable rights, in contrast, are not attached to a particular constitution or to a particular form of government. They are antecedent to the state. There could be, and are, many ways of building a government that would equally protect inalienable rights. The key is that inalienable rights cannot be taken away by the will of the majority. The majority may decide to violate inalienable rights, but it cannot take them away. They still belong to the individual by nature. The individual still owns them, even when they are being violated. (It would, of course, be irrational for a majority so to act, for in negating the inalienable individual rights of a citizen or class of citizens, the group would, by definition, delegitimize the state under whose authority such a decision is made and thereby deprive themselves of their own delegated authority to pass such legislation.)

In sum, then, human beings possess inalienable rights simply because they are human, no matter what the form of the local state. If the state fails to protect inalienable rights or tries to violate them, the state loses its raison d'être, its legitimacy, and ultimately throws into question the appropriateness of its existence.

If the inalienable rights of the people are the ground of governmental legitimacy, and therefore the state's legitimacy is subordinate to the inalienable rights of its citizens, then diagram 9 should express the objective priority of a state's and government's legitimacy, from the most fundamental to the least fundamental.

This prioritization is essential because it determines the proper end of legitimate government and distinguishes that end from the various means to that end. Protecting the inalienable rights of the people is the most fundamental end of legitimate government. This involves seeking the common good and pursuing the objective demands of justice—the

1. Inalienable rights of all citizens
2. Common good/objective demands of justice
3. Raison d'être and objective of the state
4. Legitimacy of state
5. Power to enact a constitution and/or power to actualize a specific
   form of government

Diagram 9.

second category in diagram 9. Therefore, justice and the common good must answer to inalienable rights. That is why inalienable rights are ranked first, and common good/justice second. The legitimacy of the state must be grounded in the state's proper end, protection of the common good and pursuit of justice, each of which in turn must be grounded in the inalienable rights of the governed. All four of these primary categories must be acknowledged before a constitution can be enacted.

The authors of the United States Constitution had no power, in themselves, to enact a constitution. Their power was chiefly derived from their purpose: to protect the inalienable rights of the governed, the common good, and the demands of justice. Absent that purpose, the Constitution would have been nothing more than an unenforceable collection of procedures heading nowhere.

The Constitution does not derive its legitimacy solely from the "consent of the governed"; consent, too, is subordinate to inalienable rights, the common good, and the demands of justice. The Constitution only has legitimacy insofar as it is used to protect the inalienable rights of persons and only insofar as the operative definition of "person" *is as broad as the broadest understanding of human person.* This last point is extremely important because it shows that no constitution can be legitimate without a definition of "person" that will protect the inalienable rights of all persons constituting the state. This makes the critical assumption mentioned in section I above a necessary condition for the legitimacy of the state and its constitution: *Every being of human origin must be considered a "person" with an intrinsic, unconditional dignity.* If a state fails to make this critical assumption, it risks doing unconditional harm to the persons constituting it, which, in turn, undermines its raison d'être.

The corollary to the above critical assumption is also a condition necessary for the legitimacy of the state and its Constitution: *When in doubt, err on the side of assuming and according personhood to every being of human origin, whether or not the activities of that being manifest the above unconditional qualities of personhood.*

Therefore, if a state is in doubt about personhood, it must do everything within its power to protect it until it is *certain* that such "personhood" does *not* exist. Failure to do so risks unconditional harm to the persons constituting it, which in turn undermines its legitimacy.

The Constitution deserves immense respect, but even greater respect is due the inalienable rights of persons, for such rights are the basis of the Constitution's legitimacy.

The power to bestow extrinsic rights and the power of plebiscite (voting) arise out of the authority of the Constitution. They, too, are subordinate to inalienable rights, the common good, and the demands of justice. Hence, their low ranking in diagram 9. Consequently, one cannot legitimately vote inalienable rights out of existence or pass legislation that violates inalienable rights, the common good, or justice. *Nor can one legislate or define an extrinsic right that violates the inalienable rights of the governed.*

These categories and their relationships must be kept straight. If they are not, then very likely inalienable rights, the common good, and justice will be increasingly violated by the extrinsic rights of a majority, or even a select few. This will not only undermine the legitimacy of the government; it will also create the conditions for the very "tyranny of the majority" the national founders feared, in which 51 percent of the citizenry could violate the inalienable rights of the other 49 percent. Such a result is not explicitly prohibited by the Constitution. Only our fundamental awareness that the purpose of government is to protect the inalienable rights of all citizens will allow us to see through the attractive rhetoric of special interests or issues that could be used to that end.

Much has been made of the United States being a democracy, or at least a democratic republic. This can be very misleading if "democracy" is not defined. If our analysis is correct, then democracy does not mean merely "government *by* the people"—by plebiscite or by election of legitimate representatives—but also government *of* the people and *for* the people. Currently, government *by* the people is overemphasized. Wisdom is sought in opinion polls, not in thoughtful analysis. Legitimacy is sought in majority votes, not in fidelity to the fundamental aims of government. "*By* the people" refers to the procedural elements of diagram 9: representative government and direct plebiscite. Indeed, our current overemphasis on procedure is, to some extent, culturally determined, for today's culture is particularly enamored of the expression of subjective preferences and impatient with rational constraints.

In contrast, "*of* the people" and "*for* the people" refer to the first five levels in diagram 9. "Of the people" refers to inalienable rights and the demands of justice and the common good. "For the people" reminds us that government exists for *all* the people; government does not have the right to violate the inalienable rights of any one person, let alone a specific group of persons. To do so would be to violate the objective demands of justice and the common good, and therefore to violate the state's own purpose. This, in turn, would undermine the state's legitimacy.

If "we, the people" allow the inalienable rights of any person or group to be undermined, we negate the "*we*" and surrender to the government power over "*us*" in that we allow the government to have a purpose independent of "us" and of our inalienable rights. We allow the government to be an end in itself. A government that becomes an end in itself is potentially totalitarian, whether or not it adheres to democratic procedures, for totalitarianism is not defined by its forms or procedures but by its purpose. Specifically, totalitarianism is defined by its purpose to usurp the power to alienate what is inalienable—to equate extrinsic and inalienable rights and to juggle or replace them, willy nilly. We, as educated citizens, must never lose sight of this. If we do, we will have a democratic form of government without human rights. We will have a government "by the people" that is neither "of the people" nor "for the people". We will have democratic forms, but totalitarian content.

B. Three Inalienable Rights

As noted above, all individuals are obligated to avoid unconditional harm to human persons. Two such unconditional harms are easily discernable: killing and slavery. There is a corresponding inalienable right to each unconditional harm. Since death is obviously an unconditional harm to a human being, life is considered an inalienable right.

Similarly, slavery is an unconditional harm to human beings. By "slavery" I mean either ownership of a person or not allowing someone (in principle) some measure of autonomous conduct. Inasmuch as self-possession is necessary to be a person (as defined above), whatever undermines the very *possibility* of self-possession (such as slavery) must do unconditional harm to the person. It is therefore a violation of the inalienable right to liberty. The inalienable right to liberty does not pertain to freedom of every sort, but only to what is necessary for the *possibility* of self-possession in order to pursue truth, love, goodness/justice, and faith. Hence, I do not have an inalienable right to free speech, because free speech is not *necessary* for the *possibility* of self-possession. I do, however, have an inalienable right not to be owned or to have all of my conduct controlled by another, for these two activities would undermine the very possibility of being self-possessed. Inasmuch as free speech is not an inalienable right, it must be declared to be a right by constitution, plebiscite, or some other juridical means. It is, therefore (as was noted above), an extrinsic right.

Some thinkers have included property in the list of inalienable rights. This is true to the extent that property is necessary to avoid serfdom. Property rights gave people the ability to have some autonomy within their domicile so that the lord of the realm could not control another's activities while legitimately in his domicile. (A man's home is his castle.) Hence, property rights were viewed as an extension of freedom within one's domicile, of the ability to conduct oneself as one chooses so long as one is not violating the equal or greater rights of another. Inasmuch as serfdom is defined as "not having autonomy in one's own domicile", it causes an unconditional harm to a human person because it undermines the possibility of self-possession. In this restricted sense, then, property could be considered an inalienable right. However, property is not an inalienable right in the vast majority of cases, because most property ownership is not necessary for the possibility of self-possession or life itself. Hence, I do not have an inalienable right to a Mercedes 500 E-class, because I still have the possibility of being alive and self-possessed without one.

*C. The Objective Prioritization of Inalienable Rights
and the Resolution of Rights Conflicts*

Social situations often create conflicts between inalienable rights, and if there were no objective priority of one right over another, rights conflicts would have to be resolved either by subjective mandate or by compulsive force. There is an objective hierarchical order to these three rights, however, which can be determined by considering which right is necessary for the existence of the others. This ordering may be termed "an ordering by objective necessity" or "an ontological ordering".

As might by now be obvious, the right to life is a condition *necessary* for the *possibility* of the right to liberty (the possibility of self-possession). If I am not alive, the possibility of my self-possession is a moot question. Likewise, it must also be acknowledged that the right to liberty is the condition *necessary* for the *possibility* of the right to property (ownership of one's domicile), for the ownership of property is a moot question if someone owns *me*. The contrary is not the case. One can be alive without being self-possessed, and one can be free without owning property.

From this we can draw the following conclusion: Even though all three inalienable rights are required to prevent an unconditional harm to human beings, the right to life ranks higher than the right to liberty, and the right to liberty ranks higher than the right to property, by objective necessity. By "higher rank" is meant the right that must take precedence in a rights conflict.

This prioritizing of fundamental rights is not our invention; it is intrinsic to reality. It is not only Jefferson's language in the Declaration of Independence; it is the basic logic of the American legal system. To violate this structure—which is based on objective necessity, not on subjective assertion—is to remove rights conflicts from the realm of reason and reality and open them to adjudication by raw power or arbitrary whim. Subjective assertions of rights, without a basis in objective necessity, are arbitrary and fall prey to the legal adage "arbitrarily asserted, arbitrarily denied". But more, reducing the law to whim and the dictates of arbitrary power conjures up Hobbes' "state of nature" in which life was solitary, poor, nasty, brutish, and short. Governments exist to deliver people from just such a brutish state.

Abortion presents a perceived rights conflict between the preborn's inalienable right to life and liberty and the mother's inalienable right to

liberty (self-possession with respect to her own body). This is a legitimate rights conflict that must be resolved objectively. Objective necessity requires that the child's right to life supersede the mother's right to
liberty, because life is the necessary condition for the possibility of liberty.

Obviously, this resolution of the conflict has not been law in the
United States since 1973. Instead, judicial thought has resolutely avoided
considering questions of personhood and has strenuously avoided applying the logic of the rights structure upon which the law is based. By
intellectual abdication to political pressure, the courts have unnecessarily reduced this area to a conflict of subjective assertions backed by raw,
arbitrary, and irrational power.

There are limits to irrational judicial power. When a state asserts a
subjective ranking of rights that violates objective necessity, human beings of common sense will eventually recognize this and will also recognize that not only has the state put its subjective and arbitrary will
above reason, it is in fact claiming the power to bestow and deny inalienable rights. Such a claim is a breathtaking usurpation with grim
logical consequences, for no matter how carefully written the Constitution, when interpretation of the Constitution departs from reason
and objective necessity, the rule of arbitrary whim will follow, yielding
chaos or tyranny—probably both, in that order. There is no middle
ground between objective reality and arbitrary whim. Reasonable people will obey a government of reason and objectivity, but they will correctly identify a government of whim as intrinsically illegitimate.

I am not denying that a woman's control over her body during preg-
nancy is an inalienable right. Nor do I suggest that it is easy for her to
allow impingement upon this right. Nevertheless, rights conflicts must
be resolved, and they must be resolved according to an objectively necessary order subject to the demands of reality and reason. There is no
other basis for ordered freedom. To protect that order, and therefore
the inalienable rights of the people, sacrifices must sometimes be asked
of individual citizens. But these sacrifices must also be subject to objective necessity and rational order. (For example, no citizen ought to
be asked to give up the right to life when only an extrinsic right or
perhaps a less fundamental inalienable right is at stake—the sacrifice
must be commensurate with the danger.)

There are many resolutions of rights conflicts that follow this principle, such as the temporary conscription of an army at a time when a

hostile power threatens to eradicate the life and liberty of the entire populace. Obviously, the conscripted soldier not only sacrifices his Fourteenth Amendment protection against involuntary servitude (an "extrinsic right" based on liberty), but should the worst happen, the inalienable rights to life and liberty as well. Given the gravity of these sacrifices, the state is obliged to be sure that the risk to the citizenry is also to life and liberty. For the state to sacrifice citizens involuntarily for extrinsic rights, or for purposes of economic happiness or other convenience, is intrinsically wrong and violates the system described above (and upon which this country's law is based). Were such disproportion to occur, people of common sense would again ferret out the illegitimacy of imposing subjective governmental will contrary to objective necessity and rebel against it.

Rights conflicts must be resolved; otherwise they will become social conflicts. Governments are aware of this and generally attend to rights conflicts. Unfortunately, legislatures or the courts sometimes do not attend to the criteria used to resolve rights conflicts (that is, determining whether objective or subjective criteria are used). But as has been shown above, the criteria used to resolve rights conflicts are just as important, and have as many long term implications, as the specific resolution of rights conflicts themselves. To resolve a rights conflict according to a subjective criterion, when an objective criterion could have been used, is nothing more than a usurpation of inalienable rights by the state, because the state views its authority to be superior to that of objective necessity and reason. To resolve a rights conflict by a subjective criterion contrary to objective necessity is to sow the seeds of civil discontent, for people who value inalienable rights grounded in objective necessity will not easily have their rights unjustly taken away by arbitrary and irrational usurpation. A government that does so will create social conflict with only two possible outcomes:

1. collapse of governmental legitimacy and dissolution of the republic

2. tyranny, in which an illegitimate government destroys the expression of inalienable rights, ignores objective necessity, and stays in power by ruthless and deceitful application of terror

There is more at stake in the abortion issue than the annual toll of 1.5 million human lives in the United States and many millions more abroad.

D. The Universality of the State's Protection of Inalienable Rights

This section is exceptionally important, for we live in a culture that tends to subjectify principles, viewing objective principles as arbitrary, thereby making all principles violable, or at least open to exceptions. However, I would maintain that there are inviolable principles that are neither arbitrary nor open to exception or subjectification; these principles are intrinsic to inalienable rights, and without these all rights theory collapses. These inviolable principles are beyond any subjective disagreement because they are objective and can be known as logically necessary in the same way that any necessary principle can be known in logic or mathematics—that is, through the principle of noncontradiction.

In order to explain this, we must review three logical first principles:

1. *The principle of noncontradiction.* Whatever is logically contradictory is logically and ontologically impossible and, therefore, logically and ontologically false.

2. *The principle of objective necessity.* The contrary of any contradictory (and therefore impossible and false) proposition is necessarily true.

3. *The principle of objective universality.* Any proposition that violates the principle of noncontradiction cannot exist anywhere—not in any possible universe in any possible place or time—and any proposition that is objectively necessary must be true for all possible universes at all possible places and times.

With respect to the first point (the principle of noncontradiction), it is logically impossible for a "square circle" (whose boundaries are defined by Euclidean geometrical axioms) to exist in the same respect at the same place and time. Imagine, for example, a two-dimensional piece of wood. And imagine that "square" and "circle" are defined by Euclidean axioms such that a square must have four interior right angles, and a circle not have any interior angles at all. Now try to imagine the piece of wood in the shape of both the square and the circle in the very same respect (with the same internal area) at the same place and time. You are probably trying to flip back and forth between the two possible shapes without achieving any success in combining them. The reason for this by now should be clear. The *boundaries* of "square" (a shape with four interior right angles) *exclude* the *boundaries* of "circle" (a shape having no interior angles). Another way of talking about the exclusion of these boundaries is to say that they *contradict* one another. This harks back to a well-known principle considered to be the founding principle of all logic, namely, the principle of noncontradiction: No real object can possess boundary A and boundary not-A in the same respect at the same place and time.

For example, a table cannot be both three foot five (A) and three foot six (not-A, that is, *not* three foot five) in the same precise respect, place, and time. The boundary of "three foot five" *excludes* the table from also having the boundary of "three foot six" in the same precise respect, place, and time. The boundary of "three foot five" *excludes* or *contradicts* the boundary of "three foot six". Hence, any proposition that declares that three foot five and three foot six could exist in the same respect, place, and time is a contradictory proposition; this contradictory proposition is impossible and, therefore, false.

What I will show below is that there are certain propositions in rights theory that are also subject to the principle of noncontradiction and therefore subject to objective necessity and to objective universality. But I must explain these latter two concepts before we can proceed.

The second principle (the principle of objective necessity) is quite simple. It merely states that if a proposition is logically contradictory, then its impossibility must be objectively true. For example, if a square circle (as defined above) is impossible, and therefore objectively false, then the impossibility of square circles must be objectively true. If a table being both three foot five and three foot six in the same respect, place, and time is impossible and objectively false, then the impossibility of the table being both three foot five and three foot six is objectively true. The reason why the words "objectively true" or "objectively false" are used here is that no subjective disposition, no act of willing or imagination can make an impossible proposition true. Not even Albert Einstein, with all his imaginative power, could make square circles exist, as defined, no matter how hard he tried. The reason for this is not traceable to any lack of creative imagination on the part of Albert Einstein. Instead, it is traceable to the exclusionary properties of boundaries. Even if a person were to have *perfect* creative abilities, he still could not conceive of a square circle as defined above. If a person is not forced to assent to this truth, he has only one alternative: to say that he has successfully combined two contradictory boundaries in the same respect, place, and time. Any reader who can do this should report to the author at once.

With respect to the third point (the principle of objective universality), any objectively necessary truth is also an objectively universal truth. That is, it must be true for all possible universes at all possible places and times. Back to our example of the square circle, a square circle as defined by Euclidean axioms could not exist in Washington, or in Africa, or even in another universe at the "end" of a black hole. It will not exist five years from now or a billion years from now. It did not exist fifty years ago, and it did not exist eight billion years ago. The reason for this, again, is that the *boundary* of square excludes the *boundary* of circle.

The principle of noncontradiction shows how undeniability arises out of necessary exclusion. But undeniability can also arise out of necessary inclusion; that is to say, there are some "things" that are necessary for the possibility of other things. For example, a line (a one-dimensional geometrical configuration) is necessary in order for a plane (a two-dimensional geometrical configuration) to exist. And a plane is necessary for a cube (a three-dimensional geometrical configuration) to exist. One might say that if the first dimension did not exist, the second dimension *could* not exist, and if the first and the second dimensions did not exist, the third dimension *could* not exist. Another way of expressing this same truth is that the first dimension is *necessary* for the possibility of the second dimension (though not vice versa), and the second dimension is necessary for the possibility of the third (though not vice versa). No amount of willing, imagining, or sincerity will bring a two-dimensional object into being without a first dimension, or a three-dimensional object into being without the first two. Furthermore, there is no universe, place, or time where a three-dimensional object can exist without the first two dimensions, or a two-dimensional object without the first. Such is the nature of reality.

Now, inasmuch as a necessary truth is a universal one, it must apply equally to *all* possible situations. More specifically, inasmuch as the objective prioritization of rights is objectively necessary, it must apply equally to *all* people, in all nations and situations, for all time. Thus, as applied to rights, the state must protect the inalienable rights of *all* persons within its domain. If it does not do this for even one person (even one preborn person who must also possess his own present and future existence), it forfeits its legitimacy. The state cannot pick and choose which persons' inalienable rights it will protect, because its authority is contingent upon the objective necessity (and therefore, the objective universality) of inalienable rights themselves, and upon its own fidelity in protecting them for all.

There are, therefore, three *universal* duties that *every* state owes to *all* individuals constituting it:

1. Every being of human origin must be acknowledged to be a "person" (and therefore entitled to the protection of his inalienable rights). If the state does not do this, it risks doing pervasive, unconditional harm to whole groups of persons.

2. Once the state has acknowledged the personhood of all beings of human origin, it is obligated to protect their inalienable rights from those both inside and outside the state who would cause such persons unconditional harm. Recall that inalienable rights (those belonging to persons by nature) are specifically oriented toward preventing unconditional harm (that is, the destruction of a person or the undermining of the very possibility of exercising the powers of personhood). All other "rights" are extrinsic rights. Needless to say, inalienable rights take precedence over extrinsic ones, for protection of the former is necessary for the legitimacy of the state to proclaim the latter.

3. Rights conflicts (for example, the preborn child's right to life versus the mother's liberty right to custody over her own body) must be resolved according to the criteria of objective necessity (the conditions necessary for the possibility of . . .). Should a state use criteria in conflict with objective necessity, it becomes arbitrary and capricious in its use of power. This not only risks great social dissent and conflict but also undermines its own legitimacy.

In sum, the legitimacy of the state is grounded in the personhood of beings of human origin, the inalienable rights of those persons, and the objective prioritization of those inalienable rights. *Not vice versa.* The advocacy of a contrary position would mean that the state is answerable to nothing, that the state would have no raison d'être, that it would become, as it were, an end in itself. This, of course, is a recipe for arbitrary power, social conflict, unconditional harm, and tyranny. The genius of Jefferson was to recognize that the unconditional dignity of the person supersedes and therefore legitimizes the power of the state. Regrettably, he did not explicitly extend his definition of "person" to all beings of human origin (he owned slaves). This oversight perpetuated immense social injustice and perhaps even the Civil War and its aftermath.

E. The So-Called Principle of Clarity and an Example of Its Misuse

Many in the abortion debate have indicated that even though the right to life is more fundamental than the right to liberty, the preborn's right to life should be subordinated to the mother's right to custody over her own body (liberty), because the mother's right is *clearer* than that of the preborn. Preborn infants, after all, are not visible. Their appearance is different from that of full-grown human beings. Furthermore, they are far more dependent for their survival than fully grown human beings.

The bogus nature of this so-called principle of clarity can be easily exposed by considering the following:

1. Clarity is always in the eyes of the beholder. It is not objectively necessary. It is dependent upon the intelligence, acuity, perspective, and whims of the perceiver. For a person unfamiliar with mathematics, the Pythagorean Theorem may well be unclear. As noted above, this does not mean that it is invalid. For the untrained eye, an X-ray of a man's shoulder might appear to be normal, but a radiologist may see several hidden fractures. Unclarity to the novice does not mean that the fractures are not there. Millions of similar examples can be given for every aspect of reality and human knowledge. Clarity is not an *objective* principle; it is merely a skill of perception acquired through discipline and study. Much of this skill is based on definition and interpretation. Therefore, it can never be made into a principle to resolve rights conflicts. Newtonian physicists saw *clearly* that space was a Euclidean vacuum. Common sense would not permit it to be otherwise. Albert Einstein was much less clear about this view of space, and, in the end, he turned out to be correct.

2. The "principle of clarity" has been used by the elite throughout history to place their subjective priorities over those of the marginalized. The following example shows how this can be done effectively when a society decides to abandon objective principles (such as the objective prioritization of inalienable rights) to merely subjective "principles" like that of clarity.

Let us suppose that self-conscious life capable of pursuing higher level desires (love and transcendence) has been found on Mars and transported to the earth. Let us suppose that Martians do not look like Earthlings, and that because of this many Earthlings question their personhood. Let us further suppose that according the Martians liberty rights will adversely affect the property rights of many influential members of Earthling society. Not only will according Martian liberty rights destroy a potential source of cheap labor, but also Martians may begin demanding social services (which could raise taxes, unless working Martians pay enough tax to compensate for the increased services required). Martians may begin competing with Earthlings for hourly wages or buying homes in prestigious neighborhoods—which could harm property values in those neighborhoods and introduce alien (Martian) ideas into the public schools.

All of these considerations could hinder the property rights of many influential people who would like to own Martians (and industries that use Martian labor) and would be hurt economically by full recognition of Martian personhood. There is a clear rights conflict here between the Martians' liberty rights and the Earthlings' property rights. Recall that the Martians' opponents are not certain that Martians are persons and therefore are not sure that Martians deserve rights or perhaps even humane treatment.

To resolve this rights conflict, one must first decipher the rights claims and then prioritize the rights according to objective necessity. In the case of the Martians, even though much of the populace is uncertain about their personhood and hence their liberty rights, this uncertainty must be resolved according to the broadest possible understanding of "person". As noted above, failure to do so could result in the arbitrary and unjust violation of *all* the inalienable rights of *all* Martians. The broadest understanding of personhood requires that the Martians' personhood be recognized before any other societal good can be pursued. If this is done, then it must be admitted that the Martians have inalienable rights.

Once the inalienable rights of Martians are presumed, a rights conflict emerges, that is, between the liberty rights of the Martians and the property rights of the Earthlings who would like to own them.

Given that, in our case study, there are reasonable appearances of higher level desires in Martians, and given the objective hierarchy of rights we have outlined, it is clear that the rights conflict must be resolved in favor of Martian liberty, even though that resolution will necessarily entail injury to the property rights of many Earthlings. Liberty is a higher claim than property and must therefore win the conflict.

The Martians' prospective owners may allege that our objective hierarchy can apply only to rights that exist without ambiguity. This argument would assume that the law can operate solely within the limits of *clarity* (a most interesting hypothesis, given existing judicial experience) and that therefore the state should accord rights on the basis of clarity and adjudicate only between clear, unambiguous rights, without taking into account the above principles. Applying this clarity principle to our example will reveal its immediate weakness, namely, that one cannot base a decision about rights simply on the criterion of subjective clarity, but rather must base it on objectively necessary principles about rights holders and according and prioritizing rights. Failure to do this will not only detach the resolution of rights conflicts from objective principles; it will also likely produce laws that will be very clear, but will lack connection to the common good of the citizenry.

Let us analyze the conflict between the Martians and their prospective owners from the standpoint of clarity. Since it is not clear that enslaving Martians is evil, and since it is very clear that freeing them will produce measurable financial harm to their prospective owners, if the law is to operate in accordance with the greatest clarity, the Martians must be enslaved. The clear financial interest of the owners must triumph over the unclear liberty rights of the Martians.

This is not a merely theoretical concern. This nation did exactly this with respect to the *Dred Scott* decision.[1] Fortunately, the nation reversed itself before this corrosive logic gained enough momentum to destroy the idea of inalienable rights. Unfortunately, it took the Civil War to reverse the momentum of *Dred Scott*. Regrettably, the momentum of abortion moves in the same direction as *Dred Scott*. One hopes

---

[1] *Dred Scott vs. Sandford*, 19 Howard 393 (1857).

that the momentum of abortion will not destroy the idea of inalienable rights or the republic built on them. One hopes that civil strife may be avoided. It is still possible to use reason to correct this obvious denial of the principle of objective necessity. But time grows shorter as we defer reasonable resolution.

Such a result could generate considerable social evil and consequent social disturbance and drive the society to an ambiguous position that may be resolved only by conflict or war, since the principle of objective necessity has been superseded by the subjective will of those who claim to have clarity in the situation. This so-called principle of clarity must be qualified by two further questions:

1. clarity in whose opinion?

2. clarity to whose benefit?

Since those with enough power to assert their own subjective opinions in this matter may well end up answering these questions, to rely on clarity as a principle for adjudicating rights conflicts encourages autocracy, the only limits of which will become the calculated self-restraint of the powerful. The principles of objective necessity and broad definition serve the general welfare much more effectively than the subjective enforcement of "clarity".

Once again it is clear that society, the state, political structures, and law cannot be based on the subjective will of the powerful, for what they deem to be good may turn out to be good only for them and not for the people as a whole. If the common good and the objective demands of justice are to be pursued, as has been made clear, then the principles of objective necessity and a broad definition of "person" must reign supreme. This is the only way to guarantee that the good of the whole will not be subordinated to the "clarity" of the influential.

The principle of objective necessity must be used wherever possible because it:

1. stands on its own against the subjective will of any citizen or group of citizens, thereby preventing the arbitrary will of the powerful from dominating what can be objectively known to be just

2. implies objective universality, thereby looking to the good of the *whole*, indeed, the good of *all*, rather than to the good of a

few, which could maliciously or nonmaliciously arise out of the subjective whim of the powerful

These two principles stand as the guardians of liberty and justice *for all*. Other principles, such as the so-called principle of clarity, may well lead to a subjectivizing and relativizing of good, rights, and above all the common good. We must remember to stick to sound principles and act according to them if we are not to allow arbitrariness to snuff out the rights of life, liberty, and property for all.

F. Abortion, Euthanasia, and Inalienable Rights

While it is true that the state's denial of personhood to beings of human origin is a gross violation of their inalienable rights, it is also true that even the *suggestion* by the state that it has the authority to bestow such rights on any human person (such as in the *Roe vs. Wade* decision) is an equally gross usurpation.

In the *Roe vs. Wade* decision, the court sought to answer the question of when human personhood begins. This quest constitutes a usurpation of inalienable rights, because the state must assume that personhood belongs to *all* beings of human origin (the critical assumption). This assumption requires that the state *acknowledge* (not declare) the personhood of even a single-celled embryo because that embryo is a being of human origin. It does not matter whether the single-celled embryo is dependent on his mother or not, whether he is wanted or not, or whether he will have a vast array of opportunities in his childhood, adolescence, and adulthood. In order to avoid risking unconditional harm to a whole group of individuals, the state must acknowledge (not declare) that this being of human origin is a person with inalienable rights that are more fundamental than the extrinsic rights of others. If it does not do this, it undermines its legitimacy.

I am not suggesting here that the Court *intentionally* usurped the inalienable rights of the persons who constitute the state, but unfortunately, that's exactly what it did. By saying that it would *declare* when personhood or human life begins, it gave itself the power to deny personhood to any being of human origin falling outside its definition. Once the Court gave itself this unfounded and illegitimate power, it opened the possibility of denying personhood to anyone falling outside of any subsequent definition of "person" that the court might declare at any future time. Thus, in the future, a court might decide that personhood does not extend to one-year-olds. This is not farfetched. There are geneticists, doctors, and philosophers who already seriously advocate such positions. The Australian bioethicist Peter Singer, appointed the Ira W. DeCamp Professor of Bioethics post at Princeton University, holds that "if the fetus does not have the same claim to life as a person, it appears that the newborn baby does not either, and the life of a newborn baby is of less value than the life of a pig, a dog, or a chimpanzee.... If we can put aside ... emotionally moving but strictly irrelevant aspects of the killing of a baby we can see that the grounds for not killing persons do not apply to newborn infants." Singer continues, "If we must have a point at which the developing human being has the same right to life as you or me ... this right, I would suggest, emerges gradually during the first few months after birth." [2] What would happen if the Court turned to these so-called experts to make its next declaration of when personhood begins?

The reasoning in the *Roe vs. Wade* decision also gives the court the power to determine when life ends. By the same unfounded authority it gave itself in the *Roe vs. Wade* decision, it could also say that a being of human origin ceases to be a human person, say, after the age of eighty, or when he uses a heart-lung machine, or when he is incapable of articulating himself clearly.... If we as citizens allow the Court to deny personhood (and therefore inalienable rights) to beings of human origin at the beginning of their existence, then ipso facto we have granted them the power to deny personhood to beings of human origin at the end of their existence. Indeed, we have granted them such power over human beings at any point of their existence.

It must be emphasized that the Court has truly usurped inalienable rights in the *Roe vs. Wade* decision. As explained above, inalienable rights belong to the human person (to all beings of human origin). They do not belong to the Court. Therefore, the moment the Court declared some beings of human origin not to be persons, it illegitimately turned their inalienable rights into extrinsic ones and illegitimately brought these rights under its purview. This is precisely what is meant by "usur-

---

[2] Peter Singer, *Practical Ethics* (New York: Cambridge University Press, 1979), p. 169.

pation". The only way of remedying this egregious error is to acknowledge the critical assumption (Chapter One, section IV) and the two objective principles attached to this critical assumption and to declare the *Roe vs. Wade* reasoning to be inconsistent with these *most* fundamental principles. Anything short of this allows the usurpation to continue and the Pandora's box to open wider.

Euthanasia also undermines the above *most* fundamental principles. To see this clearly, we must return to the adage mentioned in the previous chapter: "One person's option can be another person's duty." Recall that the option of assisted suicide opens the door to implicit and even explicit pressures to exercise this option by people who might otherwise *not* want it. A relative, friend, doctor, or even society could put enough psychological pressure on a person to choose assisted suicide even if it were undesired. Thus, giving an option to one person could become the unwanted duty to die for another. This unwanted duty to die (whether it arises out of implicit or explicit pressure) is a violation of the inalienable rights of the person who does not "want" to die. Put in legal terms, the Court could declare the existence of a new *extrinsic* right (the option of assisted suicide), but it would inevitably lead to the violation of the *inalienable* rights of some human beings within its purview.

It must be noted that even if there were only one person whose inalienable rights would be violated by the promotion of a new extrinsic right, that extrinsic right could not possibly be legitimate, because the state would negate its own legitimacy in bestowing it. Put simply, the state does not have the right to deny even one person's inalienable rights in order to promote a new extrinsic right of many. The line of democracy must be drawn by the objective necessity of protecting the inalienable rights upon which democracy is founded.

Of course, the inalienable rights of many are at stake. Indeed, a very good case could be made that there are far more people whose inalienable rights would be violated by legalized euthanasia than people who would "benefit" from having this new extrinsic right (after all, many of our compatriots are subject to depression, internal compulsions, financial pressure, low self-esteem, and all forms of subtle persuasion). But this is not a question about numbers; it is a question about the priority of principles upon which our republic is founded. Consequently, I reassert that every extrinsic right, even if it involves the entire population, is *always* subordinate to any inalienable right, of even one single individual. Given this ontological subordination of extrinsic to inalienable rights, the case for euthanasia can never be legitimately made. Conversely, maintaining laws against euthanasia is perfectly compatible with the state's legitimate function of protecting inalienable rights, for inasmuch as it prevents an option that could undermine inalienable rights, it acts to protect the personhood of each and every one of its citizens.

The above treatment of rights and personhood may seem exceedingly philosophical for what appears to be a purely legal issue. It might seem as if we should restrict ourselves to legal method, reasoning, and precedence, instead of straying into the larger philosophical domain. It may be tempting to think that if we keep ourselves locked into the narrow definitions and reasons of contemporary precedence, we can achieve great clarity. Unfortunately, clarity is not all we seek in trying to come to the truth. Completeness and groundedness are also just as important. Recall the old philosophical cliché: "There are far more errors of omission than commission." Sometimes the pursuit of clarity can intentionally exclude the pursuit of completeness. Too many details can cloud up the perfect clarity that can be achieved through the elimination of "irrelevant" data. We can never afford, as a nation, to get legal clarity at the expense of unconditional harm and the ignoring of objective necessity. We would have clarity, but certainly not truth, respect, and integrity.

At the end of the day, clear *and* complete legal reasoning will have to be based on objective necessity, and this objective necessity on the inalienability of rights (which can never be turned into extrinsic rights), and these inalienable rights, in turn, on the presumed unconditional dignity of every being of human origin. Anything short of this legitimates arbitrary power and puts the arbitrary will of the state above the unconditional dignity and inalienable rights of human beings.

If our courts do not embrace the personhood of all beings of human origin and the criterion of objective necessity, we allow our government to declare our personhood and our inalienable rights *out of existence*. It's time for our justices to move outside the confines of narrow legal methodology and to reexamine the objective foundations and presumptions upon which the legitimacy of our state and its Constitution depend.

G. *The Legitimate State and the Objectively Necessary*
Proscriptions of Its Powers

In conclusion, there are ten actions that a state cannot take without
jeopardizing its legitimacy, because it will act against the inalienable
rights of its individual citizens and against the common good:

1. It cannot *explicitly* violate an inalienable right (for example,
   "all people under six foot one should be euthanized").

2. It cannot *explicitly* declare limits to the self-possession of inalienable rights other than the natural beginning and the natural end of human existence (for example, "the inalienable
   right to personhood will take place after the second year of
   life" or "will cease after the sixtieth year of life").

3. It cannot *implicitly* declare limits to the self-possession of
   inalienable rights other than the natural beginning and the
   natural end of human existence (for example, "abortion is
   permitted up to the third trimester"—such policy constitutes
   an implicit declaration that the right of self-possession of one's
   present and future existence exists only after the second
   trimester).

4. The state cannot *explicitly* subjectivize inalienable rights, for
   this would undermine the objective necessity that belongs to
   inalienable rights by their very nature. Thus, the state cannot
   say, for example, that the right to life and liberty is still an
   open question. To declare this to be an "open question" is
   explicitly to declare that the determination of when an inalienable right begins is a matter of subjective human opinion
   and not intrinsic to objective reality.

5. The state cannot *implicitly* subjectivize inalienable rights for
   the same reason it cannot explicitly do so. Thus, for example,
   the state cannot invite people to discuss or even vote on the
   question of when inalienable rights might begin or end, for
   this would subjectivize inalienable rights. Subjectivization undermines objective necessity, which, in turn, reduces inalienable

rights to merely extrinsic rights, to be bestowed or denied by
the state, at will.

6. The state cannot sacrifice the inalienable rights of a single
   citizen to promote the extrinsic rights even of many citizens.
   The state's legitimacy rests upon its *universal* protection of inalienable rights, that is, the protection of the inalienable rights
   of all its citizens. It cannot subordinate this mandate to any
   other possible mandate.

7. The state cannot implicitly or explicitly legalize, legitimize,
   or condone any option that *could* undermine the inalienable
   rights of its citizens. This is merely a corollary of what was
   stated above in prohibition 6, for if a so-called option were an
   extrinsic right to benefit many, it could never supersede the
   inalienable rights of even one citizen.

8. The state cannot implicitly or explicitly allow a social ambiance that will allow private citizens to (a) violate an inalienable right, (b) subjectivize inalienable rights, (c) undermine
   the universality of inalienable rights, or (d) otherwise allow
   itself any option that could undermine inalienable rights.

9. A state cannot *explicitly* promote a prioritization of inalienable rights other than that which is objectively and logically
   necessary. Hence, the state cannot declare that the inalienable
   right to liberty is more fundamental than the inalienable right
   to life. This not only would violate an inalienable right; it
   also would introduce an irrational subjectivity into the structure of inalienable rights—which would constitute yet another usurpation of inalienable rights by the state and another
   blow against the state's legitimacy.

10. The state cannot *implicitly* promote an ordering of inalienable
    rights other than that which is objectively and logically nec-
    essary. For example, the state could not legitimately invite
    people to discuss or vote upon the prioritization of inalien-
    able rights. To do so would imply that the people or the gov-
    ernment had the right to make such a determination, that the
    people or the state had the power to contradict reality and

negate inalienable rights, which, in turn, could encourage them ultimately to replace more fundamental inalienable rights with less fundamental extrinsic ones.

Any state that engages in any of the above-mentioned prohibited practices acts against

1. the personhood and therefore the best interests of its citizens

2. the common good of its citizens and the objective demands of justice

3. *its own legitimacy*

This legitimacy derives partly from the subjective will of the people, but more fundamentally from the objectively necessary and universal inalienable rights of each and every one of the persons within its domain. The subjective will of the people must remain subordinate to the objectively necessary and universal inalienable rights of all persons within the state.

H. The Principles of Nonmaleficence and Beneficence

The above material on inalienable rights and personhood may now be seen in relationship to the two most fundamental principles of ethics: the principle of nonmaleficence and the principle of beneficence (see Chapter Six). As will be shown, undermining the three above fundamental *political* principles (the critical assumption of personhood, the inalienability of rights, and the objective prioritization of rights) also necessarily undermines these two most fundamental *ethical* principles.

The principle of nonmaleficence may be stated as "do no harm" or "minimize harm", and the principle of beneficence may be stated as "optimize the good for others". These rules are frequently stated in self-referential fashion as the Silver Rule ("Do not do unto others as you would not have them do unto you"—nonmaleficence) and the Golden Rule ("Do unto others as you would have them do unto you"—beneficence).

Evidently, the principle of beneficence assumes the principle of nonmaleficence and goes further. It requires seeking that which will positively enhance the other being, the other person, the human community, that which will bring about the good beyond self. The principle of beneficence has advantages over the principle of nonmaleficence both in personal conduct and in societal relations, because the principle of beneficence resolves ethical and political dilemmas beyond the reach of the principle of nonmaleficence. The principle of nonmaleficence only indicates what conduct is *proscribed* and should *not* be engaged in, whereas the principle of beneficence indicates what conduct is *prescribed* and *should* be engaged in. Even though the principle of beneficence (*summum bonum*) represents a cultural ideal that together we ought to pursue, it cannot be used to negate the principle of nonmaleficence. The principle of nonmaleficence is more fundamental than the principle of beneficence; the former is the condition necessary for the possibility of the latter, so it must take primacy and cannot be ignored.

Our first obligation is to do no harm, or, if harm cannot be avoided, to minimize it (nonmaleficence). That being accomplished, we are free to pursue a greater good (beneficence). Since the principle of nonmaleficence is logically antecedent to the principle of beneficence, we must avoid the Maoist fallacy of pursuing the "greater good of China" at the cost of "a few million individual lives". Pursuit of the greater good cannot justify the harm that is done to individuals. Conversely, we do not want to fall prey to a minimalist bias, whereby we hold that after having avoided any harm we need do nothing more: "There is no further good to be pursued." This would tempt us to think, for example, that it is not necessary to call anyone to a higher level of happiness, so long as we are not doing any harm to their life or liberty rights. That would undermine the pursuit of the common good (see below, section III).

In order to avoid extinguishing the principle of nonmaleficence in the pursuit of "the greatest good for the greatest number", two procedures must be employed before the summum bonum may be sought:

1. One must set out all of the potential harms that could accrue to any of the parties involved. A "potential harm" may be viewed as one that has a reasonable chance of occurring. This "reasonable chance" should be determined by experts acting on behalf of those who would have to pay damages or could be held criminally liable for these harms.

2. These harms must be ranked according to the objective priorities of rights (see above, section B).

At this point, the objective criteria should be able to resolve the rights conflict almost automatically. There should be little need for the discretionary powers of a judge or legislator, because objective criteria should hold sway over the subjective preferences of any arbiter. The resolution of the rights conflict should be discovered (because it is objective), not invented (because it is thought to be subjective).

Once rights conflicts have been resolved according to this procedure, one is free to seek the greatest good for the greatest number. Indeed, for the good of society, one may even feel compelled to do so. But the greatest good for the greatest number cannot be used to justify a violation of the principle of nonmaleficence.

The logical connection between the principle of nonmaleficence and our three fundamental political principles is self-evident. Therefore, if our courts or legislatures permit or advocate a violation of the critical assumption of personhood (that all beings of human origin are persons), the principle of inalienability of rights, or the principle of objective prioritization of rights, they also permit or advocate a violation of the principle of nonmaleficence. Since this principle is the underlying ground of all ethical thought, the permission and advocacy of its violation from the highest legal and political authority cannot help but undermine the conscience of our culture. The importance of this point cannot be exaggerated, for the authority of our highest political institutions carries not only legal weight but also enormous normative and pedagogical weight.

We cannot afford to deceive ourselves any longer, because virtually every group within our culture is picking up the implicit moral message that violations of the principle of nonmaleficence are sometimes permissible, even advisable, if we really "want" these violations enough. If "want" means acting according to the strongest momentary emotion, then we are truly teaching the culture that the strongest momentary emotion, even outrageous passion and anger, can justify violations of our most fundamental ethical principles and, therefore, our consciences. This "teaching" is the kind of hedonism that virtually every great political thinker feared most for the culture.

If we are to turn back from this perilous ethical and political journey, we must admit the following:

1. that our advocacy of abortion and euthanasia has undermined the three most fundamental political principles

2. that the undermining of any of these principles (let alone all three) undermines the principle of nonmaleficence

3. that the undermining of the principle of nonmaleficence is an undermining of conscience and ethics within the culture; it is teaching the culture that strong momentary emotions permit violations of conscience

If we do not admit these three truths and bring back the notion of conscience through the principles of nonmaleficence and beneficence, I cannot see how the culture will not continue on its current path of self-destruction.

It is difficult to see how a government could claim to be protecting the rights of its citizens while negating any one of (let alone all four of) the above-mentioned principles, namely:

1. the critical assumption (equating "person" with "being of human origin")

2. the principle of inalienability of rights

3. the principle of the objectively necessary prioritization of rights

4. the principle of nonmaleficence

Such negations are not only gross violations of human rights; they are also a sure recipe for political and social disaster. A republic must be consistently grounded in the above four principles, not merely in the consent of the governed. Indeed, grounding in these four principles is more fundamental than the consent of the governed; therefore, even a unanimous majority that would deny them is intrinsically illegitimate. The consent of the governed is far from absolute and must be constrained by a duty to the above four principles.

Popular will cannot abandon the above four principles; to do so would again be illegitimate, for the consent of the majority would rest on nothing more than on its own arbitrary, subjective will, not on that which can be objectively and necessarily known. Violations of these four objective principles constitute a tyranny of the influential or majority—a perversion rejected by virtually all democratic thinkers. Similarly, the popular will cannot negate nonmaleficence, even for only one person, without negating its own legitimacy. For these reasons, majority rule has never been thought to be an absolutely unconditioned principle; it must subject itself to other, more basic principles on which its legitimacy is based.

The above three fundamental political principles create the objective basis for legitimate government. Inalienable rights, which belong to human persons by nature (that is, by existence and human origin), mandate a benevolent state. That mandate also subjects the state to the principle of nonmaleficence for the reasons I have discussed. These principles are the basis of governmental legitimacy—not the Constitution or popular will. Pieces of paper can be altered. The subjective will of the majority can be manipulated by selfish interests, even to the point of choosing tyranny. The only things that stand objectively outside of government and outside of subjectivity are our critical assumption and the principle of the inalienability of the rights to life, liberty, and property, in that order. Combined with the principle of nonmaleficence, these three inalienable rights offer the means for the objective, impartial resolution of rights conflicts and the effective and just ordering of society. The only visible alternative is the rule of force, which would be intrinsically illegitimate.

II. The Pursuit of the Common Good

A culture's definition of the "common good" is its prized possession, for it constitutes its ideals, its collective goals, the breadth and depth of its individuals' collective activities, and the quality of its collective life in both the present and the future. This definition is, therefore, the intrinsic motivating principle of society's collective activity, which means that it controls the quality and efficacy of every human relationship and individual life within the polity. If we, as a society, fail to clarify this definition, if we allow it to become progressively more ambiguous, or if we feel no duty toward it, we rob our society of not only a better but also an equivalently good future.

By now three points about the common good must be obvious:

1. that it is grounded in the principle of beneficence (the Golden Rule)

2. that it therefore presumes and is dependent upon the above-mentioned four fundamental principles

3. that it goes far beyond those four principles to seeking the optimal and highest good for society, culture, and state

In the previous section, the principle of beneficence was all but ignored in order to discuss the intrinsic relationship between the principle of nonmaleficence and our three fundamental political principles. We may now proceed to a discussion of this grander principle, recalling that it can never be properly actualized without first attending to the four more fundamental principles discussed above.

No one will dispute that the common good pertains to the good of the whole group, but what is the good of the whole group? Is it merely the aggregated good of individuals? Must it not also include the good of the structure that organizes the individuals' collective activity? Would we not have to seek out the good of the economy as well as the good of the individuals laboring within the economy? Should the common good include qualitative goods, such as education and other Level 3 or 4 goods, as well as quantitative goods, such as tangible goods, money, and other Level 1 or 2 goods?

Perhaps the easiest way to untangle this definition is to borrow a principle from organizational theory: the principle of optimal stakeholder benefit. In organizational theory, a "stakeholder" is anyone vitally involved with the organization (a customer, employee, supplier, manager, stockholder, or community member). The principle of optimal benefit holds that a good for one stakeholder, which does not cause harm to other stakeholders or the unity or survival of the group, will become, in the long term, a good for all stakeholders. Thus, for example, if management pursues a good for its employees (which does not harm the other stakeholders or the unity or survival of the organization), that good will produce good will, creativity, adaptability to change, and trust on the part of those employees. These qualities of employees will, in the long term, benefit customers, suppliers, managers, and community members. Therefore, all stakeholders within the organization will want to pursue a "win-win" relationship with all other stakeholders, even if they should have quite diverse interests, because "win-lose" relationships will interrupt the actualization of optimal benefit.

How does the principle of optimal stakeholder benefit elucidate the common good? It accounts for both the good of the individuals and the good of the structures organizing the activities of those individuals in the long term. Organizations, of course, have very different objectives from societies and cultures. Some organizations try to make a profit, while others are trying to provide goods and services to the maximum number of clients. Societies and cultures cannot be limited to such quantitative and economically oriented objectives, because cultures are concerned with the greatest possible benefit for all their stakeholders. The widest conceivable benefit for stakeholders may best be described as the optimal stakeholder meaning or purpose in life. Cultures and organizations, therefore, do have one thing in common. They want to optimize the good for their stakeholders in order to promote the long-term viability of those stakeholders and the group. However, their definitions of "stakeholder good" are quite different in that cultures must define the good far more broadly than organizations.

By now it must be apparent that the above discussion about the four levels of happiness will have a profound effect on the definition of the above three all-important terms: "stakeholder", "stakeholder good", and "meaning and purpose in life". A quick review of how the four levels of happiness affect these three terms will reveal how they affect the definition of the "common good", the prized possession and intrinsic motivating principle of every culture.

I am not so interested here in reiterating the definitions of "meaning and purpose in life" and "stakeholder good" in terms of the four levels of happiness. By now you are quite capable of doing this for yourself. I am much more interested in looking at the definition of *"stakeholder"*, that is, the person with whom we want to have a "win-win" relationship. Notice that the definition of a stakeholder will be derived precisely from how we view "optimal benefit", because "win-win" relationships are supposed to lead to optimal benefit. Notice also that the definition of "optimal benefit" depends precisely on the level of happiness we have implicitly or explicitly chosen for our collective selves. As will be made clear, this interrelationship among definitions will produce the following effects: Level 1 cultures will tend toward materialism and superficiality. Level 2 cultures will tend toward elitism. Level 3 cultures will tend toward coresponsibility and generativity. And Level 4 cultures will tend toward self-transcendence, universality, and faith.

The way we view meaning and purpose in life, therefore, affects the way we view "optimal benefit", and the way we view "optimal benefit", in turn, affects who we believe to be a worthy stakeholder. Inasmuch as individuals will always want to achieve the status of stakeholder, the definition of "stakeholder" becomes the internal motivating force for the culture's future. It is therefore incumbent on all of us as citizens to make explicit our beliefs about meaning and purpose in life (and "worthy stakeholders") and to make certain that our educational systems are prepared to help the next generation to understand these beliefs. If we fail to do this, we leave the definition of "common good" in a cloud of ambiguity that an unprepared younger generation will have to discover for itself. From an objectively probabilistic point of view, this condition does not bode well for our culture.

If our society explicitly chooses, or implicitly slips into, a Level 1 view of life, it will define success for the next generation of aspirant stakeholders in Level 1 terms. These aspirants will do everything they can to achieve this status of "worthy stakeholder", though only some will make it. The bar, of course, gets higher and higher as more aspirants compete to get nearer to it. The farther from the bar certain aspirants fall, the more marginalized they become, and the more marginalized they become, the easier it is to ignore them. It is easier to relegate the nonelite to the status of loser and leave them there, because, after all, they really are not as good as we are.

If these failed aspirants have a strong Level 3 or 4 identity, they will view their lack of inclusion in the Level 1 "in group" as insignificant, or even humorous. But if they have never heard of such an identity, if they have never seen their purpose or meaning in life in terms of contribution and love, they will view themselves as inferiors, resent their lack of good fortune, or resent the elitist structures that kept them down. Now, imagine for a moment that a society has implicitly and explicitly chosen a Level 1 definition of "the common good", because this helps to sell products and because money buys enough power to sustain this kind of cultural identity. Suppose that this identity were actively propagated by the media and the workplace environment. Suppose further that many astute educators began to believe this definition of the common good as well and began creating justifications for it. It probably would not be long before a majority of our youth began to feel inferior for possessing "paltry" qualities like being contributory, compassionate, generative, loving, astute, and creative. After all, they didn't have what really mattered: an abundance of wealth. Instead of feeling inferior, another group might well feel resentment, and abandon a myriad of opportunities for education and service to pursue the symbols of wealth (say, the hottest tennis shoes). Still others might become violent in their resentments. All these groups will experience a severely hampered future unless this hypothetical culture changes its view of "stakeholder", and the only way it will do this is to make explicit and acceptable the other options that can characterize meaning and purpose in life (Levels 2, 3, and 4).

The definition of "stakeholder" of course is linked to "the common good". If the view of "stakeholder" is Level 1, and if it is providing an abundance of wealth for its stakeholders, then the culture will believe that it is accomplishing the common good. When it comes time to judge how well we are doing, the response might well be, "The RGNP (adjusted for inflation) went up x amount, which is 3 percent better than last year. Of course we are achieving the common good. Is there anything else we need to consider?"

A sense of entitlement accompanies this view of "stakeholder" and "the common good". If someone should come along and say, "We ought to make some additional job opportunities available to a marginalized group of people", the response may come back, "We did it for ourselves. Let them carry their own weight. Taxes are too high anyway, and these so-called learning opportunities don't go anywhere." Again, the sense of entitlement tends to keep the forces of culture (and therefore the forces of the economy and political system) focused on Level 1. In the days of the Industrial Revolution, the sense of entitlement blinded the elite to the abject poverty of 80 percent of the population of Europe. It was often heard quoted, "The poor wretches don't know how lucky they really are."

As I have noted many times throughout the course of this book, our collective view of the common good does not simply affect our view of the life issues. It affects economic, political, and even cultural marginalization. It can bring about materialism, materialistic reductionism, and even a complete loss of what is pervasive, enduring, and deep. It is not merely individual decisions (or lack of them) that cause the anxieties of the comparison game. The culture can produce these anxieties in whole groups of people by implicitly defining "stakeholder" in a Level 1 or 2 way.

The reader can apply the same set of consequences to a culture that defines "stakeholder" in terms of Level 2. Those who achieve a certain level of promotion or prestige will be considered stakeholders, while those falling short of the bar will be marginalized. The culture will justify this marginalization by defining "the common good" in terms of its view of "stakeholder". When asked if the culture is achieving the common good, people will respond, "Of course, we opened 70,000 new upper level management positions last year." It may forget to ask, "What happened to the people who didn't get there?" or "Are we losing a sense of Level 3 or 4 in our collective lives?" This internal motivating principle will become the standard for youthful aspirants, who will now pursue cultural acceptance by pursuing greater promotions and being associated with prestigious clubs and organizations. They will also learn the converse lesson that other qualities, such as contribution, compassion, creativity, and educational leadership, are "nice, but insignificant in the whole panoply of life". Youth will internalize these definitions and find themselves either in the elite or in the ranks of those who feel inferior, resentful, or even violent. Again, the only way out of such a strong cultural momentum is to make explicit our Level 3 and 4 definitions of "stakeholder" and "the common good". Even if we do not want to select one of the four levels for the culture, we need to make *all four* levels explicit and acceptable so that our youth will feel cultural acceptance and support for becoming Level 3 or 4 stakeholders.

What about a Level 3 or 4 view of "the common good"? This is an ideal that we are unfortunately moving away from. If we are to rekindle it within the culture, we will have to make it explicit and acceptable. This book has been devoted to defining Levels 3 and 4. It is now time to ask the reader to make it come alive within the culture. How? By taking the education in this book and bringing it to schools, community organizations, churches, and every other place where one can find an audience. The only way of making Levels 3 and 4 explicit is to get the information out there. The only way to make it acceptable is for us to form communities (localized cultures) who believe in these Level 3 and 4 definitions of "stakeholder" and "the common good". If the information is presented cogently, and if, despite our imperfections, we consistently try to live out of these beliefs, we will have created a "localized cultural ethos" that provides acceptance and support for a Level 3 or 4 view of "stakeholder" and the "common good".

But how do we move from "localized Level 3 and 4 cultures" (over which we have some direct influence) to the general culture (the culture of the United States)? How can we actively promote a general Level 3 and 4 culture without imposing our *personal* view of meaning and purpose in life on groups who may not want this influence? The difficulty with moving from a localized culture to the general culture is that there are bound to be groups who, for various reasons, do not want to make the move to Level 3 or 4. In order for Level 3 and 4 people to avoid imposing their beliefs on those who do not want them, we cannot insist that the general culture promote a Level 3 or 4 view of the common good. But we can ask that the general culture promote *all four* options.

Bearing this condition in mind, we can pursue a program of general cultural edification on five major fronts:

1. Encouraging equal time for Level 3 and 4 viewpoints within *educational institutions*. This would include books, classroom time, extracurricular activities, service learning programs, and clubs. It is not sufficient for schools simply to explicitize information about the Level 3 or 4 viewpoint. They must allow these viewpoints to enjoy equal acceptance and valuation within the schools' environment.

2. Encouraging the *media* to present as many programs devoted to Level 3 and 4 stakeholder viewpoints as they do to Level 1 or 2. This would also include responsible script writing so that characters pursuing a reckless Level 1 or 2 lifestyle occasionally experience some of the emotions of the comparison game, some of the destroyed relationships, and some of the unhappiness that ordinary people would commonly experience.

3. Encouraging the *legal establishment* to honor the four fundamental objective principles given above and to give equal time to the third and fourth levels of freedom, person, and the common good as they do to the first and second levels of these

crucial ideas. Recent court decisions have turned "freedom" into "what I want" (with "want" meaning "strongest momentary emotion"). In so doing, they have undermined a view of freedom as "commitment toward the pervasive, enduring, and deep". As was explained in this chapter, the courts have also severely undermined the view of "person", "inalienable rights", and "the objective prioritization of rights". The legal establishment not only needs to reverse much of its recent reasoning; it also desperately needs to rekindle at least a Level 3 dimension in its reflection on the ten categories of cultural discourse. The judiciary is not merely an indifferent perpetuator of good and bad precedence; it must responsibly carry out its normative and pedagogical functions, which are inseparable from its legal one.

4. Encouraging *legislators* to give equal time to Level 3 and 4 stakeholder viewpoints. This Level 3 or 4 viewpoint is essential not only in the writing of legislation, but also in the *example* given from the highest rungs of governmental authority. Our populace needs to hear this in speeches from the floor of the House, to speeches delivered at graduations and visits to one's hometown. As with the legal establishment, governmental authority also carries normative and pedagogical influence.

5. Encouraging *commercial establishments* to market their products responsibly. The intensive and immediately gratifying characteristic of Level 1 or 2 marketing makes it virtually irresistible. We need to ask marketers to give equal time to Level 3 and 4 appeals. Human beings are naturally contributory, and they want to do the good. If marketers appeal to this higher dimension of human nature, they will get an immediate and powerful response.

The professionals involved in these five areas will know far better than I how to put together practical strategies to give equal time to Levels 3 and 4. As I have explained in Chapters Two and Three, this will not be easy because Levels 1 and 2 are more tangible, immediately gratifying, and intense. They are more viscerally attractive and viscerally satisfying. They sell products better, and they even sell self-image better. But, of course, the end result of such products and self-image is short term, shallow, and nonpervasive. Hence, in order to promote Level 3 and 4 strategies, we must prepare our audiences to think for the long term and to value enduring satisfactions as much as intensive ones and, finally, to value intangibles as much as tangibles.

This brings us back to the beginning of this book. How can we encourage the culture to seek the sublimity of intangibles like love, virtue, and "freedom for", when they are being showered with products that focus their minds on tangibility, intensity, and immediate gratification (even in the virtual world)? We must make an appeal to the heart—an appeal that tugs at the strings of our desire to optimize the good with our lives, to see the good news in others, and to enter into common cause for a common good worthy of us. If we can reach these heartstrings, then the rest will follow like the night the day.

I therefore encourage every professional in the above areas to form professional communities to discuss and reflect upon these Life Principles and the practical strategies that can be used to implement them.[3] If we do not do this together, we have little hope of accomplishing this most difficult and arduous task of elevating our cultural view of "stakeholder" and the "common good".

Though it will be difficult, I am extremely hopeful about this prospect. I have met literally hundreds of people from each of the above professions who are willing to begin the process of reflection and strategizing on these principles. Like me, they are not perfect in their pursuit of Levels 3 and 4, but they do very much understand that these viewpoints represent not only a road to sanity but also a life of optimal contribution and love. They know the rightness of this for themselves, their children, their friends, and the culture. As individuals striving for Level 3, they give willingly of their time and energy to enter into common cause for a view of the "common good" that will ennoble our culture in its future.

---

[3] For those interested in either starting or participating in a reflection group in their own local community, please see page 347 below for a toll free number to call for more information.

Chapter Eight

Summary of the Ten Categories
of Cultural Discourse

Introduction

Before proceeding to a discussion of the abortion and euthanasia issues, it will be helpful to review briefly the ten categories of cultural discourse. The following table does this by distinguishing between the Level 1 and 2 view, and the Level 3 and 4 view. Notice how the first six attitudes affect one's view of "person", which in turn affects one's attitude toward rights and the common good. The combined effect of these ten categories will determine not only one's view of abortion and euthanasia but also every other cultural and political issue, for our beliefs in all such issues are mere extensions of what we hold about happiness, success, self-worth, love, suffering, ethics, freedom, personhood, rights, and the common good.

This table is set out for the purpose of helping the reader to be *consistent*. The sheer number of factors involved in a systematic philosophy of personal and cultural life is frequently too large to hold in our heads at once. Therefore, it is useful to have a checklist that one can consult periodically to test consistency and fidelity to one's convictions. The following table shows the implications of a Level 1 and 2 view of happiness for the other nine categories of cultural discourse. It does the same for the Level 3 and 4 view of happiness.

As noted above, a Level 3 or 4 view of happiness can help us move out of the destructive emotions of the comparison game and live for what is pervasive, enduring, and deep. This recipe for personal sanity is also a recipe for cultural healing. If we consistently extend our beliefs about our personal lives into the domain of our collective lives, we not only will put an end to abortion and euthanasia but also will keep safe inalienable rights, the common good, and hence the future of our culture.

I recommend that you first read all the Level 1 and 2 material in all the cells, and then go back and read all the Level 3 and 4 material. Afterward, it will be useful to return to the beginning of the table and compare the Level 1 and 2 side of each category with its Level 3 and 4 side. Reading the table in this way will help you to see how all ten categories of cultural discourse hang together in the Level 1 and 2 view, and then the Level 3 and 4 view. After seeing the intrinsic intelligibility of these two views, you can then appreciate the contrasts in each individual claim and position.

HAPPINESS	
Level 1 and 2 (L1/2)	Level 3 and 4 (L3/4)
1) Materialistic (L1), ego oriented, and comparative (L2).	1) Contributory (toward love—L3), self-transcendent, transcendent (faith—L4).
2) Not pervasive, enduring, and deep.	2) Pervasive, enduring, and deep.
3) Tangible, apparent, immediately gratifying, and intense.	3) Less tangible (requiring search and education), delayed gratification, less intense.
4) Emotive problems associated with the comparison game.	4) Relief of emotive problems associated with the comparison game.

SUCCESS	
Level 1/2	Level 3/4
1) The successful life is accumulation of possessions (L1), comparative advantage, and admiration for having achieved comparative advantage (L2).	1) The successful life is optimizing the difference one can make to family, friends, community, work, church, and world (L3) and contribution to and involvement in what has ultimate, unconditional, and eternal significance (growth in faith—L4).
2) Progress in life (going somewhere) equals obtaining the above objectives.	2) Progress in life (going somewhere) equals obtaining the above objectives.

SELF-WORTH	
Level 1/2	Level 3/4
1) Object self, thingified self, materialistic ("clump of chemicals"—L1); and egocentric, esteemable self (*my* achievements, winning, popularity, and control as ends in themselves—L2).	1) Subject, likable, lovable self (intangible, interpersonal, empathetic, connective presence to others—L3); and mysterious, self-transcendent, transcendental (*soul*) in *interpersonal* relationship with God (faith), having unconditional dignity (L4).

SELF-WORTH (continued)

Level 1/2	Level 3/4
2) Therefore, self-worth occurs only when one accumulates more things (L1) or more achievements, winning, popularity, or control (L2).	2) Therefore, self-worth occurs when one either broadens (quantitatively) or deepens (qualitatively) love (L3); or when one broadens or deepens faith (L4).
3) Therefore, compulsive, because external accumulations are not ultimately satisfying. Implicit recognition of undervaluation of self-worth.	3) Therefore, zealous (to optimize), but not compulsive.

LOVE

Level 1/2	Level 3/4
1) Reduction of "love" to physical affection, sexual feelings, and sexual gratification (L1); or to ego high ("I am desirable") or conquest (L2).	1) Love seen fundamentally as "gift of self"— looking for good news in other and entering into unity with other such that doing the good for other is easier than doing good for self. This unity is not reducible to sexual gratification, though in marriage sexual feelings are compatible with it. Feeling desirable is subordinated to the good of the other.
2) Intangible components of love are almost unrecognizable, hence little distinction between romantic love and non-romantic love (e.g., delight or energy arising out of accomplishing the good together). Also, love not necessarily associated with commitment, therefore, difficulty distinguishing between *eros* (sexual), *philia* (friendship), and *agape* (self-sacrificial) love.	2) Intangible components of love are recognizable, therefore commitment is associated with love (L3); so also is faith in a loving God (L4). Relevant distinctions are made between *eros*, *philia*, and *agape*. Differentiation between nonromantic feelings and romantic feelings is also evident.

SUFFERING

Level 1/2	Level 3/4
1) Little value to suffering. Therefore, must be compensated by additional pleasure or possession (L1); or some value of suffering in obtaining achievement, winning, popularity, or control as ends in themselves (L2).	1) Suffering has value for the sake of wisdom, forgiveness, humility, growth in love and compassion, and other seven qualities (L3—see Chapter Five); and growth in faith (trust in, and relationship with, God—L4).

SUFFERING (continued)

Level 1/2	Level 3/4
2) When one cannot see good in suffering, it leads to depression, listlessness, self-pity, outrage, and despair. These emotions are frequent in an L1/2 lifestyle.	2) Since one can see good in suffering for self (e.g., growth in love), for others (compassion, self-sacrifice), for community, world, and kingdom of God, suffering can lead to greater openness (through vulnerability) instead of closedness, greater horizon for life instead of bitterness, greater spirit and resilience instead of self-pity, and greater patience instead of anger.

ETHICS

Level 1/2	Level 3/4
1) L1/2 attitudes emphasize comparative advantage instead of contribution/love/faith (higher ends). Therefore, it is very difficult to understand the reasons for virtue (means to higher ends) and for avoiding vice (which undermines higher ends).	1) Higher end of life is clear (e.g., contribution/love/faith). Therefore, the reasons to pursue virtue (means to higher ends) and to avoid vice (which undermines higher ends) are also clear.
2) Without understanding the rationale, it is difficult to acquire the habit and discipline of virtue and to believe in inviolable principles. "Integrity" and "character" seem vague. Ethics can even seem useless and counterproductive.	2) In light of the understood rationale, it is natural to love virtue and to want to avoid vice. This makes it easier (though not easy) to develop the habit and discipline necessary for integrity and character. Ethics is seen as desirable and noble.

FREEDOM

Level 1/2	Level 3/4
1) "Freedom from." Freedom is associated with what I want, and "want" is associated with the strongest momentary emotion.	1) "Freedom for." Freedom is oriented toward making the most of my talents, energy, and time. Thus, it is oriented to what is most pervasive, enduring, and deep.
2) Therefore, it tends to be hyper-emotive, impulsive, escapist, anti-discipline, and anti-commitment. Oriented toward the short term.	2) Therefore, it tends to be oriented toward commitment, the discipline necessary to achieve one's commitments, education, and virtue. It does not align itself with emotional satisfaction that is inconsistent with commitments, and it is oriented toward optimizing one's time and talent in the long term.

PERSONHOOD

Level 1/2	Level 3/4
1) L1/2 attitudes stress what is tangible, exterior (L1), and comparative (L2). Therefore, L1/2 attitudes tend to orient people toward *appearance* definitions (a thing is what it looks like). They tend not to emphasize *essential* definitions (which define according to the perfection of a thing's powers—see Chapter One). "Perfection" seems like a future quality instead of a real guiding force operating in the present. Even if such a perfection is viewed merely in terms of genetics (instead of "soul"), this group tends to see the perfection as not yet existing (as something that has not yet appeared and therefore does not yet exist). As a consequence, L1/2 tends to define personhood according to appearance and present capacity. These definitions can frequently be *subjective*. Therefore, for this group, "person" frequently seems to be a subjective, assignable quality instead of an intrinsic, *objective* one.	1) L3/4 attitudes stress using one's time, talent, and energy for the optimal positive effect among family, friends, work, community (L3); and the kingdom of God (L4). They are, therefore, oriented toward the *ultimate perfection* of both self and all human beings. The group embracing these attitudes views essential definitions as not only real but also most significant. *Appearance* definitions are seen as less significant and sometimes even as superficial. This group views the guiding force toward perfection (whether genetic or soul) as a present, objective, well-designed reality. The perfection of a thing (its design) is a real part of a real guiding force to that perfection. Therefore, this group defines "person" in terms of the real guiding force toward human perfection (unconditional Truth, Love, Goodness, Beauty, and Being). This guiding force is seen to be present at the moment a human being begins development, that is, at the moment a human being's development is guided by this force (i.e., at the stage of a single-celled embryo). Since this group sees the guiding force as objectively real, it views the definition of "person" to be *objective* instead of *subjective*.
2) L1/2 attitudes deemphasize *intangibles*. Therefore, they tend to ignore the *intrinsic* unconditional dignity, lovability, mystery, and transcendentality (i.e., intangibles) of beings of human origin. L1/2 advocates also find it difficult to understand the perfection of human beings to be *unconditional* Truth, Love, Goodness, Beauty, and Being, because these perfections seem abstract. Furthermore, this group (oriented toward the tangible, exterior, and comparative) interprets "intrinsic", "perfection", and "unconditionality" to be mere concepts.	2) L3/4 attitudes emphasize love (L3) and transcendentality (L4) in human beings. Therefore, the group embracing these attitudes is not only open to intangibles, but acutely aware of them through their effects. This group is therefore aware of the specific transcendental perfections of human beings (i.e., unconditional, perfect, and ultimate Truth, Love, Goodness, Beauty, and Being). As such, it is not difficult for this group to identify the objective reality of intrinsic, unconditional dignity. Intangibility does not indicate unreality for them. Indeed, the intangible can reflect the full reality of a person far more than the tangible.

PERSONHOOD (continued)

Level 1/2	Level 3/4
3) Therefore, L1/2 advocates find the essential definition of "person" to be quite perplexing and abstract. Recall this essential definition from Chapter One: "person" is a "being possessing an intrinsic guiding force (whether genetic, and/or soul) toward fulfillment in perfect, unconditional, ultimate Truth, Love, Goodness, Beauty, and Being".	3) Therefore, L3/4 advocates find the essential definition of "person" to be virtually self-evident. Recall this essential definition from Chapter One: "person" is a "being possessing an intrinsic guiding force (whether genetic and/or a soul) toward fulfillment in perfect, unconditional, and ultimate Truth, Love, Goodness, Beauty, and Being".
4) Inasmuch as this group does not understand the reality of this essential definition of human beings, it will have difficulty recognizing the *intrinsic, unconditional dignity* of human beings. This, in turn, will make it difficult to recognize the *unconditional harm* that is done if one such being is killed, jeopardized, or taken for granted.	4) Inasmuch as this group finds the essential definition of "person" to be self-evident, it will also find the *intrinsic, unconditional dignity* of beings of human origin to be self-evident. This, in turn, will make self-evident the *unconditional harm* that would be done if such a being were killed, jeopardized, or taken for granted.
5) Therefore, this group will find it difficult to accept the critical assumption of humane culture, namely that every being of human origin be considered a "person" (with an intrinsic, unconditional dignity). To ignore this assumption, even in one instance, is to risk unconditional harm to this unconditionally dignified being, which is a gross violation of both the Silver Rule (minimalistic ethics), and inalienable rights.	5) Therefore, this group will see the critical assumption (necessary for humane culture) to be both self-evident and an inviolable principle: that every being of human origin be considered a "person" (with an intrinsic, unconditional dignity). *To ignore this assumption, even in one instance, risks unconditional harm to this unconditionally dignified being.* Even though this group may not be aware of the Silver Rule or inalienable rights, it is acutely aware that such an unconditional harm is deeply threatening to the culture.

PERSONHOOD (continued)

Level 1/2	Level 3/4
6) In conclusion, the L1/2 group (inclined to overlook the intangibles) so fixes upon appearances in its approach to definition, that it tends to overlook the critical assumption necessary for the survival of humane culture. If the L1/2 mentality sets our cultural agenda, it will cause unconditional harm not only at the beginning and end of human life, but also in the middle.	6) In conclusion, the L3/4 group (inclined to look for the perfection and highest power of human beings to optimize good in the world) sees the "guiding force toward unconditional and perfect Truth, Love, Goodness, Beauty, and Being" to be real. In so doing, it is inclined to assume that every being of human origin be considered a "person" (possessing this guiding force) from the very moment of the beginning of development, to the very moment of natural death. This group is acutely aware of the consequences of ignoring this critical assumption, and feels a strong moral obligation to adhere to it. If the L3/4 mentality is allowed to set our cultural agenda, it will not only protect the beginning and end of human personhood, it will also direct the culture to a flourishing of the middle through contribution, love, virtue, and the common good.

RIGHTS

Level 1/2	Level 3/4
1) L1/2 attitudes (focusing on the tangible, external, and comparative) will view "inalienable rights" as abstractions, that is, as inventions of the human mind. The group embracing these attitudes will therefore believe that inalienable rights (contrary to the meaning of these words) do not objectively belong to human beings, but rather are merely subjective qualities, invented by human beings, and assigned to them by a polity, state, or constitution.	1) Inasmuch as the L3/4 mentality views intrinsic, unconditional dignity as self-evident and objectively real, it is also inclined to view inalienable rights similarly. A very elementary education in rights theory will be sufficient to manifest to this group the objective reality of inalienable rights. After education, this group is likely to find the existence of inalienable rights in all beings of human origin. It will not be inclined to believe that such rights are mere inventions of political theorists, nor will it be inclined to believe that they are assigned to people by a polity, constitution, or plebiscite. It will generally hold that inalienable rights cannot be bestowed on persons by a polity any more than intrinsic dignity can.

RIGHTS (continued)

Level 1/2	Level 3/4
2) Inasmuch as L1/2 attitudes restrict personhood to beings who *appear* to be fully human (appearance definitions), they also tend to restrict inalienable rights to the same group. For this group, the clarity principle (see Chapter Seven) is more important than the critical assumption. Since this group believes that inalienable rights need to be assigned by polities in order to exist, and that such rights should not be assigned until it can perceive a *clearly* apparent person, it tends to restrict rights to whoever conforms to *its perception* of a clearly apparent person. Needless to say, this can lead to the removal of inalienable rights from any group that does not happen to fall within the elite's perception of clearly apparent personhood (e.g., mentally and physically disabled or economically marginalized).	2) The L3/4 group is inclined toward the critical assumption. Therefore, it will recognize inalienable rights in all beings of human origin lest it cause unconditional harm to a being of unconditional dignity. This group will not restrict its recognition of inalienable rights to human beings in any way. Its universal recognition of human rights supersedes the clarity criterion. Given the consequences of subordinating universal recognition of rights to the clarity criterion (e.g., an elitist, arbitrary removal of human rights from the "unfavored"), this group will generally consider such subordination to be a gross violation of minimalistic morality (the Silver Rule). If L3/4 attitudes set the political agenda, inalienable rights will be protected and fostered within both the culture and the polity.
3) L1/2 attitudes (in their search for what is tangible, external, and comparative) ignore objective necessity not only in the ranking of inalienable rights but also in mathematics and logic. This group may frequently be heard to say that the Pythagorean Theorem is nothing more than a set of human definitions. It would hold that the theorem does not have an intrinsic, objective necessity which cannot be other than it is. As such, this group would prefer to resolve rights conflicts on the basis of clarity rather than on an objectively necessary prioritization. Hence, this group might say, "The mother is a more clearly apparent 'person', than her preborn daughter. Therefore, the mother's right to liberty should be viewed as more important than her preborn daughter's right to life." Needless to say, this could lead to the subordination of life rights to liberty rights (or liberty rights to property rights) any time the elite do not clearly perceive the personhood of the rights holder.	3) The L3/4 group does not require that reality be tangible. Therefore, it is more willing to accept objective necessity in mathematics, logic, and other areas. As such, it is willing to accord greater priority to life rights than to liberty and property rights. It sees that life rights are more fundamental than liberty rights because the former are *objectively necessary* for the latter, but not vice versa. This group will, therefore, not subordinate this *objective* ranking to the merely *subjective* clarity criterion. This group will view such a subordination as a gross violation of minimalistic morality (the Silver Rule). By adhering closely to objective necessity, this group will keep the prioritization of inalienable rights safe from the arbitrary whim of a powerful elite.

COMMON GOOD

Level 1/2	Level 3/4
1) In its search for what is tangible, exterior, and comparative, the L1/2 group will find the common good to be unspecifiable and vague. It will generally view this as the dream of idealists who are not acquainted with the true reality of socio-economic life (e.g., that everything is comparative and competitive and that it is a "dog-eat-dog world out there"). Though there is some truth to this, it becomes a life philosophy for the L1/2 group, leading to a rather pessimistic appraisal of the future. The common good, therefore, seems not only vague and unspecifiable but also completely unrealistic and unactualizable.	1) Inasmuch as the L3/4 group seeks contribution, love, and self-transcendence as meaning and purpose in life, it will also see the common good as concrete, specifiable, and actualizable. Even though some participants in the culture may want to take advantage of the benevolence offered by others, this group will generally not despair of the future. It will protect itself from the bad will of others while still reaching out to a future of greater love, compassion, commitment, and peace.
2) Therefore, the best we can hope for is to protect our rights (our autonomy) and to tolerate everyone else's rights (their autonomy). Since the L1/2 mentality always prioritizes toleration and autonomy above the common good, it absolutizes them and, in so doing, reduces the common good to them. In this view, the culture can strive for nothing more than the tolerant pursuit of individual desires.	2) The L3/4 group will hold to the importance of toleration and autonomy, but it will not elevate them to "all we can hope for". This group hopes for a greater level of mutual concern, while tolerating those who are less concerned. It hopes for a future of greater compassion while tolerating those who are inclined toward less compassion. It hopes for a greater sharing of the world's resources, while tolerating those who would want to have more of their "rightful share". How far does the toleration go? Toleration stops at the violation of another's inalienable rights. In this way, the common good and inalienable rights can be blended in a mutually protective partnership that allows at once for the fullest manifestation of toleration and the pursuit of the highest possible collective ideal.

PART THREE

THE LIFE ISSUES:
ABORTION AND EUTHANASIA

Introduction to Part Three

As can be seen from the previous chapter, this book and the Life Principles project is attempting to restore and enhance six major cultural principles which have fallen onto hard times through the loss of intangibles and the advocacy of abortion and euthanasia:

1. Restoration of the third and fourth levels of happiness and purpose in life to the awareness of the general public

2. Restoration of the uncompromisability of the principle of non-maleficence

3. Restoration of the uncompromisability of critical assumption of personhood (that all beings of human origin are persons)

4. Restoration of the inalienability of the rights to life and liberty

5. Restoration of the objectivity of the prioritization of inalienable rights

6. As a consequence of the restoration of principles 1 through 5, a restoration of the uncompromising protection of the life and liberty of the preborn, elderly, and terminally ill from conception to natural death

No culture can survive without the objectivity, rationality, care, concern, and co-responsibility of these six principles. It may take a long time for the absence of these principles to produce cultural decadence and eventual demise, but this will inevitably take place; for culture is not dependent solely upon a great constitution, government, or legal system, but above all on a conviction about human dignity, personhood, rights, and the common good. Though this cultural conviction be intangible, it is the reality behind the constitution's, government's, and legal system's ability to pursue the common good and a benevolent society. Without it, the road to decline will be filled not only with negligence, but with ever-increasing degrees of disrespect and even cruelty.

The first five principles have been discussed in detail in the previous two parts. It now remains to discuss the sixth principle as integral to the other five, and therefore, to the very survival and growth of the culture itself.

Chapter Nine

Abortion

Introduction

If the vast majority of people aspire to Level 3 and/or 4, then why would they negate the critical assumption about personhood (every being of human origin is a person)? Inasmuch as the critical assumption is grounded in the principle of nonmaleficence (ethical minimalism), and Level 3 and 4 people are generally beneficent (ethical maximalism), advocacy of abortion is culturally and ethically perplexing. Is it because people only *aspire* to Levels 3 and 4, but when crunch time comes, they move toward the greatest convenience? I do not think so. Over the course of my life, I have seen very little reason to be cynical about human aspiration. Despite many evident human failings, there appears to be an ongoing capacity not only to protect but also heroically to foster love, virtue, compassion, justice, and the common good.

Then why would Level 3 and 4 aspirants advocate a gross violation of the principle of nonmaleficence, an unconditional harm to a being of unconditional dignity? It must be evident that each abortion affects not only the individual preborn child but also the whole future of the family, friends, and community who would have surrounded that child. Inasmuch as each of us contributes positively to the emergence of the history of our families, friends, community, and even the world, each abortion has negative "world changing" consequences. Then why would Level 3 and 4 aspirants be so benign to such a harm?

As was explained in the introduction to this book, the problem began under the guise of metaphysical materialism (the problem of relegating intangibles to the status of unreality—see box 1 in diagram 10). This led to two cultural assumptions, which paved the way for abortion and euthanasia (box 2):

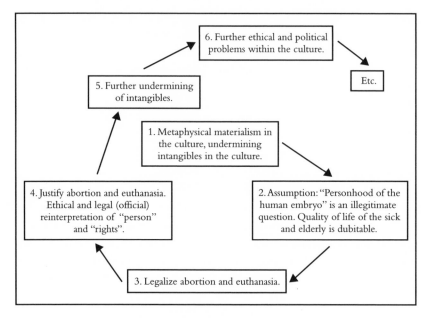

Diagram 10.

1. The "personhood of the human embryo" is a bogus question.

2. The quality of life of the sick and elderly is dubitable.

These assumptions led to the legalization of abortion and the limited legalization of active euthanasia (box 3).

In order to maintain the intrinsic connection between ethics and the law, many influential members of society (educators, the media, the judiciary, government officials) attempted to justify abortion and euthanasia *ethically* (box 4). In order to avoid the ethical problem of "murder" (the intentional, premature termination of the life of an innocent *person*), the idea of "person" had to be changed. Instead of associating "person" with its objective ground (that is, a being of human origin), the culture embarked on a reeducation program to associate "person" with a specific *kind* of human being (a human being outside the womb). The unfortunate effect of this program is the so-called slippery slope, which has been fantastically and deliberately underestimated. The moment the courts separated "person" from its objective ground, they empowered any influential interest group subjectively to redefine "person" whenever it is convenient. Why couldn't the courts just as easily declare that a person doesn't exist until the first month after birth? Many philosophers have already made such a declaration.[1] They have even added that a limited form of infanticide would help the culture economically, while providing a postnatal way of eliminating birth defects and retardation.

Recall that as the definition of "person" goes, so goes the definition of "inalienable rights". The more narrow the definition of "person", the more narrow the definition of "inalienable rights". One might object that such narrow definitions of "person" would always be viewed as morally repugnant. Hence, our ethics will save us from circumscribing the rights of "real persons" out of existence. This is a fine, optimistic thought, but it does not seem to jive with the contention of many anthropologists, namely, that "what becomes legal becomes normative, and what becomes normative becomes moral". What if there were only a 10 percent probability that these anthropologists are correct? Then, instead of our ethics protecting our rights, our narrower definition of rights would undermine our ethics.

I would contend that this has already occurred. Our ethics (our view of "virtue") has declined significantly. Our youth in particular understand well all the signals the culture is giving them about personhood, rights, and virtue. This undermining of "virtue" has led to an undermining of freedom, love, and the ability to deal with suffering, embarrassment, or even slight teasing. In short, all ten categories of cultural discourse have been undermined and continue in their decline (box 5). I see at least ten ways in which this decline has occurred.

A. the redefinition of "person" in the attempt to justify abortion

B. neglect of inalienable rights arising out of the redefinition of "person"

C. neglect of the objective ordering of rights arising out of A and B

D. neglect of the principle of nonmaleficence arising out of A–C

---

[1] See Peter Singer quote on page 252 above.

   E. superficiality of "freedom" arising out of A–D

   F. superficiality of "virtue/ethics" arising out of A–E

   G. superficiality of "love" arising out of A–F

   H. superficiality of "self-worth" arising out of A–G

   I. superficiality of "happiness/success" arising out of A–H

   J. inability to suffer well resulting in a culture of self-pity and
      despair arising out of A–I

If this continues, it will affect every other ethical and political issue
within the culture (from famine and violence, to simple care and concern for the marginalized—box 6). Without a concerted effort to reverse this cycle, the culture will continue in its dramatic decline.

As long as we continue to justify abortion and euthanasia, we will
continue to erode the ten categories of cultural discourse. This mal-
adjustment could eventually cause the culture to move toward Level 1
and 2 with such intensity that Levels 3 and 4 could be altogether forgotten. The net result would be that our culture would call us to our
lower selves and away from our higher selves.

Reversing the above-mentioned cycle will require not only a reversal
of legalized abortion and euthanasia but also a broadening and deepening of the ten categories of cultural discourse. In order to recognize
the magnitude of this project, it would do well to examine the decline
that has already occurred and is likely to occur in each of them. This
is best expedited by explaining the ten logical steps mentioned in the
list above.

I. The Redefinition of "Person" in the Attempt
to Justify Abortion

Inasmuch as abortion intentionally terminates the human mystery in
our midst, the attempt to legalize it forces the culture to explain its
violation of the most basic ethical principle (the principle of nonmaleficence—"Do no harm"). People who operate at Levels 3 and 4
(contribution toward others and the common good, and faith) will not
knowingly legislate a harm. Therefore, they must be under some mis-

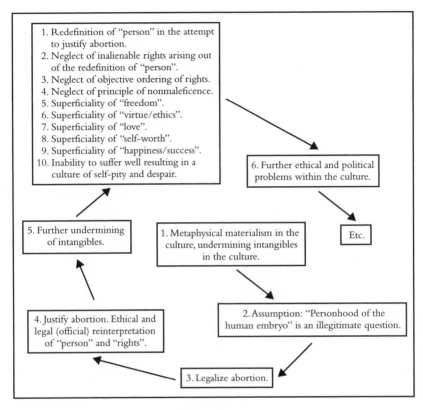

1. Redefinition of "person" in the attempt to justify abortion.
2. Neglect of inalienable rights arising out of the redefinition of "person".
3. Neglect of objective ordering of rights.
4. Neglect of principle of nonmaleficence.
5. Superficiality of "freedom".
6. Superficiality of "virtue/ethics".
7. Superficiality of "love".
8. Superficiality of "self-worth".
9. Superficiality of "happiness/success".
10. Inability to suffer well resulting in a culture of self-pity and despair.

6. Further ethical and political problems within the culture.

Etc.

5. Further undermining of intangibles.

1. Metaphysical materialism in the culture, undermining intangibles in the culture.

4. Justify abortion. Ethical and legal (official) reinterpretation of "person" and "rights".

2. Assumption: "Personhood of the human embryo" is an illegitimate question.

3. Legalize abortion.

Diagram 11.

impression about the existence or nature of the harm. This misimpression is linked to the redefinition of "person" arising out of the *Roe vs. Wade* decision.

Shortly after the Court's ruling in *Roe vs. Wade*, the opinion emerged in the popular and academic press that "person" was distinct from human life. The attempt to justify abortion required that "person" be divorced from human life because it could not be denied that a human life existed at conception. It is clear that the conceptus is a life (for it is metabolizing, growing, subdividing, and surviving). It is also clear that the conceptus is uniquely human, for it possesses the complete genetic structure of a unique human being and even the sequencing of cell divisions leading to that fully developed human being.[2] Therefore a single-cell embryo is a unique human *life*. Prior to the *Roe vs. Wade* decision a "person" was implicitly identified with a "unique human life". But after the abortion decision, this was not possible, because the killing of a unique human life would have been the killing of a person (who would have had inalienable rights, and therefore been deserving of protection under the law). If a person was a "unique human life", then the courts would have been abandoning their most fundamental mandate—to protect inalienable rights.

However, in order to justify abortion, human personhood was distinguished from "unique human life". It became almost commonplace to hear that "even though a unique human life is present, human *personhood* is not". Since it was further contended that rights belong only to "persons", it fell to the courts to define when personhood occurs, which, as was explained above, had the effect of subjectivizing the definition of both "person" and "inalienable rights".

The Court's subjectivization of "person" is completely unwarranted, because there is an obvious objective ground for it, namely, "human life", that is, the existence of a being of human origin. Once the Court detached personhood from this obvious objective criterion, it allowed the definition of human personhood to float in a subjective continuum. Nobody can really know what a "person" will be tomorrow. It all depends on what the courts think, or what experts the courts consult. All this ambiguity is absolutely unwarranted and unnecessary. Why? Because minimalistic ethics (the principle of nonmaleficence) requires that every being of human origin be considered a person lest unconditional harm be done to a whole population of people. In other words, minimalistic ethics requires that the courts attach themselves to the objective criterion of "human life equals human person". I truly believe that every member of the Court intends the principle of nonmaleficence from the very core of their being, and out of this belief, I ask the members of the Court consistently to apply the mandates of this minimum ethical principle to the definition of "person" as was done during the two hundred antecedent years of its existence. If the Court treats this

[2] See Jerome Lejeune, M.D., in *Junior L. Davis and Mary Sue Davis vs. Ray King, M.D., d/b/a Fertility Center of East Tennessee, Third Party Defendant,* "Custody Dispute over Seven Human Embryos", Aug. 1989.

matter seriously, it will be clear that it will have to embrace the critical assumption mentioned above (when in doubt, it is morally obligatory to assume the existence of personhood lest one commit an unconditional harm to a being of unconditional dignity). This would entail a reversal of the *Roe vs. Wade* decision and the legal "rationale" underpinning it.

As noted above, the separation of "person" from human life also affects our view of "inalienable rights", which opens a cultural Pandora's box. If rights do attach themselves to persons, and there is no *objective* ground of the definition of "person" (such as, the occurrence of a unique human life), then personhood (and inalienable rights) could be defined in any *arbitrary* way that a legitimate or powerful authority wills it. By changing the definition of "person", one can define who should get rights and who should not. By losing the objective ground of personhood (that is, the occurrence of a unique human life), one automatically undermines the inalienability of the right to life and all other subordinate rights.

We have placed our most important social possession (the source of our freedom and protection within society) in the control of an external authority. What once belonged to us in virtue of our existence now belongs to the courts. Will it stop merely with the abortion issue? Could a court someday define person as "a being who has reached the age of reason" or "a being who has a reasonable degree of independence" or "a being with a minimum 98 IQ" or even "a being incapable of being depressed"? Why not? The *Roe vs. Wade* decision and its aftermath have allowed any of the above subjective definitions of "person" to become a future reality. According to the Court, we are no longer *intrinsic rights holders* at the moment our unique human life occurs. We are *extrinsic rights recipients* at the moment the Court declares our personhood to exist.

Moreover, as was explained above, legal definitions of "person" find their way back into the definitions of the other nine categories of cultural discourse, because what becomes legal becomes normative, and what becomes normative becomes moral. For example, if the legal system should define personhood in terms of "degree of independence from others", then less independent people, by implication, would have to have a lesser quality of life. This lesser quality of life, in turn, would further imply less opportunity for happiness and success, which could be viewed as a life of intrinsic suffering. Should we allow these more

290 THE LIFE ISSUES: ABORTION AND EUTHANASIA

dependent people to come into a world filled with such a burden? Would it not be the more "loving" and "virtuous" thing to head their inevitable misery off at the pass? Would it be "ethical" to use scarce resources to benefit them when there are other more independent people in the world? It seems that the "common good" would dictate that we ought to subordinate the life rights of the more dependent to the liberty and property rights of the more independent. At this juncture the life of the more independent has been deemed by the culture to be more worthy than the life of the more dependent. Any number of negative social consequences, including genocide, can follow from this reasoning.

This reasoning, with all of its negative consequences, abounds in our contemporary culture. It can be found in current journals of ethics, law, and medicine and heard daily on the radio and television. If the culture as a whole is going to move out of this mindset, it must recover the above principles of personhood and make a concerted effort to bring itself back to Level 3 and 4 thinking. Perhaps the reverse is more appropriate. We must first recover Level 3 and 4 thinking so that our hearts will be disposed to looking for the objective truth about personhood. This is precisely the purpose of the Life Principles program.

II. Neglect of Inalienable Rights Arising Out of the Redefinition of "Person"

Since inalienable rights attach themselves to persons, the subjectivizing of persons had to result in the subjectivizing of inalienable rights. Whatever implicit recognition the Court had of the distinction between an inalienable and an extrinsic right seems to have been lost. The Court began to proliferate rights, and popular rhetoric took this to an even greater extreme. People had rights to hot coffee or rights not to have coffee "too hot", rights to have a place to smoke and rights not to have smoke in the atmosphere. The very narrow definition of inalienable rights, that is, of the obligation we have not to cause unconditional harm to a being of unconditional dignity, seemed to slip away into silliness. Not only did all rights seem to be equal; inalienable rights seemed indistinguishable from rather superficial, extrinsic ones.

As was noted above, the state's legitimacy is grounded in inalienable rights, while extrinsic rights are declared to exist by the legitimate state. The loss of the notion of inalienable rights, therefore, opens the door to a state that is responsible to nothing except the will of the governed. Not only can this lead to a tyranny of the majority; it can also foster the state becoming an end in itself (having the power to define when and where *all* rights occur). I am certain that this usurpation of rights was unwittingly propagated by the Court in the *Roe vs. Wade* decision. It can hardly be imagined that the justices were deliberately attempting to grab absolute authority and power for the state. Nevertheless, they did in fact do this and have opened the way to all kinds of interesting renditions of "Big Brother" in our midst.

As the Genome Project nears completion, this inattentiveness to inalienable rights will become progressively more important, for the Court now has the power, by its own self-declaration, to declare who is a person (having inalienable rights) and who is not. Could the Court declare that a preborn child with a disposition toward lung disease should not be considered a "person" deserving of inalienable rights? Of course it could. It has already used this logic thoroughgoingly in the *Roe vs. Wade* decision. If we, as citizens, feel uneasy about this kind of authority being vested in the state (whether it be in the executive, legislative, or judicial branches), then we ought to demand that the notion of "person" be once again linked to an objective criterion. We should demand that the definition of "person" be put not into *our* hands but back into the hands of an objective criterion. This demand will have to be made strongly, because even though the courts may have unwittingly usurped this power, the system of precedence requires that this egregious error be perpetuated until better reason can be found.

III. Neglect of the Objective Ordering of Rights Arising Out of A and B

In the previous chapter, much was said about how the *Roe vs. Wade* decision subordinated the preborn child's right to life to the mother's right to liberty. This was also done in the *Dred Scott* decision where the liberty rights of Blacks were subordinated to the property rights of white Americans. Again we see a further subjectivization of rights and personhood. The courts (unwittingly) took the prioritizing of rights out of the domain of objective necessity and placed it squarely in the subjective domain of their own intention. They did this ostensibly for the sake of clarity, but as we saw, clarity is a subjective principle that can differ substantially from one person to the next depending upon mental acuity, education, and experience.

Perhaps worse than this, the courts have opened up the nation to social conflict. As we have seen in other cases where objectively higher rights were subordinated to objectively lower ones, people seem instinctively to recognize the impropriety of this move. They implicitly resist it and finally explicitly fight it. The problem will not go away because the objective evidence of contradiction continues to haunt the people attending to it. For example, if I know that *Pi* equals 3.14159 . . . , the Indiana State legislature will not be able to convince me that it equals 3.2, as it attempted to do in 1897. Arbitrary judicial or legislative decree will never be able to overcome the constancy and universality of objective criteria. Not only will the misprioritization of rights in *Roe vs. Wade* be continuously before us; it also will be provocative, for this misprioritization is not simply mathematical, or theoretical. It has grave practical implications that reach to the core of objective injustice, the violation of inalienable rights, and even the violation of the principle of nonmaleficence. The Court has opened the door of social disturbance and conflict, and it will never be closed until the objective evidence is respected in the way it should be.

IV. Neglect of the Principle of Nonmaleficence
Arising Out of A through C

In the previous chapter, it was said that the critical assumption (every being of human origin must be considered a person) was based on the principle of nonmaleficence, which is the most basic (and minimum) ethical principle. When the Court detached "person" from "human life", it also unwittingly undermined the critical assumption and therefore the principle of nonmaleficence. Working backward through its logic, the Court is implicitly telling its citizens that they do not have to associate personhood with human life and, therefore, that they can risk unconditional harm to whole groups of individuals possessing unconditional dignity. In short, the Court intimated that it was all right to do harm if you were unclear about whether a harm was being done. But as was seen in the previous chapter, the principle of nonmaleficence requires precisely the opposite. It is not all right to do unconditional harm in the absence of clarity. One must *avoid* unconditional harm in the absence of clarity.

If the culture picks up the implicit cues from the Court's reasoning (when in doubt, unconditional harm is permissible), it might lead to a rather strange cultural view of ethics: "I released the *E. coli* bacteria into the stream because I was uncertain that it would cause any real harm. To be honest, I really believed that it would be so diffused in the water that it couldn't possibly hurt anyone. I was really amazed to hear that it annihilated an entire population center. And I've come to realize that I should've done some tests first to see if the bacteria would have multiplied in the ambiance in which I released it." If the principle of nonmaleficence does not hold, this person ought to be excused for his slight oversight. This kind of "excusability" not only undermines the duty for responsible conduct in both adolescents and adults; it also perpetuates reckless and dangerous behavior that will one day come back to haunt us. It is therefore incumbent upon our justices to redirect the notion of excusability back toward the duty of responsible and intelligent conduct by rekindling the principle of nonmaleficence undermined in the *Roe vs. Wade* decision.

V. Superficiality of "Freedom" Arising Out of A through D

As noted in Chapter Six, abortion has had a profound effect on our culture's view of "choice" and "freedom". Any culture must choose between two competing notions of freedom:

1. "freedom from", which tends to be grounded in strong momentary emotion (such as avoiding a particular pain or pursuing a particular pleasure)

2. "freedom for", which pursues what is most pervasive, enduring, and deep and therefore frequently delays gratification, makes sacrifice, and sometimes even endures pain

"Freedom from" tends to promote short term or immediate gratification. "Freedom for" pursues longer term gratification of the whole person in his deepest cognitive, emotive, and spiritual states. "Freedom for", therefore, tends to promote commitment, while "freedom from" tends to shy away from it.

We cannot afford to underestimate the role the culture plays in defining "freedom". From the day we are born our parents, teachers, friends, and the media give signals about when we should feel enslaved and when we should feel fulfilled and free. They tell us about either the importance of commitment and sacrifice or the foolishness of them. They create structures of expectation and anticipation about fulfillment and success. Children, adolescents, and adults all seek some form of approbation, acceptance, and esteem and, because of this, seek to imitate what the culture considers "smart" and avoid what the culture considers "dumb".

In its attempt to justify abortion, the Court used the terminology of "choice" and "freedom", but if one reads between the lines, not only in the *Roe vs. Wade* decision but also in its various legal, philosophical, psychological, and anthropological interpretations, one will notice that the implicit definition of "freedom" is based on choosing in accordance with one's strongest emotion at a particular moment. Women are not encouraged to think about what is most pervasive, enduring, and deep. They are not even encouraged to take some time off to reflect on what this decision will mean for their future and the future of others around them. The question of freedom is about what I want in the moment, which forces "want" to be viewed as the strongest emotion (the pain to be avoided or the pleasure to be pursued).

Our youth, as well as our adult population, have picked up these signals. Instead of viewing "want" in terms of a future filled with contribution, common cause, character, love, creativity, intelligence, and spirit, it is viewed as "emotive fulfillment now". This frequently produces an inability to delay gratification, to commit oneself to worthy goals, to discipline oneself, and to carry oneself through the hard times. It promotes low frustration thresholds, easy loss of temper, occasional unmitigated rage, and despair about life arising out of minute failures.

The attempt to justify abortion has moved "freedom" away from pursuing what is pervasive (good for the other or the culture) toward "getting what's mine". The thought of many abortion proponents has brought this nonpervasive thinking to its radically autonomous culmination by suggesting that the human embryo is a "parasite" upon the woman, creating hostility and opposition between what is naturally most intimate. This radical autonomy is also a radical form of "freedom from", which is being proposed to the culture as a proper and significant definition of freedom.

A further cultural problem arises out of the justification of abortion: the Court's decision places the woman's custody over her body over the embryo's right to life. In so doing, the Court turned "freedom from" (choice as the strongest momentary emotion) into a virtual absolute. The Court not only fostered the radicalization of "freedom from"; it also made "freedom from" a virtual moral imperative. This new moral imperative was picked up by the media and made the central theme for hundreds of television serials and movies. The point was not lost on our youth. Their own vocabulary revealed not only their desire for radicalized autonomy and the right to have their strongest momentary emotions fulfilled; they showed genuine moral outrage when these desires were not fulfilled. The culture had not just disappointed them; it had violated their rights. Even though many young people recognized the incompleteness and danger of these propositions, the culture has seen a rather marked change and radicalization of "freedom from" among its youth.

If this trend is to be averted, the "pro-choice" movement will have to stop using it as one of the fulcrums of its justification of abortion. Barring this, it will be incumbent upon all of us within the culture who do not share this radical belief in "freedom from" to educate our youth and our peers in the efficacy of "freedom for" and its pursuit of what is pervasive, enduring, and deep. The dividends (in terms of love, interpretation of suffering, virtue, quality of life, rights, and the common good) will be immense, indeed, and therefore very much worth our while.

VI. Superficiality of "Virtue/Ethics" Arising Out of A through E

As noted above, the attempt to justify abortion has made considerable use of the "clarity argument". If one is in doubt about whether there is a person present, one is not obliged to assume the affirmative. Rather, one is released from moral obligation if there is unclarity. Needless to say, this "reasoning" has far-reaching consequences beyond the abortion movement. In all honesty, it could be used as an excuse for any form of bias, disrespect, or denial of rights, for we can find ambiguity in virtually every ethical situation. Part of moral responsibility is knowing what one has to assume if one is uncertain. Are our youth aware of these moral assumptions, or, rather, are they being trained to excuse themselves whenever ambiguity arises? Obviously, many young people will never fall into the behavior of using ambiguity to excuse irresponsible assumptions and actions, but are we as a culture giving implicit sanction to this? Is the "clarity argument" undermining our capacity to take responsibility in the midst of ambiguity? Is it undermining the fine art of good judgment?

A second ethical problem arising out of the abortion decision is connected with the problem of freedom mentioned above. If our youth are not being exposed to what is pervasive, enduring, and deep, if they have only a superficial acquaintance with Level 3 happiness and purpose, then they will see little reason to pursue "means virtues" that will lead to these ends. We live more than ever in a culture that demands explanation for everything requiring effort. We are not likely to pursue difficult means virtues like self-discipline, humility, or courage because our parents or a wisdom figure encourages it. We would like to see a reason for it. Obviously, if we are looking only for Level 1 or 2 reasons (which will promote physical possessions, ego fulfillment, or comparative advantage, etc.), we will not be able to understand the reason for patience, self-discipline, courage, and especially humility. If, however, we are aware of and in some way living for Level 3 and/or 4, then the reason for difficult means virtues is patently evident.

The same holds true for the avoidance of vice. Most people in our culture do not want to be told "no". We don't want to hear the words "should not". Perhaps most importantly, we don't want to use the words "you should not" with respect to anyone else. This does not mean we cannot talk about moral vices (such as drunkenness, greed, avarice, anger, sloth, and pride). It means only that we cannot talk about them by using the words "you should not".

How can we talk about moral vice without using "you should not"? By *explaining* why such conduct leads away from a life that is pervasive, enduring, and deep. If, for example, our youth believe that love is a pervasive, enduring, and deep reason for living, and one can show that certain moral vices (such as cowardice, pride, undisciplined behavior) undermine such love, then they can be encouraged to avoid such vices in order to be free to pursue this end. However, if our youth are living only for the strongest emotion of the moment, if they have very little awareness of what is pervasive, enduring, and deep, if they have little sense of the third level of love or the third or fourth level of happiness, they will most likely not see the reasons to avoid the abovementioned vices. Instead, they will likely pursue them, because they are commensurate with the strongest emotion of the moment. In order to prevent them from harming themselves, we are forced to use "you should not", forced to bribe them with Level 1 and 2 rewards, and, in the end, forced to punish them for acting in the way we have encouraged. Avoidance of vice will not be seen as loving advice leading to the end of love, but only as another demand made by parents, authority figures, and society. Where's the motivation to follow through on that?

If we are to recover the ability to teach about virtue and vice, we will have to recover our view of freedom as the pursuit of what is pervasive, enduring, and deep. So long as freedom is viewed as the strongest emotion of the moment, the third level of love will seem impossible, if not unintelligible. So long as this level of love seems unintelligible, means virtues and vices will seem like mere abstractions. Tangible, immediately gratifying, strong emotions will seem much more poignant and realistic. Virtue will lose in this battle.

In the previous section, we saw what was required to recover the notion of freedom, namely, that the "pro-choice" movement, the media, educators, and all other participators in the culture refrain from interpreting "choice" in terms of immediate want, spontaneous emotion, and radical autonomy. This cannot be done in isolation from a Level 3 and/or Level 4 education, which points the way to what is pervasive, enduring, and deep. If we can come together as a community around such pervasive and enduring values, we will be able, in an atmosphere of love and rationality, to explain the truth about virtue and vice, about nonmaleficence and beneficence, and most of all, about what assumptions we ought to make in the midst of ambiguity.

VII. Superficiality of "Love" Arising Out of A Through F

As noted in Chapters Two through Four, Levels 1 and 2 can frequently be more intensive, immediately gratifying, and tangible than Levels 3 and 4, which are more pervasive, enduring, and deep. This holds true for the area of sexuality and love. If one does not make an effort to pursue what is pervasive, enduring, and deep, one is likely to define love in terms of sexual gratification and ego enhancement rather than gift of self, mutual support, common cause, intimacy, and commitment. I am not here suggesting that sexuality cannot be related to these fundamental areas of love. Indeed, sexuality finds its completion and purpose in these areas.

I suspect that the increasing rate of divorce and other domestic problems is not simply attributable to a decrease in social pressure to remain married. The enhanced focus on comparative identity and ego gratification (Level 2) within the marriage may also play a significant role. As explained in Chapter Three, as people become more focused on their Level 2 identity, jealousy, contempt, fear, inferiority, suspicion, and emptiness can frequently replace mutual support, intimacy, common cause, and commitment. The same holds true for friendships outside of marriage.

Diagram 12 shows how the emphasis on Level 1 and 2 within the culture combines with the abortion movement to produce a cyclic decline in the capacity for Level 3 and 4 love.

As noted above, cultural materialism has led to an increased pursuit of Level 1/2 desires because they are more tangible, intensive, and immediately gratifying (box 1). This has led to a Level 1 and 2 interpretation of sexuality (box 2), which emphasizes the pleasure and ego dimensions of sexuality while deemphasizing the Level 3 and 4 view of sexuality (support, long-term commitment, common cause, intimacy, and romance within this long term context). This emphasis on the Level 1 and 2 viewpoint necessarily affects the way one views love outside the context of sexuality (with friends, family, and acquaintances—box 3).

This understated view of love and sexuality became a cause célèbre in the 1960s. It became a foundation stone for the challenging of tradition and authority, which, in its turn, represented a new view of freedom. As explained above, this freedom is essentially "freedom from", which emphasizes the strongest momentary emotion while disengaging

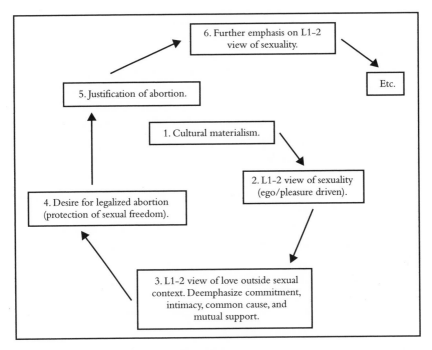

Diagram 12.

from what is pervasive, enduring, and deep. Popular culture defined this new "freedom" as real progress, giving it a strength and momentum sufficient to challenge long-standing traditions. This new freedom felt empowering. It decidedly moved a person's locus of control from community and commitment, to self and autonomy. Never before had such radical autonomy been embraced by a culture, and for a while, the youth of the culture basked in it and even made it their raison d'être. Levels 1 and 2 sexuality were a foundation and symbol of radical autonomy, and radical autonomy was the support and symbol of Level 1 and 2 sexuality. This new freedom, this progress, needed to be protected and promoted. The courts did this by legalizing abortion and declaring it to be a "right" (box 4). Abortion then became the symbol of radical autonomy, radical self-empowerment, and cultural progress. Even though it was clear that this self-empowerment was creating a "cult of self" that could undermine the fabric of family and community, popular culture decided to move headlong into it as if it were a panacea for social problems. Level 3/4 views of love and commitment seemed passé, naïve, and more trouble than they were worth. We had progressed to the pinnacle of Level 2 and were proud of it. Many elements of the women's movement recognized the association between Level 1 or 2 sexuality and radical autonomy. Inasmuch as abortion symbolized both the new sexuality *and* radical autonomy, the women's movement lent their full support to it. Abortion was now a reality in our culture, and it was heralded as the manifestation of new freedom and progress (box 5).

There seemed to be, in the culture, an almost staunch refusal to recognize the consequences of this "progress". Though people lamented the higher divorce rate, the breakdown of the family, the increase in youth violence, and the loss of commitment, they did not want to examine the root of this in the sexual revolution and its offspring, legalized abortion. Indeed, when even sympathetic critics tried to show a connection between the sexual revolution and the undermining of Level 3 and 4 love, they were blown off the proverbial public stage. They were treated as outcasts and traitors to the cause and branded as "antiprogress".

During the 1970s parents began to show far greater permissiveness about premarital sexual conduct. Many did not want to become countercultural; others did not want to use "should not"; still others did not want an unpleasant confrontation. The unfortunate consequence of this was that many youth began to view sexuality as an end in itself instead of as a means to solidifying a commitment and family. The person involved in the sexual act frequently became less important than the sexual act itself. Love on the third and fourth levels (support, intimacy, common cause, and commitment) was recognized as a kind of "romantic ideal", but never set into the context of patience, discipline, gratuitous kindness, forgiveness, deep mutual respect, and the time it takes to cultivate these. It seemed as if these characteristics were replaced by the language of "needs". Instead of asking what was necessary to develop intimacy and common cause within the relationship, we seemed to be asking, "Does this person fulfill my needs?" Though acknowledgment of need can be quite healthy, it must be admitted that this perspective became virtually all important.

The rhetoric used to justify abortion ran parallel to the rhetoric of the sexual revolution, inasmuch as both were grounded in, and promoted, radical autonomy. As noted above, radical autonomy is essentially a Level 2 characteristic (ego gratification), which gives great emphasis to "freedom from" (box 6). We cannot escape the fact that the justification of abortion and the sexual revolution necessarily promote Level 2 views of sexuality, love, and freedom. They take attention away from Levels 3 and 4 views and put an accent on competitiveness in relationships rather than complementarity. This frequently makes forgiveness and compromise a weakness rather than a strength and, in so doing, undermines the possibility of growth, intimacy, and mutual support.

Today's youth have picked up the signals of radical autonomy and Level 1 and 2 sexuality from our ardent popular defense of the sexual revolution and abortion. Many of them embrace it wholeheartedly, but many are beginning to resist it. They recognize that something is missing from their friendships and their aspirations. They know that love has to be deeper and more authentic than what the popular media makes it out to be. This group of youth is, in its own quiet way, starting a counterculture of its own. Many youth have already had disappointing sexual encounters. Others have only heard about such disappointments. But reality is beginning to break the myth. The deep and sophisticated Level 3 or 4 yearnings within the minds and hearts of our very informed and experienced youth are beginning to well up in the midst of disappointment, to challenge a myth that we, as a culture, refuse to face. This movement, in my view, needs to be empowered by Life Principles. Our youth need to see why their instincts are correct. They need to identify their higher yearnings and allow their desire for what is pervasive, enduring, and deep to prevail over mere strong, momentary emotions. Our youth are not superficial. When they hear the truth, they will seek it because they miss, perhaps more than any other segment of our society, the stability, permanence, depth, generativity, and purpose intrinsic to Level 3 and 4 love.

Though the Life Principles can provide a clarification and justification of Level 3 and 4 love, it must be reinforced within the culture. Parents, teachers, societal leaders, and, above all, the media must become integral partners in this effort. This will entail some self-critique, which may eventually result in a curtailing of the rhetoric of the sexual revolution and abortion. If this self-critique goes far enough, it may move from the *rhetoric* to the *reality* of the sexual revolution and abortion. This could form the basis of a further critique of radical autonomy and cultural materialism, which lie at the root of the contemporary decline in Level 3 and 4 purpose in life. We cannot afford to stop our cultural critique until we get at this tap root, for failure to do so would mean repeating the process in but a few years.

VIII. Superficiality of "Self-Worth" Arising Out of A Through G

By now it must be clear that our implicit views of freedom, ethics, and love significantly influence the way we look at and judge ourselves. If we implicitly believe in a Level 2 view of sexuality and love, we will tend to reduce our self-image to it. If we view freedom as the capacity to choose our strongest momentary emotions, we will likely forget what is pervasive, enduring, and deep. If we see very little purpose in virtue, we will simply leave it out of our view of self-worth. In short, our implicit views of freedom, ethics, and love define the narrowness or broadness of our categories of self-judgment, and these, in turn, define our horizons of possibility, our goals, and our identity. Notice that one need not have an explicit view of freedom, ethics, or love, and one may never have reflected on these ideas. Nevertheless, one always has an implicit view of them, and one uses these views to determine one's worth and to judge one's quality of life.

As stated many times above, an adequate sense of self-worth (capable of fostering friendships and deep relationships) cannot be grounded merely in comparisons. It must also be grounded in self-love and self-respect. Self-love consists in a sense that one is worthy of love, support, commitment, and decent treatment. These characteristics, in their turn, are grounded in Level 3 attitudes and purpose in life (see Chapter Four, section III). Self respect is focused on one's *intrinsic* dignity; therefore, it stands alone and cannot be grounded only in comparisons.

If one seeks self-worth solely from comparative advantage (Level 2), one is likely to reduce one's self-worth to the status of "winner" or "loser". Both groups lack a sense of intrinsic dignity. Since they have very little sense of *intrinsic* lovability, they tend to believe that they must "earn love". Their smile, kindness, affection, and attentiveness are seen to be insignificant next to comparative advantage. As a result, they tend to undervalue these same qualities in others, significantly underestimate affection and love in themselves, and tend to reduce relationships to "more or less", "higher or lower", and "better or worse".

If one derives a sense of self-worth from extrinsic sources alone, one will tend to lose sight of one's *intangible* qualities (love, justice, wisdom, capacity for contribution, and so on). This has a double effect:

1. It leads to "thingification" of self, that is, a view of self that is essentially external, sensible, and therefore merely physical and chemical.

2. It reinforces materialism (the loss of intangibles) within self and culture, which undermines more pervasive, enduring, and deep purposes in life while exaggerating the first and second levels of purpose or meaning (see the introduction of this book).

Without repeating what was said above, it is worth noting that these two consequences form a reinforcing cycle: the more one views oneself as a "thing", the more one will live for "thingly" purpose and meaning in life; the more one lives for "thingly" purposes, the more one will view oneself as a "thing". This materialistic cycle tends to continue until finally one's intrinsic dignity, mystery, lovability, and "soul" are completely eclipsed. When this occurs, one almost habitually acts for merely material and comparative meanings in life. The question of contribution and making a difference and the value of one's intrinsic presence lie so dormant that they emerge only in one's dreams. At this point, one is in incipient, if not explicit, despair. One desires only esteem because love is unintelligible. Indeed, one is likely to be unable to distinguish between esteem and love and hence believe that someone's esteem or admiration is, in fact, care, empathy, and appreciation of intrinsic dignity! At the very least, this is a replacement of lovability with esteemability; at worst, it is a suicide of one's lovable self-worth.

I am not suggesting here that our culture's justification of abortion has led directly to this all too frequent phenomenon, but it has certainly enhanced it. As noted above, materialism (the loss of intangibles) preceded abortion and euthanasia by many years. This was sufficient to initiate the undermining of intrinsic dignity and the lovable self. However, as explained above, the attempt to justify abortion has led to Level 1 or 2 interpretations of "person". This materialistic view of "person" has certainly led to an increased "thingification" of self-worth. Furthermore, the view of freedom as "the strongest momentary emotion" has led away from the pervasive, enduring, and deep meanings in life, which ground intrinsic dignity and the lovable self. Most ironically, the Level 1 or 2 perspective of love, which leads to a Level 1 or 2 view of sexuality, has convinced many that they are mere "sexual objects". As a result, sexuality has been viewed less as a symbol and reinforcement of commitment, romance, and mutual care and more as a symbol of one's comparative beauty and comparative performance. Thingification of sexuality leads to thingification of self-worth. Inasmuch as abortion has been justified as integral to "sexual freedom" (Level 1 or 2 sexuality), it has led to a thingification of self-worth.

The impact of our culture's increasing thingification of self-worth, leading to a loss of the lovable self and intrinsic dignity, should not be underestimated. The effects will be felt most poignantly by our youth because they are more dependent for their self-worth on love than esteem. They have neither the experience nor the developed capacities to ground a full blown esteemable self-worth. Therefore, they need, more than anyone else, to know and understand the adequacy of their "*lovable self-worth*". The more the culture signals to them that lovable self-worth is either meaningless or unreal, the more they will have to depend on their inadequate esteemable self-worth to take its place. At the very least, this will cause our youth increasingly to seek their self-worth from peer esteem. This will lead to a chameleonlike identity that changes with every set of peer expectations they encounter. Instead of remaining true to an identity they believe worthy of themselves, they are likely to have twenty identities throughout any given day imposed on them by the many audiences they encounter. This is a recipe for insecurity. To what lengths will our youth go to get peer respect and esteem? To what extent will they change their identity to get the attention and esteem they crave as a replacement for love? I have a suspicion they could innocently find their way into violence and self-destructive behavior in order to achieve self-worth. After all, no one can survive without self-worth. No one can bear to think that they, and their life, are going nowhere.

If we are to reverse this cultural trend, it will not be sufficient simply to cease justifying abortion. We will have to rekindle Level 3 and 4 views of self-worth, love, lovability, sexuality, freedom, and ethics. We will have to stop the trend toward greater materialism and reinforce meanings that are more pervasive, enduring, and deep.

The reverse is also true. If we are to stop the crisis of thingification of self, we cannot simply attempt to rekindle Level 3 and 4 self-worth, for the attempt to justify abortion will continue to have the same dramatic effects on personhood, sexuality, and freedom, which will rise up against our new attempts to reinstate Level 3 and 4 self-worth. The culture, particularly our youth, will pick up the contradiction and eventually brand it as hypocritical. We might be able to get away with inconsistency between our rhetoric and our reality in the short term. In the long term, our hypocrisy will devolve into cynicism.

IX. Superficiality of "Happiness/Success" Arising Out of A Through H

Since so many pages have been spent on the notion of happiness and success, I will treat only the characteristic alluded to in the previous section. The justification of abortion did not initiate the movement toward Level 1 or 2 views of happiness and success. Incipient and explicit materialism "accomplished" this many years before. However, the justification of abortion has intensified the move to Level 1 or 2 views of happiness and success through its effects on the notion of person, freedom, ethics, love, sexuality, and self-worth. The way one views self-worth affects the way one views progress in life. The way one views progress in life affects the way one views success. And the way one views success affects the way one views happiness (see Chapter Four, section I).

Inasmuch as the justification of abortion has intensified the thingification of self-worth leading toward the loss of the lovable self and intrinsic dignity, it also undermines our view of a successful life, and this view of a successful life, in turn, negatively impacts our happiness and moods. Recall that our view of a successful life creates a set of expectations within our conscious and subconscious psyche. When these expectations seem to be fulfilled, I feel happy. When they do not, I feel discontented, disappointed, frustrated, jealous, fearful, and even depressed. My *mood* can be frequently altered by this implicit sense of life corresponding to expectations. Suffice it to say that the more our youth thingify themselves, the more they will fix their expectations of success on Level 1 or 2 characteristics. Inasmuch as they feel that their expectations are being met, they will feel happy. Inasmuch as they *believe* these expectations to be unmet, they will be frustrated, jealous, depressed, and worse. Put yourself back into the school system you once experienced. Now, realistically assess how often you felt that your Level 1 or 2 expectations were being met. What is your general mood? How do you feel about your future? Enough said. We have been setting our youth up for a fall.

As mentioned above, a reversal of the trend toward a greater fall lies not only in ceasing to justify abortion, but also in giving our youth and adults a greater awareness of Level 3 and 4 meanings in life and a rationale for why they are more pervasive, enduring, and deep. Again, the reverse is also the case. We cannot impart Level 3 and 4 meanings in life while continuing to justify abortion through materialistic and comparative views of person, freedom, ethics, love, sexuality, lovability, dignity, and self-worth. The contradiction will be discovered and so, therefore, will the hypocrisy. The resultant cynicism will undermine the very Level 3/4 goals (noncontradictory love) that we are trying to accomplish. I believe we must undertake this twofold remedy quite soon, for our youth's individual and collective happiness depends on it.

X. The Inability to Suffer Well Resulting in a Culture of Self-Pity and Despair Arising Out of A Through I

As noted in Chapter Five, suffering can lead to lower *or* higher meaning and purpose in life. If suffering is found to have very little value (producing little or no good for anyone or anything), it tends to lead to discouragement, depression, and dread of the future. Recall that Level 1 or 2 meaning in life tends to view suffering as either negative or valueless (see Chapter Five, section I).

Conversely, if suffering is seen to have a higher purpose, or to produce some good within the world, it tends to help one grow in the nine ways mentioned above (capacity for love, forgiveness, common good, faith, and so on). This higher meaning generally comes from Level 3 and 4 meanings in life.

To repeat the example given in Chapter Five, a Level 1 or 2 meaning in life can frequently lead a hospital patient to discouragement because he will have suffered a loss to his physical stamina and ambulatory ability so important for his Level 1 or 2 identity. Conversely, Level 3 and Level 4 meaning in life can lead the hospital patient to resilience, spirit, love, forgiveness, patience, humility, wisdom, courage, self-discipline, friendship, and faith, because the suffering can lead this predisposed person to let go of Level 1 or 2 meanings in favor of Level 3 and 4 meanings.

The culture's movement to Level 1 or 2 meaning in life, therefore, is leading to a loss of the capacity to suffer well. Indeed, we don't even *know how* to find meaning, depth, virtue, freedom, and love through our suffering. We don't even know *that* we can find these qualities in our suffering. For this reason, we will become far more fragile and inclined toward self-pity and far more likely to give up in the face of adversity. The obvious consequences of this with respect to the euthanasia movement will be taken up in the next chapter. I am here concerned not so much with the cultural death wish manifest in the euthanasia movement, but with the more generic effects of "useless suffering" inherent within our culture.

If all there is to life is Levels 1 and 2, and suffering is virtually meaningless in this perspective, then suffering has the capacity completely to debilitate the sufferer. This debilitation not only prevents deep personal growth through suffering; it also actually undermines and weakens the individual person and the culture. It is not simply a waste of potential growth; it is a useless, even absurd agony. It will lead not only to a culture of self-pity, but eventually to a culture of cynicism and despair. If one cannot see a way through the absurdity of useless pain, one is likely to lash out at anyone who can see such meaning. Perhaps we will all become ultrasophisticates in our proclamation about the absurdity of life. This angst would be a tremendous shame for a culture that started out with such optimism, hope, creativity, and spirit. We have definitively planted the seed of cynical self-pity within our culture. We would do well to remove it from the ground before it grows too far.

The reversal of this cultural angst must occur in the same twofold way mentioned above, namely, by (1) rekindling and reinforcing Level 3 or 4 meaning within the culture and (2) ceasing the justification of abortion, which has reinforced the culture's inclination toward the first and second levels of meaning.

Conclusion

The rhetoric of abortion has not simply affected the political and legal establishment; it has severely impacted the culture. The effect of detaching "person" from "human life" did not stop at supporting the Court's legal reasoning; it found its way into the popular culture through politicians, educators, the media, and Madison Avenue. This unfounded distinction did not simply have the effect of undermining inalienable rights within the courts and our political system; it also led to the acceleration of materialism within the culture. The rhetoric of "choice" defined as "being able to do what I want" (with "want" being identified with "strongest momentary emotion") not only made abortion more palatable to our young people; it also undermined their ability to commit themselves to the more pervasive, enduring, and deep. Similarly, the rhetoric of "sexual freedom" did not stop at making abortion seem more progressive. It also led to the objectification and undervaluation of sexuality in its relationship to love. The same can be said for all ten characteristics mentioned above.

In sum, the justification of abortion has accelerated the culture's move toward materialism and Level 1 or 2 meaning in life. If we are to reverse this self-destructive trend, we will have to put an end to the rhetoric of abortion, which means putting an end to the justification of abortion, which ultimately means putting an end to the reality of abortion. Then, and only then, will our words about Level 3 and 4 meaning leading to a culture of respect, intrinsic dignity, inalienable rights, the fulfillment of "persons", and the common good carry with them the authenticity necessary to effect cultural transformation.

Chapter Ten

Euthanasia

Introduction

Euthanasia (from the Greek for "good death") may be defined as the deliberate, artificial ending of a life, so as to end suffering. It may take one of two forms:

1. *physician-assisted suicide*, in which death is induced by a lethal dose of "medication" provided by a physician or other health professional and self-administered by the patient

2. *direct euthanasia*, in which death is administered actively by a physician or other health professional, with the primary intention of killing the patient[1]

Euthanasia and/or physician-assisted suicide have recently been the subject of unsuccessful referenda in the American states of Washington and California and unsuccessful legislation in various parts of the United States, Canada, New Zealand, and Australia. Aside from the Netherlands, where euthanasia is technically illegal but now formally tolerated if carried out in accordance with written safeguards, the state of Oregon remains the only place in the world where euthanasia is legal.[2]

Robin A. Bernhoft, M.D., is the co-author of this chapter.

[1] A third category, so-called passive euthanasia, has been used, chiefly by the right-to-die movement in an apparent attempt to blur the distinction between euthanasia and the natural course of illness. In passive euthanasia attempts to delay inevitable death are ceased and the patient dies of the underlying disease. Examples would include stopping heroic measures in hopeless cases. This modality is generally agreed to be ethically distinct from the two forms of euthanasia in that no active measure is taken to end life and the patient dies of natural causes.

[2] Although referenda intended to legalize euthanasia failed in Washington State (1991) and California (1992), as of this writing Oregon's successful public measure has been upheld by the courts. The measure legalizing euthanasia in the Northern Territory of Australia was repealed by the national Parliament on March 24, 1997.

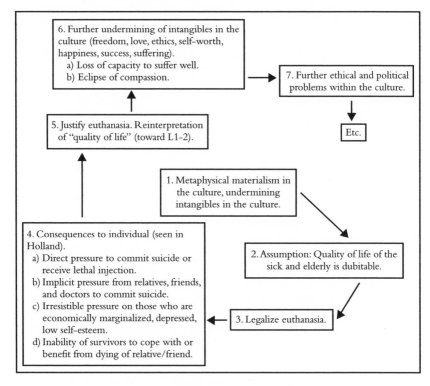

6. Further undermining of intangibles in the culture (freedom, love, ethics, self-worth, happiness, success, suffering).
 a) Loss of capacity to suffer well.
 b) Eclipse of compassion.

7. Further ethical and political problems within the culture.

Etc.

5. Justify euthanasia. Reinterpretation of "quality of life" (toward L1-2).

1. Metaphysical materialism in the culture, undermining intangibles in the culture.

4. Consequences to individual (seen in Holland).
 a) Direct pressure to commit suicide or receive lethal injection.
 b) Implicit pressure from relatives, friends, and doctors to commit suicide.
 c) Irresistible pressure on those who are economically marginalized, depressed, low self-esteem.
 d) Inability of survivors to cope with or benefit from dying of relative/friend.

2. Assumption: Quality of life of the sick and elderly is dubitable.

3. Legalize euthanasia.

Diagram 13.

Diagram 13 shows the negative impact of euthanasia on both individuals and the culture. Like abortion, euthanasia begins with cultural materialism (the loss of intangibles) and proceeds to a Level 1 or 2 assumption about quality of life, which, in turn, initiates a cycle of legislation and justification resulting in a more intransigent Level 1 or 2 culture.

This discussion will be divided into two parts:

1. the negative effects of euthanasia on individuals (section I)

2. the negative effects of euthanasia on the culture (section II)

I. Negative Effects of Euthanasia on Individuals

The negative effects of euthanasia on individuals may be seen through the rhetoric of the euthanasia movement in the United States.[3] In essence, their argument has four parts:

1. Without active euthanasia, uncontrollable *pain* is likely to accompany terminal illness.

2. Even if pain can be adequately controlled, the debility of terminal illness will likely preclude an acceptable *quality of life*.

3. Active euthanasia is a *right*. Therefore, people who do not want this option should not be permitted to prevent those who want it from obtaining it.

4. Active euthanasia will provide a variety of *social benefits*, such as helping to curb the costs of treating the terminally ill.

Each of these arguments contains flaws, which I will discuss, relating each, as appropriate, to the principles elucidated throughout this book.

A. First Argument of Euthanasia Advocates: Without Active Euthanasia, Uncontrollable Pain Is Likely to Accompany the Dying Process of the Terminally Ill

In the early stages of the euthanasia debate, this argument was one of the most powerful and emotionally persuasive points in favor of legalization and was used frequently by proponents to build support for their position. More recently, advances in pain and symptom management have rendered it increasingly false. It has been replaced generally by

---

[3] The primary national advocate of active euthanasia is the Hemlock Society (cofounded by Derek Humphry in 1980). Humphry resigned from the Hemlock Society in 1993 and then started a new, smaller organization called ERGO (Euthanasia Research and Guidance Organization). Choice in Dying is another national organization dedicated to euthanasia. It has testified in favor of assisted suicide in Canada, though it has backed away from active euthanasia as a raison d'être in the United States. Choice in Dying arose out of two other groups: Society for the Right to Die (which came from the Euthanasia Society of America, going back to the 1930s) and Concern for Dying (which came from the Euthanasia Education Council). There are several state and local organizations promoting active euthanasia.

quality of life or rights arguments. The reasons proponents have largely abandoned this point are clear from a brief review of the terminal care literature.

Martin L. Smith notes that "*ninety to ninety-nine percent* of terminal cancer pain can be controlled with the use of hospice and palliative care units".[4] Michael H. Levy affirms similar statistics in his 1993 study.[5] Even Derek Humphry (cofounder of the Hemlock Society and author of *Final Exit*, the controversial "self-help" suicide book) admits that "only *a small percentage* of terminal physical pain cannot be controlled today".[6] In the same vein, Dr. Pieter Admiraal (an anesthesiologist, clinical pharmacologist, and leading Dutch advocate of legalized euthanasia) admitted to Dr. Carlos Gomez that pain control and alertness can be achieved in *practically all* cases—given sufficient effort and sophistication on the part of all involved—and that euthanasia for pain control is therefore both unnecessary and unethical.[7]

Good pain control need not induce diminished consciousness. New techniques for the administration of morphine and other drugs allow virtually complete pain control, with alert mentation thoroughly supportive of work or of relating with friends and family. That this is now the standard of care is evident from many articles of (among others) the *Journal of Pain and Symptom Management*.

Good palliative care can generally be done as easily at home as in a hospital. Patients can approach a natural death comfortably and consciously in their own homes surrounded by family and friends. Hospice (an organization dedicated to outpatient treatment of terminally ill patients) has the capacity to treat not only pain but also depression and social difficulties in patients' homes. Morphine drips (which can be automatic or left to patients to control for themselves), liquid morphine (which can be easily swallowed or given by means of a feeding tube), sublingual morphine (administered under the tongue to provide immediate relief to patients experiencing sudden acute pain), and pain-relief

---

[4] Martin L. Smith et al., "A Good Death: Is Euthanasia the Answer?" *Cleveland Clinic Journal of Medicine* 107 (1992): 59 (emphasis added).

[5] Michael H. Levy, "Medical Management of Cancer Pain". in *Principles and Practice of Pain Management*, ed. Carol A. Warfield (New York: McGraw Hill, 1993), p. 235.

[6] Derek Humphry, *Let Me Die Before I Wake: Hemlock's Book of Self-Deliverance for the Dying* (Los Angeles: Hemlock Society, 1984), p. 76 (emphasis added).

[7] Carlos Gomez, M.D. Personal communication from Pieter Admiraal.

patches (which can be applied directly to the skin) are just a few examples of the ways in which outpatient pain treatment can be administered. None of these treatments is in any way life threatening, despite the allegations of euthanasia advocates.[8] Various new anesthetic techniques are also useful, and other drugs may benefit those who are allergic to morphine or who have conditions such as nerve or bone pain, which often require specific alternatives.

Pain treatment is a relatively inexpensive medical procedure because it is essentially pharmacological and can be administered by hospice nurses. The cost of palliative care is a fraction of the cost of life-prolonging measures.

Unfortunately, palliative care is also a distinct medical specialty in which most physicians are not trained. Consequently, large numbers of terminally ill patients suffer unnecessary pain because they are given inadequate doses of medication, either because of physician or nursing ignorance of pharmacy options and techniques or because of "narcophobia" on the part of the physician, nurse, patient, or patient's family.[9] Requests for euthanasia are not rare in patients who receive substandard treatment, but *virtually all* such requests are reversed when pain and depression are adequately treated.[10]

Horrifying anecdotes relating uncontrollable terminal pain have several causes:

1. Pain and symptom management has reached its current state of efficacy only in the last ten to fifteen years.[11]

---

[8] Morphine drips, for example, can be safely self-managed by patients for months. Arguments that they inevitably produce coma and death reflect either the intention to produce coma and death through overdose or a naïve lack of technical sophistication.

[9] *Cancer and Palliative Care*, Bulletin of the World Health Organization, Geneva, 1990.

[10] See, for example, Kathleen M. Foley, M.D., "The Relationship of Pain and Symptom Management to Patient Requests for Physician-Assisted Suicide", *Journal of Pain and Symptom Management* 6 (1991): 290 (hereafter referred to as "Foley"). "We frequently see patients referred to our Pain Clinic who have considered suicide as an option, or who request physician-assisted suicide because of uncontrolled pain. We commonly see such ideation and requests dissolve with adequate control of pain and other symptoms, using combinations of pharmacologic, neurosurgical, anesthetic, or psychological approaches."

[11] Ibid., pp. 290–291. "National and international organizations like the American Pain Society, the International Association for the Study of Pain, the American Society of Hospice Physicians, and the International Psycho-Oncology Society have all only been formed in the last 5–15 years."

2. Physicians and nurses are frequently untrained in pain and depression management. Hence, even with today's technology, pain medication is frequently underprescribed in hospitals not having pain and symptom management specialists or hospice units.[12]

3. Many physicians underprescribe pain medication because of unfounded fears of addiction and other side effects or because of regulatory constraints on appropriate prescribing tactics.[13] John V. Hartline sums up the real problem of pain management quite well, saying, "Nevertheless, use of inadequate amounts of pain medication has been implicated as the most significant form of 'drug abuse' in the care of the terminally ill." [14]

Clearly, from a public policy standpoint, the answer to uncontrolled pain is not to kill[15] those who suffer but to improve the quality of terminal care through ensuring:

1. adequate education in pain and symptom management for health care professionals

2. the accessibility of hospice care for all who desire it

These ends have already been largely accomplished in Britain.[16]

---

[12] Ibid. "At the present time, there are few highly trained physicians in cancer pain management or psycho-pharmacology whose main interest is to place a high priority on pain management, symptom control, and psychological support for these patients with far-advanced disease." See also J. Hamilton and Al Edger, "A Survey Examining Nurses' Knowledge of Pain Control", *Journal of Pain and Symptom Management* 7 (1992): 18–26.

[13] Russell K. Portenoy, M.D., "Cancer Pain: Epidemiology and Syndromes", *Cancer* no. 11, 63 (1989): 2300. "... The data reviewed above suggest that inappropriate, misapplied, or under-utilized clinical techniques of pain management underlie most of the problem. This disheartening observation can largely be attributed to two factors: ignorance of the pharmacology of analgesic drugs; and inappropriate concerns about psychologic dependence on opioids." See also his notes 1, 26, 28, and 29 on pp. 2306–7.

See also Foley, p. 291. See also Ronald Melzack, "The Tragedy of Needless Pain", *Scientific American*, no. 2, 262 (Feb. 1990), 27–33.

[14] John V. Hartline, "Compassionate Alternatives for the Terminally Ill", *Journal of the Michigan Medical Society*, (Apr. 1993): 26–27.

[15] "1. to cause the death of; to put to death; to slay": *Webster's New Universal Unabridged Dictionary*, 2d ed. (New York: Dorset and Baber (1983), p. 1001. The word *kill* conveys no information on intent; attempts by proeuthanasia advocates to conflate *kill* and *murder* ignore the dictionary meanings of the two words.

[16] Sandol Stoddard, *The Hospice Movement* (New York: Vintage Books, 1978), pp. 254–55.

Pain is, of course, only one sort of suffering. Others will be discussed in the section below on quality of life. Pain and suffering have other uses, as I have discussed, notably serving on occasion to speed entry into Happiness 3 and 4.[17] This is not, however, an aspect of terminal care that lends itself easily to the sound byte ethos of public debate.

B. Second Argument of Euthanasia Advocates: Even if Pain Can Be Adequately Controlled, the Debility of Terminal Illness Will Likely Preclude an Acceptable Quality of Life

Euthanasia for pain relief is increasingly being seen by the general public as unnecessary and unethical. Consequently, euthanasia proponents have fallen back to invoking quality of life as their favored justification for legalization. The public deeply fears disability. One commonly hears statements like "Who cares about being comfortable and alert? If I'm bedridden and can't do anything, I'd rather be put to sleep. When you're like that, you're as good as dead."

Such statements are, of course, based on implicit Happiness 1 and 2 assumptions about what constitutes quality of life. Such assumptions need not be taken at face value or left unchallenged. Every human being has desires for all four levels of happiness. In our experience of presenting the principles of this book in public formats, this desire is usually close to the surface, often in the least likely people. People can easily be called to higher levels of quality of life.

As we have seen,[18] one's understanding of quality of life is determined by one's habitual level of happiness and by the concepts of personhood and suffering associated with that level of happiness. Definition of quality of life, in turn, has a major impact on attitudes toward euthanasia. For example, persons in Happiness 1 and 2 see quality of life in concrete terms that afford immediate physical or ego gratification but provide little long-lasting fulfillment and little or no good beyond the self. Individuals in these levels generally favor euthanasia, for they are unable to find meaning in deprival of their habitual means to happiness.

[17] See chap. 5.
[18] See chap. 4.

Life in Happiness 1 is an accounting process, in which pleasures and pains are measured against one another. Good quality of life is maintaining a positive balance, in which pleasures outweigh pains. When the balance is negative, quality of life is negative and euthanasia may be "rationally" sought.

Happiness 2, similarly, sees quality of life in terms of achievement or comparative success. Rising above mediocrity, making more money, gaining more status, or otherwise feeding the ego fills life with exhilaration and a sense of progress and accomplishment. Of such is the quality of life. When competitive ability wanes, so does quality of life. When one is "unable to do anything" (say, while lying in a hospital bed), one has "no quality of life" and would be "better off dead". Hence most of the public support for euthanasia.

In contrast to these, Happiness 3 and 4 are less concrete and require delayed gratification, but their effects are deeper and longer lasting and usually produce good beyond the self.

Happiness 3 sees quality of life in communicating with or caring for others and doing a good beyond the self. Quality of life could include helping family and friends muddle through the ups and downs of life; listening or being present to others; inspiring others with courage, hope, and love; or sharing faith, friendship, or other matters of the heart. These are all activities that can be carried out from a hospital bed. They are perfectly compatible with terminal illness and may be augmented by any form of weakness or deprivation.[19] Love has a peculiar way of coming alive the moment one takes one's focus off things, toys, achievements, and competitions. Love can be stronger in the last few weeks of life than in all the years of perfect health preceding it. Indeed, healing of broken friendships or family relationships often needs the "nudge" of impending death to overcome residual pain and anger.

Happiness 4 is usually combined with Happiness 3. Faith not only enhances communication with others; it also responds to God's desire to communicate with us. Quality of life comes from participating in the ultimate Good beyond the self. God dignifies us not only through relationship with him but also through the privilege of sharing his presence with friends and family. Disability is more likely to promote than hinder the actualization of this ultimate quality of life, for the more one

[19] See chaps. 4 and 5.

is in need, the more one "lets God in". One is most in need when one is dying.

Clearly, Level 3 and 4 quality of life transcends functional status; euthanasia for functional deprivation holds little appeal to those in Happiness 3 and 4 and would be counterproductive of their quality of life.

I cannot tell you how many times as a hospital chaplain, I (RJS) saw terminally ill people make family and friends aware of new meaning and worth in life, new breadth of love, and new depth of spirit. These friends and family members reported to me that being with this newly transformed, terminally ill person was like a redemptive experience. They felt themselves walking away with a new sense of the goodness and mystery of humanity, as if something transcendent from the terminally ill person had rubbed off on them.

Clarifying these four views on quality of life has enabled me to help patients in several ways. Perhaps most importantly, it has given patients an awareness of the good that they can do even in their more restricted state. This, in turn, has allowed them to see that the most poignant and deep contribution that they can leave behind in this world can come in their last days. They no longer need façades, external adornments or manifestations of power, to relate to human beings. For many, this is the first time in their lives that they have been able to relate to another human being as an intrinsically good, intrinsically lovable, transcendent being. Sometimes it is the first time they have made direct contact with the mystery (indeed, the soul) of another. This experience of deep love and friendship (and the good that comes from it) gives the terminally ill a sense of their own lovability.

Most patients have also reported to me that when they see the third and fourth levels of quality of life in contrast to the first two, they know that the third and fourth levels are "right". They know what to live for and how to live for it. Frequently, they know what they have done "wrong" in their past pursuit of the quality of life. They have also told me that they have a new understanding of themselves, their past, and what really matters in life. In short, these patients are happy. Most are happy in ways that they have never been before. And despite their restricted ambulatory ability, many are happier than they have ever been before. We can help them achieve this new happiness by helping them clarify their view of the quality of life.

I believe that every human being has at least a tacit awareness of the above four levels of the quality of life. However, they need to be brought explicitly to consciousness and then clarified. I have not found it necessary to persuade people of the desirability to move to higher levels of the quality of life. Once I have explained the four categories, most patients come to a better understanding of what makes life worth living and, as a consequence, seem to know what to do with their remaining days. Perhaps this discussion may best be summed up by paraphrasing Paul's First Letter to the Corinthians: "[The quality of life is to be found ultimately in] faith, hope, and love, and the greatest of these is love." Some true anecdotes may further illustrate the above points.

The first anecdote concerns an older gentleman (call him Joe), in a hospital with a terminal illness. He had previously severed relationships with his two closest friends. Despite continued ill feelings, his friends came to visit him because they wanted to patch things up and say good-bye. Joe at first was cool to the idea of seeing them, but because they had come a considerable distance he allowed them into his room. When he saw them, Joe's need for their friendship overcame his anger, and they sat in the room together for about six hours. Not only did "things return to the way they once were", they improved dramatically. The urgency of impending death forced them to swallow their pride and reconcile with one another. Their spirits came alive. Friendship, care, mutual insight, and spiritual awakening became intense. One of Joe's friends summed up the experience profoundly: "Impending death allows friendship to conquer anger." Impending death revealed the intrinsic and even transcendent goodness of each to the other, healing their hearts and bringing mutual joy.

None of that would have happened had Joe been euthanized prior to their visit. Joe's friends would have been bereft of his forgiveness, friendship, and the profound love that they had discovered within themselves through him.

Another anecdote involves a fifty-seven-year-old man (call him Frank), also terminally ill. His adult son came to visit him in the hospital. Frank had neither touched his son nor expressed any love since the son was ten years old. The son had been so deeply affected by this apparent lack of paternal love that it had blighted his life. With death near, Frank no longer felt he had to treat his son "as a man". The urgency of impending death broke through his façade, and he threw his arms around his son and kissed him. The son stayed in the room for several hours with his father, discussing all the need, love, and support that had passed them by and the hurt this had caused them *both*. The two were not only reconciled; they were elated. Frank and his son found themselves through their expressed love of one another. When the son left the room, he reported, "Now I can finally live my life in peace. Now I know that my father has always loved me." Again, one might ask what would have happened had active euthanasia been an "option". Certainly it would have deprived both father and son of the most meaningful, caring, and transcendent moment of their lives.

Two more anecdotes are not so much concerned with terminal illness as with illustrating that weakness (in ourselves or others) can help bring about the highest possible quality of life. The first involves a story told by the father of a child in California with Down syndrome:

> I have a Down syndrome boy. We worked hard to "mainstream" him in the school system. Because he was older than all the other children, they at first made fun of him. But after a while, they began to see that he was really quite defenseless, that he did not have aggressive instincts with which to respond to them, and that he *needed* them. Slowly but surely, they began to look out for him and even to take care of him as a sibling.
>
> The teacher wrote us a letter that our child had been an invaluable contribution to the school, because he had singlehandedly lowered the aggression level of the other students. "Before he came, the children compared themselves to one another in a way that left room for only winners and losers (mostly losers). After his arrival, the care which they began openly to display toward him lessened their focus on themselves, and most seemed to be happier. They actually enjoyed looking after him more than they enjoyed getting the upper hand!" He was later pulled out of the school for medical treatments, at which point the aggression level in the school began to reemerge.[20]

This child was not outstandingly beautiful or blessed with valuable clothes or toys or gifted with excess functional capacity or other competitive advantages. He came to school armed only with his being and with his ability to elicit love, care, and friendship from the other children. In contrast, the "normal" children went to school equating self-worth with possessions, external adornments, functional capacities, and

---

[20] As told to the author, Van Nuys, Calif., Sept. 1992.

success—goods largely out of reach for the boy with Down syndrome. The "normal" children wanted more and more of these goods in order, ultimately, to have more self-worth than any of the other students in school.

Since the boy with Down syndrome was unable to compete with the other children in Happiness 1 and 2 terms, he was free to elicit a more "pure" friendship from them, precisely because they had to relate to him in terms other than material, empirical, and functional. There was something latent in the other children that was awakened *by the mere presence* of that boy. He kindled in them a desire for a love premised on intrinsic goodness and lovability, not on goods and services. He called these children to transcend their Happiness 1 and 2 preoccupations and experience their higher nature. He called them into Happiness 3— interpersonal personhood—and showed them a horizon of love unrestricted by performance, to which we are called by our highest levels of desire. For a time, he helped them find and really enjoy their higher personhood—not as an escape from the comparison game, but as a joy in itself, as the fulfillment, or *perfection*, of their desire for unrestricted love. He showed them a richness of life that they had been unable to see through all their anxieties about pleasure and success.

What does the above story have to do with euthanasia? It helps to illustrate how compassion (expressed in caring for the helpless) can profoundly affect the help*ers* as well as those being helped. It shows how compassion can civilize the most aggressive groups, indeed, how the weak of this world can frequently perform much more important functions than the most intelligent and talented. Inasmuch as the needy elicit love, and love tames the overly aggressive soul, the needy can frequently do more for the world in bringing peace, care, and unity than the strong. They can even make up for the domination and destructiveness of the unvirtuously strong. We need neediness and weakness to make the world strong in heart, civility, and virtue. Neediness is the linchpin of civilization's progress. Inasmuch as all of us have needs and weaknesses, we can all contribute to the progress of civilization through the compassion we elicit.

Suppose the Genome Project were capable of producing a new generation of beings without need or weakness. Suppose further that advancements in technology were able to remedy all problems of energy production, food production, and distribution of goods and services.

Do you think this would be a perfect world? Could you imagine that as people's needs and weaknesses diminished, there might also be a concomitant diminishing of compassion and care? A decline or collapse of contributory identity? Would people then become more aggressively Level 2? Would they assess marginal differences in intelligence and physical capacity in exaggerated ways? Would they make the school yard filled with talented, aggressive children seem like a microcosm of a world predicated on the comparison game? Could such a world be filled with far more psychological and spiritual anguish than the contemporary world, with all of its deficiencies? Could this world be insufferable to "normal people" by comparison with the world of weakness, neediness, compassion, care, dependency, giving, and receiving?

Again, one might ask, what does this have to do with euthanasia? It points to the very real plight of elderly and medically vulnerable people, who have much to give and live for on the third and fourth levels, with very little to give on the first and second levels. Of particular concern are those affected by Alzheimer's disease and other forms of dementia. These people evidently lack the capacity to remember *facts* and the capacity for abstraction and verbal *production*, but they retain their ability to relate effectively to other people and to remember emotionally significant moments (Level 3). Moreover, if they were religious prior to the onset of the disease, they maintain an acute sense of their relationship with God and are able to love God through their traditional religious expressions (for example, Catholics could still relate to God through receiving Holy Communion, Protestants through paging through a Bible, and Jewish people through wearing a prayer shawl— Level 4).[21]

Because Alzheimer's patients lack the capacity for *rapid* verbal production, relatives, friends, and health care workers frequently misinterpret their lack of rapid response to questions as a sign of absent mentation. Thus, a health worker might say, "How are you feeling today?" No immediate reply would come, so the health care worker would leave. Five minutes later, long after the health care worker had left the room, the patient would respond, "Fine." Relatives and friends visiting

[21] Steven R. Sabat, "The Deconstruction of Self in Alzheimer's Disease: A Constructionist View", *Life and Learning III: Proceedings of the Third University Faculty for Life Conference*, ed. Joseph W. Koterski, S.J. (Washington, DC: University Faculty for Life, 1993), pp. 151–76.

Alzheimer's patients would assume they could not understand and would ask and answer questions for the patient, for example, "How are you doing today?" No reply. "I can tell that you're doing just fine. Do you need anything?" No reply. "I can see that you want someone to put your makeup on for you." (Husband then proceeds to put makeup on for wife, who would prefer to do it for herself but cannot form the words quickly enough to prevent her husband from making an embarrassing mess.)

The point is clear here. The verbal slowness of the Alzheimer's patients either makes visitors impatient or makes them believe Alzheimer's patients incapable of thought or relationship. This prevents staff and family from relating to the patients and blunts the patients' sense of their own social selves.[22] These patients want an interpersonal self. They want to express their feelings and, above all, their love. Unfortunately, the world of "normal people" either cannot see this desire, or are unwilling to spend the time necessary to allow it to be expressed.

When Alzheimer's patients are joined with helpers who have the patience and love to allow them into dignified interpersonal relationships, the anger level of the patients decreases, while the care, compassion, and contributory identity of the helpers increases. Jean Vanier discovered this over forty years ago and used it as the fulcrum for the L'arche movement.[23] He grouped the mentally and physically disabled together with volunteers from around the world to live in community. Throughout many years of successful encounter, he found that the disabled call forth the deepest dimensions of the volunteers' hearts, producing joy and transformation. The benefits of this relationship extend to the benefactors and associates of the communities, as well as the many high schools, universities, and community centers they visit. There are hundreds of L'arche communities throughout the world today, which bring the light of compassion and hope to a world struggling to see beyond the comparison game.

These L'arche communities reveal something to all of us if we take the time to notice, namely, that the human soul and human personhood are grounded not merely in acts of physical prowess and theoretical intelligence but also in the ability to look for the good news in the

---

[22] Ibid.

[23] Jean Vanier, *Community and Growth: Our Pilgrimage Together* (New York: Paulist Press, 1979). See also Vanier, *Man and Woman He Made Them* (Mahwah, N.J.: Paulist Press, 1985).

other, to do the good for the other, and to be in unity with the other. In other words, human personhood is grounded in love. These little communities reveal purely and poignantly that human personhood and human worth are conditioned or determined not by functionality or possessions but rather in acceptance of the other and in gift of self. All of this makes us come alive—not just in the here and now, but in the future—not just in the immediate future, but in eternity. It shows us the true meaning of life, namely, that love, transcendence, and eternity are what matter and that our functional skills are merely means to those ends.

Jean Vanier has given us an example of how to allow the disabled to make love and compassion come alive in our midst. Imagine the level of heart and hope that could be actualized if we formed communities among high schools and nursing homes, among universities and the medically vulnerable, indeed, among grade schools and Alzheimer's care facilities. Such communities could transform the heart and conscience of a nation. They could probably singlehandedly rescue the destiny of personhood and inalienable rights in a culture all too willing to remove these inalienable properties from the weak and vulnerable.

Readers with faith may also be interested in two true stories that show how the vulnerability of sickness can lead to an increase in faith, which, in turn, can positively affect both those who are dying and those surviving them.

The first concerns my grandfather's death. My grandfather might have been succinctly described as intelligent and hardworking. During the second world war, he was chief naval architect of the Pacific with headquarters at Pearl Harbor. He was objective and remained so well into his nineties. He would continue to read books in five different languages every day to "keep his mind alive". Naturally, my family was quite amazed to hear that during the last few days of his life he claimed to be "talking to the angels". Everybody thought he was just hallucinating, but he insisted that they were right there in the room. He would intermittently carry on a conversation with the angels, then with the people in the room, then back to the angels, and so on. On his dying day, he was again having one of these conversations with the angels, and he abruptly, but peacefully, looked up and asked, "May I go now?" Everyone said, "Well, sure." He died right then and there. This had a profound effect on all of us. I am convinced he knew that he would die at the instant he was "given permission". The angels told him that he would be with them, and his serenity revealed his confidence in their promise.

Such stories are not specific to my family. They happen all the time, and they make us survivors acutely aware of the mystery of each human being in relationship to God and the divine order. Survivors frequently experience these events as profoundly as the dying. They dignify us. They help us to know in our most forgetful moments that we are not simply a clump of chemicals, but spiritual mysteries loved by God into eternity.

My last story concerns an elderly woman (call her Mary) who was diagnosed with terminal cancer. Mary was a woman of faith. She prayed frequently, but always felt as if something were missing in her relationship with God. As Mary progressed in her illness, she found that she needed God more and, as a consequence, allowed God to come more deeply into her heart. She no longer kept God at a distance out of fear and shame. Her need overcame her fear and shame, and as a consequence she began to understand that God had not rejected her, but, rather, wanted to be with her. As she allowed God to be with her, she noticed that she was able to trust God more and more. In the course of time, her need was transformed into trust, and her trust became a felt awareness of God's love and care. When she spoke of this, it was not like someone mouthing truisms. Her statements revealed a serenity opening upon certitude, which, in turn, opened back upon serenity. Her children claimed that they almost did not recognize her, and penetratingly observed, "She has changed so much for the better. We can sense that she loves us more because she loves herself. We know that this love for herself did not come from us, but from the God of love, who showed her how to love."

The conclusion I drew from this episode refers back to what I said above. I am most affected by God when I "let him in", and I "let him in" most when I am in need. Though I have not had the experience of terminal illness, I suspect that this will be the time when I need him most. Dying is a route to self-transcendence or rather to the God who comes, the God who transforms and redeems us in his love, if we but "let him in" in our need.

Clearly, Happiness 1 and 2 views of quality of life are not only extremely limited; they also leave many dimensions of the human person unfulfilled. Euthanasia for Level 1 and 2 reasons leaves many important dimensions of life unlived. In contrast, when quality of life is seen in terms of love and faith—self-communication and self-transcendence—the last few weeks of life may well be the most important. They can be an avenue to undreamed-of dignity and goodness beyond the self. This culture needs to consider seriously all of its options for quality of life before it exercises such a "choice" as legalizing euthanasia.

C. Third Argument of Euthanasia Advocates: Active Euthanasia Is a Choice, an Option, a Fundamental Right; Therefore, People Who Do Not Want This Option Should Not Be Permitted to Prevent Those Who Do Want It from Obtaining It

Proponents of assisted suicide and lethal injection frequently claim that it is their right to have this *option*. Those who do not want this option, it is contended, do not have to avail themselves of it. Why take it away from those who want it? Is this not another instance of pro-lifers unjustly interfering in the lives of others?

The answer to these questions lies in what by now is an old sociopolitical and legal cliché: "One person's *option* can become another person's *duty*." This cliché correctly acknowledges that new options can carry with them an implicit or explicit duty. Once society legalizes the option of euthanasia, certain groups within the society might feel that it is not simply an option but also a duty. Vulnerable people could be pressured to avail themselves of an option that they would not have otherwise wanted. What could be the source of this pressure? Feelings of being a burden to their family, a burden to society, a burden to the doctor, or an illegitimate consumer of resources. In short, people can feel obligated by an option if others or the society suggest that it is the moral or appropriate thing to do. The new option opens the way for a new duty imposed on those who would formerly not have been inclined even to think about suicide.

The people who would be most vulnerable to this new unwanted duty would be those who have judged themselves to be less worthy to live. These would include the clinically depressed, the marginalized or economically deprived, those with low self-esteem, those who feel themselves a burden to their families, and those with a heightened sense of anxiety from their illness. Indeed, even those suffering from reversible depression[24] could also find themselves vulnerable. Hence a significant portion of the population could find itself pressured to commit suicide when they are not suffering, depressed, or desirous of the option.

The matter of options for some becoming the duty to die for others may also be analyzed in terms of inalienable and extrinsic rights (see Chapter Seven). As noted above,[25] inalienable rights are fundamental to all of our rights and to our entire legal system. By definition, they cannot be alienated. To argue that they can be is to reduce them to extrinsic rights, which are not absolute but subject to political creation and nullification.

Creation of a new extrinsic right must be subject to the principles of objective prioritization of rights and nonmaleficence. If, for example, the state wants to create an *extrinsic* right to active euthanasia, it must first:

1. Assess the *potential* harms that may accrue to other parties by offering such a right.

2. Rank potential harms and benefits under the principle of objective prioritization of rights. Is the potential harm caused by making euthanasia an extrinsic right greater than the potential harm caused by not making it an extrinsic right?

Assuming, for the moment, that creating a new extrinsic right to be euthanized would benefit a limited class of people who desire the right to have their lives ended, could that extrinsic right potentially lead to the violation of the inalienable right to life of other persons? Euthanasia has considerable potential for abuse, as has been shown in the Netherlands (where *involuntary* killing by physicians is common, despite tight safeguards).[26] In assessing potential abuse, one does not need to compare the number of potential "beneficiaries" and victims. Under the objective prioritization of rights, the violation of *inalienable* rights outweighs any conceivable benefit from creation of an *extrinsic* right to euthanasia.

[24] Elizabeth Kübler-Ross, M.D., *On Death and Dying* (New York: Macmillan, 1969). The whole of the chapters devoted to anger and depression are quite elucidating with respect to this issue.

[25] See chap. 7.

[26] *Medische Beslissingen Rond Het Levenseinde* (*Medical Decisions About the End of Life*), 2 vols. (The Hague, 1991).

We may see how this principle operates in Oliver Wendell Holmes' famous statement about restrictions of freedom of speech. Though this is an almost unlimited extrinsic right in the American constitutional system, one cannot shout "fire!" in a crowded theater; freedom of speech (an *extrinsic* right) is constrained here by concern that shouting "fire!" might harm innocent parties. Someone might be trampled to death in the rush to escape the "burning" theater, thereby threatening the *inalienable* right to live. No extrinsic right can legitimately cause harm to an inalienable right. Hence, if it can be reasonably expected that violations of the inalienable right to life will result from the legalization of euthanasia (an extrinsic right), then euthanasia cannot be legitimately legalized. I will show below that harm to the inalienable right to life can arise directly out of the legalization of active euthanasia for almost half the population. Consequently, the standard we have set would almost certainly be met. Let us look more closely at the practical application of a "right to euthanasia" and weigh the costs against the benefits.

Proponents of euthanasia admit that beneficiaries will be few, that in competent medical hands there are very few patients who will find pain and depression adequate reason for euthanasia.[27] However, as noted above, the victims will be many, and they will come from virtually every stratum of the population. How many potential victims might there be?

Given the existing standard of terminal care in the United States and most other countries (with the possible exception of the United Kingdom), many people would choose to die unnecessarily, for untreated depression and pain.[28] The "free choice" of such persons is compromised by the absence of full information on effective treatment alternatives. We are here dealing not with malicious abuses, merely with the well-intentioned but uninformed practice of many physicians.

Most agree that when victims exceed beneficiaries, public policy loses its enthusiasm—and indeed, such has been the considered opinion of every governmental body that has addressed the issue so far.[29] But the list of potential victims is even longer than it might seem.

The first category of potential victims is those with *low self-esteem* who have no strong religious or philosophical beliefs against suicide.

[27] See no. 10 above.

[28] Y. Conwell and E. D. Calne, "Rational Suicide and the Right to Die: Reality and Myth", *New England Journal of Medicine* 325 (1991): 1100–3.

[29] In the state of Oregon euthanasia was legalized by plebiscite.

Such individuals are not rare. Individuals with low self-esteem, by definition, are predisposed to hear, and receive, the most negative suggestion made by an authority figure (such as a doctor). If a doctor gives a person with low self-esteem the choice between palliative care and euthanasia, that person will hear a subliminal message: "The doctor thinks I deserve to die. I'll take euthanasia."

Such an individual is not psychologically free to "choose" euthanasia. The sheer number of people suffering from low self-esteem within this culture manifests clearly the potential harm. Their psychological deck is stacked in favor of death.

A second category of potential victims is those suffering from *reversible depression*, a state that is common—and commonly reversible—in terminal illness.[30] The depression and anger that seem to be intrinsic to some cases of terminal illness (that is, not secondary to inadequate care) generally, in Kübler-Ross's experience, subside or disappear altogether as patients move closer to death.

Obviously, we are "not ourselves" when we are upset or depressed. The mood swings inherent to anger and the hopelessness, emptiness, and bleakness associated with depression can make us do what we otherwise would not. Euthanasia "voluntarily chosen" by someone with reversible depression would be irreversibly tragic. Terminal patients commonly report times when they would have "chosen" to die had euthanasia been legal and great relief that the "choice" had not been available, for they regained their desire to live and benefited greatly from continued life. Temporary depression can make life seem permanently intolerable; in the midst of such a depression *an* option can appear to be *the only* option. "Freedom of choice" here is again found misleading both on psychiatric grounds and on practical grounds given the low standard of psychiatric care available to the terminally ill and elderly.[31]

A third psychological type psychiatrically predisposed to "choose" euthanasia is the *stoic hero*. Such individuals loathe dependency and weakness and would rather die than admit either, preferring to "end it all while I'm still strong". Such an individual could easily "choose" euthanasia in

---

[30] Kübler-Ross. The whole of the chapters devoted to anger and depression are quite elucidating with respect to this issue.

[31] Conwell and Calne.

the early stages of terminal illness, before any functional compromise, and die without consulting friends or family, to "avoid burdening them". This, of course, would load the survivors with all the trauma of a suicide and ignores the possibilities that the hero and his survivors might together discover the higher levels of meaning and purpose in life.

A fourth group are the victims of *inadvertent cruelty*. Perhaps a mother, given a terminal diagnosis and the option of palliation or death, turns to her daughter for advice. The daughter, not wishing to impose her values on her mother, says, "Whichever you think is right, Mom. We'll support whatever you want to do." The mother thinks, "That's all I mean to her!? She doesn't care if I live or die?! Then why go on? I'll end it all." What was intended to be supportive and nonjudgmental was construed as the ultimate rejection. Again "choice" not freely entered into but compelled by extraneous factors.

A fifth group of likely victims are the *elderly*, and especially elderly women. The elderly consistently express support for euthanasia, citing their concern "not to be a burden" and their desire not to consume unnecessary resources. Presumably the elderly in this culture are also subject to self-assessment in Happiness 1 and 2 terms. Euthanasia chosen "to get out of the way" appears to be a form of compulsion through guilt—again radically less "free" than the "free choice" euthanasia proponents advocate.

Each of these categories of victims represent ways in which "choice" becomes a form of "duty"—"an available option" becomes "the only acceptable option". Large segments of our population are vulnerable to these mistaken interpretations and could, as a result, turn this new option into a new compelling duty. One need only look at the percentages of people who live through depression, low self-esteem, and stoic heroism to see the victims piling up, victims who will have felt themselves compelled to cut short what could have been the most poignant and healing part of their lives for themselves and for their loved ones.

We have not yet considered the category of euthanasia courtesy of malicious family members, friends, or physicians. That will be dealt with below. Here, it suffices to point out that governments have legislated for centuries against "options" with unwise applications. This has often been done with great clarity in the interest of the common good. Hence, incanting the word "choice" ought not to constitute a form of political blackmail. Unwise options that harm the vulnerable have been and ought to be regulated or forbidden by law.

*D. Fourth Argument of Euthanasia Advocates: Active Euthanasia
Will Provide a Variety of Social Benefits, Such as Helping
to Curb the Costs of Treating the Terminally Ill*

There are other means of curbing treatment costs. Heroic treatment
need not be done for every terminal patient; indeed, it is often med-
dlesome. Our insurance system has encouraged heroic treatments and
inpatient hospital treatments and neglected outpatient and home hospice care. That situation is changing. Hospice and other palliative care
is usually quite inexpensive, as are the most effective pain medications.
Consequently, advocating euthanasia to trim health care costs seems
unnecessarily cold blooded.

Discussion of cost, however, raises another group of victims: individuals shunted into euthanasia by economic pressure. The trend in the
United States toward managed health care has led to de facto rationing
in many areas. Dr. Laurel Herbst, medical director of Hospice of San
Diego, has had numerous referrals of patients with treatable cancer who
have never been told they have treatable cancer.[32] They have been sent
for palliative hospice care because it is less expensive, without being
told all their options. If euthanasia is legalized, many victims will never
be offered effective palliation.

There will also be numerous victims of medical paternalism. In Holland, the Dutch government report cited thousands of cases of *involuntary* euthanasia in 1990, initiated and carried out by doctors without
patient knowledge or request, because *the doctors* thought it appropriate.[33] This, despite carefully thought out written safeguards supposedly
insuring patient control and fully informed consent.

Evidently, given the Dutch experience, euthanasia appears to be uncontrollable. Their situation should have been a best-case scenario: a
small country without significant racial conflict or economic pressure
on the health care system, with carefully constructed safeguards (much

---

[32] In "Your Health Care: Who Calls the Shots?" (video), Evergreen Freedom Foundation, Olympia, Wash., 1994.

[33] Richard Fenigsen, M.D., "The Report of the Dutch Governmental Committee on
Euthanasia", *Issues in Law and Medicine* 7 (1991): 339–44, I. van der Sluis, M.D., "The Practice of Euthanasia in the Netherlands", *Issues in Law and Medicine* 4 (1989): 460–71. B. A.
Bostrom, J.D., "Euthanasia in the Netherlands: A Model for the United States?" *Issues in Law
and Medicine* 4 (1989): 471–86. *Medische Beslissingen Rond Het Levenseinde.*

tighter than any proposed thus far in the English-speaking world). And yet, perhaps one in ten deaths there is *involuntary*, at the hands of doctors.[34]

The common good recoils at the thought of encouraging such destruction of the right to live. Also, love conquers death. Dying can enhance love and faith and thereby enhance quality of life, freedom, and personhood. Conversely, active euthanasia allows death to conquer dying, thereby allowing death to conquer love. This is perhaps the worst cost-benefit aspect of the entire euthanasia debate.

II. Negative Effects of Euthanasia on the Culture

Let us now go to diagram 14, describing the effects of euthanasia on the culture. As can be seen, euthanasia not only creates an implicit, explicit, and irresistible duty to die for almost half the population; it also alters our view of the quality of life. It implicitly says that those who experience the limiting symptoms of terminal illness have an equally diminished quality life. As noted above, this statement is true *only* in the perspectives of Levels 1 and 2. It is patently false in the perspectives of Levels 3 and 4, which see poignancy of life for both the dying and their survivors arising out of forgiveness, reestablishment of friendships, growth in humility, love, intrinsic dignity, and faith. Hence, to justify euthanasia on the basis of quality of life is an unqualified advocacy of the first and second levels of meaning in life.

Recall that what becomes legal becomes normative, and what becomes normative becomes moral. The sick and elderly will be the first to experience our culture's moral sanctioning of the first and second levels of meaning through euthanasia. But the signal will not stop there. After the directly affected population has been given the message, euthanasia will have to be justified through the usual cultural vehicles (politicians, the media, educators, Madison Avenue, and others).

These agencies will likely run with the new option (the new moral sanction) in the ways that they did with respect to abortion. This will require making the new option more palatable and desirable. One might expect, therefore, that some television shows, advertisements for insurance

[34] Ibid.

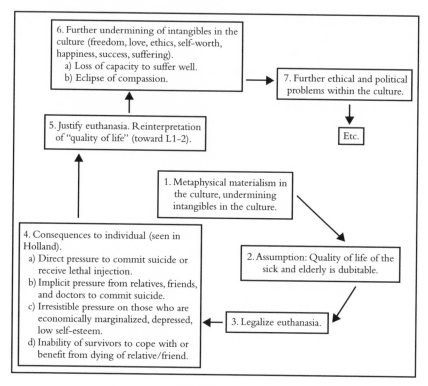

Diagram 14.

companies, and educators might begin to "forget" Level 3 and 4 meanings of life in an attempt to make the "beauty" of euthanasia more pronounced. These vehicles of the culture might also take it upon themselves explicitly to advocate the benefits of Level 1 and 2 meanings so that loss of ambulatory ability will seem even more debilitating and euthanasia, therefore, more attractive. As television programs, advertisements, magazine articles, and classrooms begin to manifest the "beauty" of the new option, youth and young adults can be fully expected to become convinced of its goodness for them. The culture will again have inadvertently crusaded for Level 1 and 2 meanings in life.

Much has been said above about how the justification of abortion became a justification for a Level 1 or 2 view of person, inalienable rights, freedom, ethics, love, self-worth, success, and suffering. The very same can be said for the culture's new push of Level 1 and 2 meaning with respect to the advocacy of euthanasia. The negative effects within the culture will go far beyond the dying and their survivors. It will affect our youth in virtually every way and, in the end, affect our culture's ability to reach new heights of civilization. Indeed, it may also affect our culture's ability to survive.

Special mention must be made of suffering, here, for the advocacy of euthanasia will be particularly debilitating to our ability to suffer well. Two points should be mentioned here. They will be covered briefly, because a fuller treatment has been given in Chapter Five:

1. euthanasia as a self-fulfilling prophecy

2. the eclipse of "compassion"

Diagram 15 illustrates the first point (euthanasia as a self-fulfilling prophecy). As noted in diagram 15, euthanasia inevitably incites the elderly toward a Level 1/2 quality of life. The culture will incite the rest of the population toward this viewpoint if it decides to promote its moral sanctioning of the new option. Level 1 and 2 perspectives make suffering seem meaningless because they exclude love, lovability,

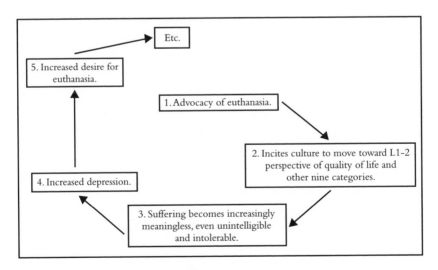

Diagram 15.

contribution, faith, and the like from their purview. The meaningless-ness and intolerability of suffering, in turn, increase the depression of the person suffering, for it seems as if no good is coming out of this ultimate life deprivation. This depression, in turn, makes euthanasia seem like a more attractive option.

Though it is a more attractive option, it is not necessarily a freer one. Recall that freedom can be viewed in one of two ways: (1) as the stron-gest momentary emotion or (2) as the ability/commitment to move toward what is most pervasive, enduring, and deep. Euthanasia pro-motes freedom only in the first sense (Levels 1 and 2). In its promotion of death, euthanasia obviously militates against the second perspective, which anticipates and moves toward a future of growth in love for oth-ers and oneself. When advocates of euthanasia are promoting its freeing qualities, it would be helpful for them to make their definition of "free-dom" *plain*, for these implicit definitions are quite literally killing not only our elderly but also others within our populace who are unable to suffer well.

The second negative cultural effect arising out of euthanasia's under-mining of the ability to suffer is the eclipse of compassion. Compassion means the ability to "suffer with" another. As was indicated in Chapter Five, this quality is closely tied to empathy, the close connection with another such that one can feel what the other feels. This close connec-tion gives rise to the energy and desire to make sacrifices and to dem-onstrate friendship on an extraordinary level. Affection, tenderness, connectedness, and contributory behavior are so heightened that both the giver and recipient of compassion find themselves to be living on a wholly different plane. It is frequently described as a supernatural experience.

Advocates of euthanasia have dramatically changed the meaning of "compassion" in their attempt to justify this new "option". Even though palliative care is able to alleviate 90 to 99 percent of pain in terminally ill patients,[35] physicians are made to look "more compassionate" when they offer assisted suicide. This decidedly redefines "compassion" in terms of "putting someone out of misery (or a substandard quality of life)". If compassion is viewed in this extremely Level 1 or 2 way, it will eventually lose its original meaning, which is completely contrary to

---

[35] See n. 4 above.

this new interpretation. But what if we as a culture lose sight not only of the original meaning of "compassion", but also of the *reality* of compassion? Could our loss of the ability to suffer well amidst our unmitigated promotion of the Level 1 or 2 perspective lead to the loss of empathy, superconnectedness, and compassion's heightened state of love? If it did, would this not be the greatest loss of civility and civilization? Would this not constitute a loss of heart within the culture? Would the sun finally fail to dawn on our civilization?

Conclusion

Let us return to diagram 13, at the beginning of this chapter. The ongoing cycle of materialism within the culture will now, hopefully, be evident. The advocacy of euthanasia seems to be related directly to this cultural materialism, which, in its Level 1 or 2 perspective, assumes that the quality of life for the elderly, the terminally ill, and the vulnerable is very low. This conviction has driven many within the culture to pursue a new option, a new freedom, which, at first glance, may appear to be compassionate, but in the final reckoning not only undermines compassion but also puts incredible pressure on the economically marginalized, the depressed, and those with low self-esteem to commit suicide. This pressure will be felt even though most people in this situation would reverse any such desire for suicide if their pain and depression were properly treated. The grand irony of this "new freedom" is that it is creating an *unnecessary, unwanted,* pressure, if not *duty,* to die. If I am not mistaken, death is the end of freedom. Hence, this new freedom is producing an unnecessary, unwanted duty to end freedom.

The harm of euthanasia is not limited to individuals. It is also producing three devastating cultural effects:

1. It accelerates the culture's obsession with a Level 1 or 2 view of freedom, love, ethics, self-worth, happiness, success, and suffering.

2. It undermines our ability to suffer well and therefore to grow from suffering.

3. It allows a radically false view of "compassion" to eclipse its true, profound meaning grounded in the highest dimensions of empathy.

The ultimate effect of these consequences to the individual and the culture is a heightened materialism that could spell the demise of love and with it all hope.

I, for one, do not believe that the culture will end in this negative way, because I am convinced that human beings, in their intrinsic desire to make a difference with their lives, will come to a realization of what's missing. The evident generosity and goodness within our youth, adults, and elderly population betoken a resurgence and deepening of love within the culture, even in the midst of our current decline. But if this solution is to occur, we must *name* the problem and give its solution specificity and practical steps. We will have to take an uncomfortable message courageously to a culture that is growing increasingly more comfortable in decline. We may even have to be the gadflies of the good news of redemptive, responsible love.

The Life Principles project is one such attempt among many others. Its primary function is not merely to *name* a problem but also to point the way to a solution. The solution may seem somewhat "intangible" in its concern for ideas and ideals, but who ever said that "intangibles" were bad? Unfortunately, the culture has. It is now time to resist the impulse to flee from the intangibility of ideas and ideals and to return to them as if they were the very safeguards of love within the culture. If we do not redress this with our youth, and indeed ourselves, the decline will continue. However, if we do redress it through ideals similar to those mentioned in this book, then our hearts will reignite, and in so doing, we will together find a path to allow love to prevail over death.

Epilogue

Though this final section represents a conclusion to this book, it is really a beginning and a call to action. There is no one more suitable than yourself to begin reversing the effects of cultural materialism; no one better to tell a story about how living for what is pervasive, enduring, and deep leads to greater happiness, love, fulfillment, and cultural participation. Though you may have not formally studied philosophy and its related enterprises, though you may not have imagined yourself as a champion of inalienable rights and the common good or seen yourself as a defender of the intrinsic dignity of personhood within the culture, there is no one more suited to the task of rescuing the culture than you. You are irreplaceable within your family, group of friends, workplace, church, and community organization. No one can replace your story about the road from Level 2 to Level 3. And no one can take away your conviction about the intrinsic dignity of every person of human origin.

What can you do? In some contexts, all you can do is talk about your perspective on a Level 3 or 4 lifestyle. Sometimes you can share this with your children. Perhaps you can give this book away or bring the Life Principles videotape series to your community organization or church.[1] Sometimes all we can do is say to a colleague at work, "I think there is more to life than that." Some of us will have the opportunity to take this message to middle school and high school students. Some will even have the opportunity to adapt it to a grade school audience. Whatever our call might be, no matter how grand or small, we must commit ourselves to doing something, for this is true freedom.

There is only one problem with having a Center for Life Principles. People might think that the Center is the agent of cultural transformation. Unfortunately, it is only a transmitter of information. The agents of cultural transformation are the individuals who get this information into churches, community centers, hospitals, nursing homes, middle

---

[1] For information, see page 347 below.

schools, high schools, the workplace, and even the hallowed halls of universities, courts, and legislatures.

As has been noted repeatedly throughout this book, transformation of the culture cannot occur solely through spreading the word about Levels 3 and 4. We will have to rectify our self-creation of two of the most powerful agents of cultural materialism: abortion and euthanasia. If we allow these two "new options" to continue to gain momentum, we will give credence to the assumptions on which they are based. Allowing these assumptions to persist not only will cause great individual harm but also will accelerate the move to Level 1/2 within our culture. This will lead ultimately to the demise of happiness, self-worth, love, ethics, freedom, personhood, rights, and the common good.

I do not want to draw a superficial parallel to the *Dred Scott* decision here, but I think it is worth mentioning that the abolitionists' espousal of the ideas of human dignity never took root within the general culture until slavery was finally abolished after the Civil War. The abolition of slavery was not simply a rectification of a particular evil; it resulted in a cleansing of the culture that enabled us to see clearly the rights and dignity of human beings in ways that eluded the attention of many in times past. Wars are, of course, a terrible way of rectifying injustice. Education is obviously the better path. All we need do is attend to this education as if it were taking place in the aftermath of a war, giving it the same credence, urgency, and zeal that we would give the lessons of war.

Why this urgency? Because the ten great categories of cultural discourse, which should be the most inspiring, beautiful, vital, and creative ideas for individuals, culture, and community, have been coopted and even eclipsed by political agendas furthering mere egocentricity. I am not suggesting here that the advocates of these political agendas intended this consequence; indeed, I suspect they may have intended the opposite. Nevertheless, the decline has *in fact* occurred. Many within the culture now believe that "the ultimate freedom is death" or "freedom is doing what I want" (with "want" meaning "strongest momentary emotion"). The culture is *in fact* becoming more adverse to commitment. It is becoming more superficial about happiness and life's purpose. It is, despite our best intentions, shifting from the contributive to the comparative with each passing day. It is becoming more relativistic in its view of ethics. It is trying to seize control over when inalienable rights begin (as if it had this power!). Indeed, it is at the point of losing its whole sense of personhood. I do not mean, here, losing a Level 3 or 4 sense of personhood (grounded in truth, love, goodness, beauty, and being). I mean losing the sense of personhood altogether. We are at the brink of considering personhood to be a meaningless abstraction. If we do this, we *will* eventually lose the sense of intrinsic dignity upon which all true respect, freedom, and love depend.

When I look at this cultural decline head on, I do not become consumed with discouragement. Rather, I believe that human beings, in their fundamental capacity for love, can overcome even the most radical decline. But if this love, in its individual and cultural manifestation, is to be given a chance, it must be grounded in the critical assumption upon which this book and all healthy cultures are founded:

When in doubt, we must accord personhood, unconditional dignity, and inalienable rights to all beings of human origin, lest we cause unconditional harm to both individuals and the culture.

MANIFESTO OF CULTURAL SURVIVAL

To preserve, protect, and promote:

1. The third and fourth levels of happiness and purpose in life

2. The principle of non-maleficence

3. The critical assumption of personhood

4. The inalienability of the rights to life and liberty

5. The objective prioritization of inalienable rights

6. The protection of the right to life and liberty of the preborn, elderly, and terminally ill from conception to natural death.

Appendix I

Powers, Perfection of Powers, and Quantum Systems

The following is another rather fascinating manifestation of the real components signified by the three kinds of real definition discussed in Chapter One. A quantum system is the basis of electrical energy and light energy, the electron and the photon, respectively. As the reader may know, a quantum system can manifest itself as either a particle or a wave. Particles are self-enclosed, conserve momentum, and, therefore, collide, displaying the dynamics and mechanics of collisions. They are described by the mathematics of eigenstates. Waves act in just the opposite fashion. Instead of being self-enclosed, they are diffuse. Indeed, with the passage of time, they get more and more diffused as the wave spreads out. Again, instead of colliding as two particles might, two waves will blend with each other, creating interference patterns much like what one would see in a wave tank. Finally, we cannot use the mathematics of eigenstates to describe a wave. We must use a mathematics appropriate to wave mechanics. As you can see, waves and particles contradict one another. Therefore, we cannot postulate a phenomenon like a "wavicle". The self-enclosedness would contradict the diffusedness. The collision mechanics would contradict the interference mechanics. When the quantum system has not yet taken the form of a wave or a particle, it must be more elementary than either waves or particles. Whatever it is, it is not a "wavicle".

How can we go about defining a quantum system? First, we want a "what" definition. Not merely its appearance, but its powers. So a quantum system has the power for electromagnetic interaction. In order to produce real electromagnetic effects, however, it must be either in a wavelike form or a particlelike form. As mentioned above, it cannot be in both of these forms simultaneously, for that would be contradictory. Therefore, it must be in some more fundamental or elementary form when it is in its potential state.

We now proceed to the "perfection" definition. In order for a quantum system to do anything (to move from potentiality to activity), it must take the form of either a particle or a wave. Its perfection, therefore, is to be particlelike or wavelike. Given that the system could display either wavelike or particlelike characteristics, it must have some information within it that would cause its transformation into wavelike behavior or particlelike behavior when the conditions call for them. This information must specify which conditions will elicit wavelike behavior and which ones particlelike behavior. We cannot, however, say that the system is a wave or a particle before those conditions occur. It exists with the potential for both contradictory states.

One would not want to say that there is no wavelike aspect in the quantum field, because if there were not, the quantum field would not become wavelike. So also, one would not want to say that there are no particlelike aspects of the quantum field, for this would preclude its becoming a particle. Its future wavelike or particlelike state is already infused in the field. It really exists. It is the future perfection of the field. It simply has not yet been actualized. When information is introduced into the quantum system, it will stimulate either particlelike behavior or wavelike behavior, at which point the system will have achieved its perfection, its *to ti en einai*, its "what it was meant to be".

It is a little bit more difficult to isolate what this information (which leads to the system's perfection) is like prior to its actualization, because unlike genetic information, which is molecularly coded, quantum information seems to be billions of times more elementary. Nevertheless, it is *real* information existing in *real* quantum systems before those systems have manifested themselves in their perfected states (that is, either a wavelike or particlelike way).

Again, the "perfection" definition is grounded not merely in my knowledge of what the future holds for this quantum system but more importantly in the information within the quantum system itself, which gives rise to particles or waves in accordance with the conditions of its surrounding environment. If this information about the perfection of the system were not in the system itself, I would not have any knowledge about its future as a wave or a particle, for it would not transform itself into either.

Every other active entity can be defined through these real modes of definition. Protons, electrons, positrons, alpha particles, beta particles, space-time, cellular metabolism, animal consciousness, rocks, trees, birds, planetary motions, whatever one wishes. The point is that nominalistic definitions are subjective descriptions. Real definitions are explanations grounded in power, conditions of powers, and perfections of powers. They are, therefore, fundamentally objective.

Appendix II

The Necessity of Finite Past Time and, Therefore, a Creator

This rational judgment can be seen from an insight of David Hilbert (the father of finite mathematics). Hilbert recognized a difference between a potential infinite sequence and an actual infinite sequence. A "potential infinite sequence" is one that can keep on going but is never achieved. An "actual infinite sequence", however, would be tantamount to achieving a terminus after traveling an infinite span.

Now, let's apply this insight to past time and future time. If there were such a thing as "infinite past time", it would have to be an actual infinity, because past time has already occurred, and therefore an infinite span would have had to have been traversed in order to reach the present moment. This would not be the case for infinite future time, which is only a potential infinity. Recall that a potential infinity really never occurs. It is simply the potential to keep on going without limit. Needless to say, future time does not yet exist. The future can keep on going, but at any given point only a finite amount of it has occurred from any given present moment. Hence, when we say "infinite future time" we mean that an infinite span was not traversed, but when we say "infinite past time" we mean that an infinite span was traversed (it has occurred).

Returning to Hilbert's insight for a moment, an actual infinite sequence is impossible, for it is absurd to say that an infinite span was actually traversed. This would imply that the unachievable was achieved (a contradiction). Notice that an infinite sequence by its very nature is unachievable, for infinity implies a continuation without limit, which implies more than whatever can be achieved. Hilbert therefore recognized that the only noncontradictory way of speaking about an infinite sequence was a "potential infinite sequence", because this does not imply that an infinity (the unachievable) was in fact achieved.

345

Now, if we apply Hilbert's insight to the problem of past and future time, it is clear that past time must have occurred, that is, it must have been achieved. So the phrase "infinite past time" suggests an achieved unachievable! Infinite sequences are by nature unachievable, and past time must be achieved. If we put "infinite" together with "past time" we have an achieved unachievable—a contradiction. Therefore, it cannot be said that past time is infinite, meaning that it must be finite. Now if past time is finite, then it must have a beginning. Prior to that beginning, it could not have existed. Therefore, it could not have caused itself. Hence, some other causative force outside of past time must have caused it to exist and to begin. This causative force outside of past time is frequently referred to as a "Creator", which is intuitively associated with the unconditional fulfillment of our nature. Hence, it is referred to as "God".

Is infinite future time possible? Why not? Because future time has not yet occurred. Unlike past time (which must always be achieved), future time must always be unachieved. Again, an infinite sequence is unachievable. But when we combine this unachievability with the unachieved status of future time, we have only an unachieved unachievable which is perfectly legitimate. Hence, we cannot use infinite future time as an analogy for infinite past time. They are as different as apples and oranges. The former is contradictory and therefore impossible, requiring a beginning and a Creator. The latter is simply the potential to keep on going.

More Information about the Life Principles Project

The Center for Life Principles was founded by Robert J. Spitzer, S.J., Ph.D., in 1993 as a project of Human Life of Washington Education Foundation. Directed by Camille E. De Blasi, M.A., its purpose is to share the message of the Life Principles philosophy in as many forums as possible.

To facilitate Life Principles education in a wide variety of audiences, the Center for Life Principles has developed several useful tools available to individuals, organizations, and groups. They include videos, audiotapes, books, and curriculum materials.

To order materials, schedule a speaker, or establish a Life Principles educational program in your area or for more information, please contact:

Center for Life Principles
c/o Human Life of Washington
  Education Foundation
2601 151st Place NE
Redmond, WA 98052
Toll free: (877) 345-LIFE
www.lifeprinciples.net
mail@lifeprinciples.net